Second Edition

EDUCATIONAL
FOUNDATIONS

Second Edition

EDUCATIONAL
FOUNDATIONS
An Anthology of Critical Readings

Editors

ALAN S. CANESTRARI
Roger Williams University

BRUCE A. MARLOWE
Roger Williams University

Los Angeles | London | New Delhi
Singapore | Washington DC

For information:

SAGE Publications, Inc.
2455 Teller Road
Thousand Oaks, California 91320
E-mail: order@sagepub.com

SAGE Publications India Pvt. Ltd.
B 1/I 1 Mohan Cooperative
  Industrial Area
Mathura Road, New Delhi 110 044
  India

SAGE Publications Ltd.
1 Oliver's Yard
55 City Road
London EC1Y 1SP
United Kingdom

SAGE Publications Asia-Pacific
Pte. Ltd.
33 Pekin Street #02-01
Far East Square
Singapore 048763

Printed in the United States of America

Library of Congress Cataloging-in-Publication Data

Educational foundations: an anthology of critical readings/edited by Alan S. Canestrari, Bruce A. Marlowe.—2nd ed.
    p. cm.
Includes bibliographical references and index.
ISBN 978-1-4129-7438-7 (pbk.)
    1. Critical pedagogy. 2. Teaching. 3. Teachers. I. Canestrari, Alan S. II. Marlowe, Bruce A.

LC196.E393 2010
370.11'5—dc22   2009004840

This book is printed on acid-free paper.

09   10   11   12   13   10   9   8   7   6   5   4   3   2   1

Acquisitions Editor:	Diane McDaniel
Editorial Assistant:	Ashley Conlon
Production Editor:	Brittany Bauhaus
Typesetter:	C&M Digitals (P) Ltd.
Proofreader:	Theresa Kay
Indexer:	Michael Ferreira
Cover Designer:	Janet Foulger
Marketing Manager:	Christy Guilbault

Contents

Preface

Context

The ideological clash over what students should learn and how they should learn it continues unabated—although the conflict, in many ways, resembles more of a rout than a clash. Since the first edition of *Educational Foundations: An Anthology of Critical Readings* was published in December 2003, the neoconservative reform agenda has come to dominate American public education. An "at-risk" mind-set, characterized by an almost singular focus on how our schools are failing, has resulted in narrow directives now firmly embedded within public education. What once appeared as isolated news stories and cause for local embarrassment—teaching to the test, scripted curricula, mindless repetition of facts—is now openly advocated without chagrin by local and state school officials. Yearly test results have emerged as the most important measure of the worth of our schools despite the fact that the numbers such assessments provide obfuscate the complexity of schooling and serve to short-circuit deeper understanding of student learning and high-quality teaching. Can such an at-risk educational vision serve to renew and sustain our nation, our democracy, and our schools? Does the current model of accountability serve the public interest? Is there another way to frame reform?

Fortunately, there are still many thoughtful, progressive administrators, teachers, and parents. You will read their words in the pages that follow. In different ways, and at different times, they have refused to blindly accept an "at-risk" perspective, questioned uncritical compliance, and challenged the notion that there is, of necessity, a singular path to learning that requires rigid adherence to state directives. We have chosen these authors because, like Thoreau, they worry that public education is in jeopardy of making "a straight-cut ditch of a free, meandering brook."

But, how does one begin to walk down an alternative path? Why aren't teachers at the forefront of the debate? How can we prepare beginning teachers to move purposefully in another direction, to ask questions, to challenge assumptions . . . to be involved? What questions should teachers ask? What answers should teachers accept?

We hope that new teachers will consider asking whether their instruction promotes the status quo. We would like them to ask themselves how deliberate their efforts are to promote equality and to include the experiences of traditionally marginalized groups in the curriculum. We would also like them to ask themselves whether their instruction is implemented at a transformational, social action level. New teachers need models of critical reflection (and even dissent) in order to help them develop their own critical questions and voices.

Purpose

Like the first edition of this text, the major purpose of this second edition is to help teachers develop habits of critical reflection about schools and schooling before entering the classroom. It is for this reason that we have deliberately chosen authors with strong views that reflect these particular biases. We hope that these readings will offer a platform for discussion and debate that may be used by instructors to increase student knowledge of pedagogy and to provide authentic opportunities for potential teachers to think critically about teaching and learning. For example, we are very concerned about the current trend toward standardization of curriculum and instruction a trend that we believe devalues teaching and increases the distrust of teachers. We believe, like Deborah Meier, that this trend had manifested itself in schools organized around testing and that it is imperative for teachers to actively critique such events and recapture some of the control and power over their work.

We assembled this book because we believe that the current textbooks written on the foundations of education are too broad and too politically cautious to engage students or to help them develop their own critical voices. Such texts do a good job of providing a survey of practices, but with very limited reference to the social contexts of teachers and their students and without taking a strong stance in favor of one practice or another. In these texts' attempt to cover everything in a curriculum, students have little opportunity to delve deeply into any substantive issues. Instead, they are exposed, in only the most superficial ways, to the important issues facing the field. While the scope of the typical course has become broader in the last several years, the tone has become more dispassionate. As textbook content demands expand, students become responsible for knowing less and less about more and more. Like textbooks in many fields, the texts available for courses in educational foundations and/or introduction to education are so cursory that they leave professors few options other than assuming highly didactic, teacher-directed approaches to instruction. The available texts also tend to promote practices that are antithetical to meaningful instruction: lecture, memorization, and multiple-choice assessment. Finally, because of their size and scope and their neutral stance, available texts foster acceptance of the status quo without opportunity for in-depth examination, reflection, and discussion.

What you have in your hands is a book that we hope you will find as exciting as we do—an anthology of critical readings for students about to enter the teaching profession and for students interested in carefully examining schools and schooling. We feature provocative, engaging authors whose views are politicized but whose writing and opinions matter not simply because they are gadflies, but because their ideas work and because their achievements as teachers, principals, and policy shapers are so notable.

Organization

The anthology continues to be organized around essential questions. They are: Why Teach? Who Are Today's Students? What Makes a Good Teacher? What Do Good Schools Look Like? How Should We Assess Student Learning? How Does One Develop a Critical Voice? Our authors' answers continue to be bold and refreshing. They eschew the unquestioning compliance so characteristic of new teachers and by taking a hard look at traditional educational practice they serve as models for the kind of reflective practitioners we hope our students will become when they enter the field. We frame each chapter with a very brief introductory vignette that provides context for the issues that the authors' essays address and that also serves to raise probing questions about teaching and learning.

Changes to the Second Edition

We have had plenty of feedback to the first edition of *Educational Foundations: An Anthology of Critical Readings*. While the response to our book has been overwhelmingly positive, we also received a number of very specific, constructive recommendations from valued colleagues, critics, and the students with whom we have had the pleasure of working. Principal among these were recommendations that essays more directly "answer" the questions posed at the outset of each chapter. To address this suggestion, we removed essays that were only tangentially related to each chapter's opening question and substituted them with essays that more directly address the content of each chapter's focus. In addition to most of the fine essays contained in our original edition, you will now also find works by Herbert Kohl, Frank McCourt, Deborah Meier, Carol Ann Tomlinson, and Lois Weiner. We also commissioned two new pieces by imaginative teacher educators—Kelly Donnell and Ann Gibson Winfield—both of whom have long experience working in schools, and with children and young people.

How Not to Use This Book

If you are a professor who adopted our first edition and hold our second edition in your hands, rest assured that we have not changed our perspective concerning the use of this book. If you are a professor who has adopted our second edition and are searching for some guidance in using this book well, here is fair warning: You won't find any direct instruction here. Instead, we hope that you, like those who have found the anthology useful, will think critically about the most effective ways to engage your students with these readings and the issues they raise, without simply telling. Let's once again be clear: Simply walking through the table of contents, chapter by chapter, and expounding on the views of the authors contained in these pages is not what we had in mind.

If you are a student, you hold our second edition in your hands for the first time; we challenge you to ensure that your professors practice what they preach about instruction. Are you sitting through long and boring lectures about why teachers should not lecture? Are you engaged in discussion? If not, perhaps it is time to ask your professor, "Why not?"

Acknowledgments

Our thinking regarding teaching and learning continues to be shaped, reshaped, and supported by our colleagues and our work with children. Like the first edition, this anthology is composed of the writing of those who have had a profound influence on our understanding of what is most important for learners, teachers, and schools. We also want to thank Kelly Donnell and Ann Winfield, two of our colleagues here at Roger Williams University, for agreeing to write new pieces for the second edition of this book. Kelly Donnell offers an optimistic urban education essay and Ann Winfield closes the anthology with an inspirational message to teachers.

Great teachers and writers, however, are not our only sources of inspiration or support: Special thanks to Pam and Nancy for their criticisms of the manuscript at its various stages. We are also grateful to Gary Canestrari for his artistic sense and input regarding the design of the book's cover, and to Janet Foulger at SAGE for the final product.

We are extremely fortunate to have wonderful administrative support here at Roger Williams University. Mary Gillette, as always, was extremely helpful using her manuscript wizardry and her artistic sense to make our new chapters visually appealing.

At SAGE, Diane McDaniel has been a continuous source of encouragement and support. Ashley Conlon, Editorial Assistant, was also instrumental in shepherding the project through all its phases.

Reviewers for the second edition are gratefully acknowledged:

Kenneth W. Carlson, *Shawnee State University*

Richard C. Carriveau, *Black Hills State University*

Thomas G. Greene, *University of Portland*

Philip E. Kovacs, *University of Alabama, Huntsville*

Mark LaCelle-Peterson, *Houghton College*

Timothy J. Touzel, *Coastal Carolina University*

Marsha Zenanko, *Jacksonville State University*

Reviewers for the first edition are gratefully acknowledged:

Fred Bedelle, *Lincoln Memorial University*

Christopher Blake, *Mt. St. Mary's College*

Dave Donahue, *Mills College*

Russ Dondero, *Pacific University*

Allison Hoewisch, *University of Missouri, St. Louis*

Carolyn Wemlinger, *Dominican University*

About the Editors

Alan S. Canestrari is a veteran social studies practitioner and Associate Professor of Education at Roger Williams University. He earned his EdD from Boston University. He has had a long career in public schools and universities as a history teacher and department chair, as adjunct professor at Rhode Island College, and as mentor in the Brown University Masters of Teaching Program. In 1992, he was recognized as the Rhode Island Social Studies Teacher of the Year. He is coeditor (with Bruce A. Marlowe) of *Educational Psychology in Context: Readings for Future Teachers*.

Bruce A. Marlowe is the author (with Marilyn Page) of *Creating and Sustaining the Constructivist Classroom* and of a six-part video series titled *Creating the Constructivist Classroom* (The Video Journal of Education). He earned his PhD in Educational Psychology from The Catholic University of America in Washington, D.C., where he also completed two years of postdoctoral training in neuropsychological assessment. He has taught at the elementary, secondary, and university levels and is currently Professor of Educational Psychology and Special Education at Roger Williams University.

Alan and Bruce have both taught courses in the foundations of education; neither is satisfied with any of the foundations texts currently available on the market. Both authors can be reached by mail at Roger Williams University, School of Education, One Old Ferry Road, Bristol, Rhode Island 02809, and also by telephone and email: Alan Canestrari at (401) 254-3749, acanestrari@rwu.edu; and Bruce Marlowe at (401) 254-3078, bmarlowe@rwu.edu.

PART I

Why Teach?

Students file into a crowded lecture hall at a small liberal arts college in the Northeast. The class, Foundations of Education, is a prerequisite for acceptance into the School of Education program and it is enrolled at maximum capacity. It is the first day of class. Students are expecting that the syllabus for the course will be distributed and read aloud, and if no one asks any questions about the requirements of the class, then the students can cut out early and enjoy the warm September sunshine. After all, nobody bought the book yet. The professor arrives and greets the students.

"Good morning. So, you are all interested in becoming teachers? Wonderful. We need bright, energetic, young teachers in the profession today. Teaching can be a very rewarding career, but I must warn you that it is a challenging time for teachers, especially beginning teachers. Teachers are under tremendous scrutiny. There are also increasing concerns about the deplorable condition of our schools, the lack of parental support, the disturbing behavior of the children, and the general disrespect for teachers by the public at large. So, why teach?"

A long silence fills the hall.

"This is not a rhetorical question. Tell us, why do you want to teach?"

More silence . . . long silence.

Finally, Jennifer offers, "My mom is a teacher. So is my aunt. I guess I have grown up around teaching, and ever since I can remember, I've wanted to teach, too."

Then Erin says, "I just love kids. Like, I just want to make a difference in their lives. I want to teach elementary school. The kids are so cute at that age."

1

Robert adds, "I work as a camp counselor in the summers. My cabin always wins the camp contest. I really connect with kids. I mean, I just know what they like. It is not so hard, plus teachers have summers off."

Sound good? Do Jennifer, Erin, and Robert have it right? Are these the reasons to teach?

1

Teacher Man

Frank McCourt

M*ea culpa.*
Instead of teaching, I told stories.
Anything to keep them quiet and in their seats.
They thought I was teaching.
I thought I was teaching.
I was learning.
And you called yourself a teacher?
I didn't call myself anything. I was more than a teacher. And less. In the
high school classroom you are a drill sergeant, a rabbi, a shoulder to cry on,
a disciplinarian, a singer, a low-level scholar, a clerk, a referee, a clown, a
counselor, a dress-code enforcer, a conductor, an apologist, a philosopher,
a collaborator, a tap dancer, a politician, a therapist, a fool, a traffic cop, a
priest, a mother-father-brother-sister-uncle-aunt, a bookkeeper, a critic, a
psychologist, the last straw.

The advice was wasted. I learned through trial and error and paid a price for
it. I had to find my own way of being a man and a teacher and that is what I
struggled with for thirty years in and out of the classrooms of New York. My
students didn't know there was a man up there escaping a cocoon of Irish
history and Catholicism, leaving bits of that cocoon everywhere.

My life saved my life. On my second day at McKee a boy asks a question that sends me into the past and colors the way I teach for the next thirty years. I am nudged into the past, the materials of my life.

Joey Santos calls out, Yo, teach. . . .

You are not to call out. You are to raise your hand.

Yeah, yeah, said Joey, but . . .

They have a way of saying yeah yeah that tells you they're barely tolerating you. In the yeah yeah they're saying, We're trying to be patient, man, giving you a break because you're just a new teacher.

Joey raises his hand. Yo, teacher man. . . .

Call me Mr. McCourt.

Yeah. OK. So, you Scotch or somethin'?

In the teachers' cafeteria veterans warned me, Son, tell 'em nothing about yourself. They're kids, goddam it. You're the teacher. You have a right to privacy. You know the game, don't you? The little buggers are diabolical. They are not, repeat not, your natural friends. They can smell it when you're going to teach a real lesson on grammar or something, and they'll head you off at the pass, baby. Watch 'em. Those kids have been at this for years, eleven or twelve, and they have teachers all figured out. They'll know if you're even thinking about grammar or spelling, and they'll raise their little hands and put on that interested expression and ask you what games you played as a kid or who do you like for the goddam World Series. Oh, yeah. And you'll fall for it. Next thing is you're spilling your guts and they go home not knowing one end of a sentence from the other, but telling the moms and dads about your life. Not that they care. They'll get by, but where does that leave you? You can never get back the bits and pieces of your life that stick in their little heads. Your life, man. It's all you have. Tell 'em nothing.

Joey is the mouth. There's one in every class along with the complainer, the clown, the goody-goody, the beauty queen, the volunteer for everything, the jock, the intellectual, the momma's boy, the mystic, the sissy, the lover, the critic, the jerk, the religious fanatic who sees sin everywhere, the brooding one who sits in the back staring at the desk, the happy one, the saint who finds good in all creatures. It's the job of the mouth to ask questions, anything to keep the teacher from the boring lesson. I may be a new teacher but I'm on to Joey's delaying game. It's universal. I played the same game in Ireland. I was the mouth in my class in Leamy's National School. The master would write an algebra question or an Irish conjugation on the board and the boys would hiss, Ask him a question, McCourt.

Get him away from the bloody lesson. Go on, go on.

I'd say, Sir, did they have algebra in olden times in Ireland?

Mr. O'Halloran liked me, good boy, neat handwriting, always polite and obedient. He would put the chalk down, and from the way he sat at his desk and took his time before speaking you could see how happy he was to escape from algebra and Irish syntax. He'd say, Boys, you have every right to be proud of your ancestors. Long before the Greeks, even the Egyptians, your forefathers in this lovely land could capture the rays of the sun in the heart of winter and direct them to dark inner chambers for a few golden moments. They knew the ways of the heavenly bodies and that took them beyond algebra, beyond calculus, beyond, boys, oh, beyond beyond.

Sometimes, in the warm days of spring, he dozed off in his chair and we sat quietly, forty of us, waiting for him to wake, not even daring to leave the room if he slept past going-home time.

No. I'm not Scotch. I'm Irish.

Joey looks sincere. Oh, yeah? What's Irish?

Irish is whatever comes out of Ireland.

Like St. Patrick, right?

Well, no, not exactly. This leads to the telling of the story of St. Patrick, which keeps us away from the b-o-r-i-n-g English lesson, which leads to other questions.

Hey, mister. Everyone talk English over there in Ireland?

What kinda sports didja play?

You all Callies in Ireland?

Don't let them take over the classroom. Stand up to them. Show them who's in charge. Be firm or be dead. Take no shit. Tell them, Open your notebooks. Time for the spelling list.

Aw, teacher, aw, Gawd, aw man. Spelling. Spelling. Spelling. Do we haveta? They moan, B-o-r-i-n-g spelling list. They pretend to bang their foreheads on desks, bury their faces in their folded arms. They beg for the pass. Gotta go. Gotta go. Man, we thought you were a nice guy, young and all. Why do all these English teachers have to do the same old thing? Same old spelling lessons, same old vocabulary lessons, same old shit, excuse the language? Can't you tell us more about Ireland?

Yo, teacher man. . . . Joey again. Mouth to the rescue.

Joey, I told you my name is Mr. McCourt, Mr. McCourt, Mr. McCourt.

Yeah, yeah. So, mister, did you go out with girls in Ireland?

No, dammit. Sheep. We went out with sheep. What do you think we went out with?

The class explodes. They laugh, clutch their chests, nudge, elbow one another, pretend to fall out of their desks. This teacher. Crazy, man. Talks funny. Goes out with sheep. Lock up your sheep.

Excuse me. Open your notebooks, please. We have a spelling list to cover. Hysterics. Will sheep be on the list? Oh, man.

That smart-ass response was a mistake. There will be trouble. The goody-goody, the saint and the critic will surely report me: Oh, Mom, oh, Dad, oh, Mr. Principal, guess what teacher said in class today. Bad things about sheep.

I'm not prepared, trained or ready for this. It's not teaching. It has nothing to do with English literature, grammar, writing. When will I be strong enough to walk into the room, get their immediate attention and teach? Around this school there are quiet industrious classes where teachers are in command. In the cafeteria older teachers tell me, Yeah, it takes at least five years.

Next day the principal sends for me. He sits behind his desk, talking into the telephone, smoking a cigarette. He keeps saying, I'm sorry. It won't happen again. I'll speak to the person involved. New teacher, I'm afraid.

He puts the phone down. Sheep. What is this about sheep?

Sheep?

I dunno what I'm gonna do with you. There's a complaint you said "dammit" in class. I know you're just off the boat from an agricultural country and don't know the ropes, but you should have some common sense.

No, sir. Not off the boat. I've been here eight and a half years, including my two years in the army, not counting years of infancy in Brooklyn.

Well, look. First the sandwich, now the sheep. Damn phone ringing off the hook. Parents up in arms. I have to cover my ass. You're two days in the building and two days you're in the soup. How do you do it? If you'll excuse the expression you're inclined to screw up a bit. Why the hell did you have to tell these kids about the sheep?

I'm sorry. They kept asking me questions, and I was exasperated. They were only trying to keep me away from the spelling list.

That's it?

I thought the sheep thing was a bit funny at the time.

Oh, yeah, indeed. You standing there advocating bestiality. Thirteen parents are demanding you be fired. There are righteous people on Staten Island.

I was only joking.

No, young man. No jokes here. There's a time and place. When you say something in class they take you seriously. You're the teacher. You say you went out with sheep and they're going to swallow every word. They don't know the mating habits of the Irish.

I'm sorry.

This time I'll let it go. I'll tell the parents you're just an Irish immigrant off the boat. But I was born here. Could you be quiet for one minute and listen while I save your life, huh? This time I'll let it go. I won't put a letter in your file. You don't realize how serious it is to get a letter in your file. If you've got any ambition to rise in this system, principal, assistant principal, guidance counselor, the letter in the file will hold you back. It's the start of the long downward slide.

Sir, I don't want to be principal. I just want to teach.

Yeah, yeah. That's what they all say. You'll get over it. These kids will give you gray hair before you're thirty.

It was clear I was not cut out to be the purposeful kind of teacher who brushed aside all questions, requests, complaints, to get on with the well-planned lesson. That would have reminded me of that school in Limerick where the lesson was king and we were nothing. I was already dreaming of a school where teachers were guides and mentors, not taskmasters. I didn't have any particular philosophy of education except that I was uncomfortable with the bureaucrats, the higher-ups, who had escaped classrooms only to turn and bother the occupants of those classrooms, teachers and students. I never wanted to fill out their forms, follow their guidelines, administer their examinations, tolerate their snooping, adjust myself to their programs and courses of study.

If a principal had ever said, The class is yours, teacher, Do with it what you like, I would have said to my students, Push the chairs aside. Sit on the floor. Go to sleep.

What?

I said, Go to sleep.

Why?

Figure it out for yourself while you're lying there on the floor.

They'd lie on the floor and some would drift off. There would be giggling as boy wriggled closer to girl. Sleepers would snore sweetly. I'd stretch out with them on the floor and ask if anyone knew a lullaby. I know a girl would start and others would join. A boy might say, Man, what if the principal walked in. Yeah. The lullaby continues, a murmur around the room. Mr. McCourt, when are we getting up? He's told, Shush, man, and he shushes. The bell rings and they're slow off the floor. They leave the room, relaxed and puzzled. Please don't ask me why I'd have such a session. It must be the spirit that moves.

Frank McCourt is a Pultizer Prize–winning author of *Angela's Ashes* and *'Tis*.

2

The Green Monongahela

John Taylor Gatto

In the beginning I became a teacher without realizing it. At the time, I was growing up on the banks of the green Monongahela River forty miles southwest of Pittsburgh, and on the banks of that deep green and always mysterious river I became a student too, master of the flight patterns of blue dragonflies and cunning adversary of the iridescent ticks that infested the riverbank willows.

"Mind you watch the ticks, Jackie!" Grandmother Mossie would call as I headed for the riverbank, summer and winter, only a two-minute walk from Second Street, where I lived across the trolley tracks of Main Street and the Pennsylvania Railroad tracks that paralleled them. I watched the red and yellow ticks chewing holes in the pale green leaves as I ran to the riverbank. On the river I drank my first Iron City at eight, smoked every cigarette obtainable, and watched dangerous men and women make love there at night on blankets—all before I was twelve. It was my laboratory: I learned to watch closely and draw conclusions there.

How did the river make me a teacher? Listen. It was alive with paddle-wheel steamers in center channel, the turning paddles churning up clouds of white spray, making the green river boil bright orange where its chemical

---

NOTE: From *Dumbing Us Down: The Hidden Curriculum of Compulsory Schooling* by John Taylor Gatto. Copyright 1992 New Society Publishers (www.newsociety.com). Reprinted with permission.

undercurrent was troubled; from shore you could clearly hear the loud *thump thump thump* on the water. From all over town young boys ran gazing in awe. A dozen times a day. No one ever became indifferent to them because nothing important can ever really be boring. You can see the difference, can't you? Between those serious boats and the truly boring spacecraft of the past few decades, just flying junk without a purpose a boy can believe in; it's hard to feign an interest even now that I teach for a living and would like to pretend for the sake of the New York kids who won't have paddle-wheelers in their lives. The rockets are dull toys children in Manhattan put aside the day after Christmas, never to touch again; the riverboats were serious magic, clearly demarcating the world of boys from the world of men. Levi-Strauss would know how to explain.

In Monongahela by that river everyone was my teacher. Daily, it seemed to a boy, one of the mile-long trains would stop in town to take on water and coal or for some mysterious reason; the brakeman and engineer would step among snot-nosed kids and spin railroad yarns, let us run in and out of boxcars, over and under flatcars, tank cars, coal cars, and numbers of other specialty cars whose function we memorized as easily as we memorized enemy plane silhouettes. Once a year, maybe, we got taken into the caboose that reeked of stale beer to be offered a bologna on white bread sandwich. The anonymous men lectured, advised, and inspired the boys of Monongahela—it was as much their job as driving the trains.

Sometimes a riverboat would stop in mid-channel and discharge a crew, who would row to shore, lying their skiff to one of the willows. That was the excuse for every rickety skiff in the twelve-block-long town to fill up with kids, pulling like Vikings, sometimes with sticks instead of oars, to raid the "Belle of Pittsburgh" or "The Original River Queen." Some kind of natural etiquette was at work in Monongahela. The rules didn't need to be written down: if men had time they showed boys how to grow up. We didn't whine when our time was up—men had work to do—we understood that and scampered away, grateful for the flash of our own futures they had had time to reveal, however small it was.

I was arrested three times growing up in Monongahela, or rather, picked up by the police and taken to jail to await a visit from Pappy to spring me. I wouldn't trade those times for anything. The first time I was nine, caught on my belly under a parked car at night, half an hour after curfew; in 1943 blinds were always drawn in the Monongahela Valley for fear Hitler's planes would somehow find a way to reach across the Atlantic to our steel mills lining both banks of the river. The Nazis were apparently waiting for a worried mother to go searching for her child with a flashlight after curfew, then *whammo!* down would descend the Teutonic air fleet!

Charlie was the cop's name. Down to the lockup we went—no call to mother until Charlie diagrammed the deadly menace of Goering's Luftwaffe. What a geopolitics lesson that was! Another time I speared a goldfish in the town fishpond and was brought from jail to the library, where I was sentenced to read for a month about the lives of animals. Finally, on VJ Day—when the Japanese cried "Uncle!"—I accepted a dare and broke the window of the police cruiser with a slingshot. Confessing, I suffered my first encounter with employment to pay for the glass, becoming sweep-up boy in my grandfather's printing office at fifty cents a week.

After I went away to Cornell, I saw Monongahela and its green river only one more time, when I went there after my freshman year to give blood to my dying grandfather, who lay in the town hospital, as strong in his dying as he had ever been in his living. In another room my grandmother lay dying. Both passed within twenty-four hours, my grandad, Harry Taylor Zimmer, Sr., taking my blood to his grave in the cemetery there. My family moved again and again and again, but in my own heart I never left Monongahela, where I learned to teach from being taught by everyone in town, where I learned to work from being asked to shoulder my share of responsibility, even as a boy, and where I learned to find adventures I made myself from the everyday stuff around me—the river and the people who lived alongside it.

In 1964, I was making a lot of money. That's what I walked away from to become a teacher. I was a copywriter on the fast track in advertising, a young fellow with a knack for writing thirty-second television commercials. My work required about one full day a month to complete, the rest of the time being spent in power breakfasts, after-work martinis at Michael's Pub, keeping up with the shifting fortunes of about twenty agencies in order to gauge the right time to jump ship for more money, and endless parties that always seemed to culminate in colossal headaches.

It bothered me that all the urgencies of the job were generated externally, but it bothered me more that the work I was doing seemed to have very little importance—even to the people who were paying for it. Worst of all, the problems this work posed were cut from such a narrow spectrum that it was clear that past, present, and future were to be of a piece: a twenty-nine-year-old man's work was no different from a thirty-nine-year-old man's work, or a forty-nine-year-old man's work (though there didn't seem to be any forty-nine-year-old copywriters—I had no idea why not).

"I'm leaving," I said one day to the copy chief.

"Are you nuts, Jack? You'll get profit sharing this year. We can match any offer you've got. Leaving for who?"

"For nobody, Dan. I mean I'm going to teach junior high school."

"When you see your mother next, tell her for me she raised a moron. Christ! Are you going to be sorry! In New York City we don't have schools; we have pens for lost souls. Teaching is a scam, a welfare project for losers who can't do anything else!"

Round and round I went with my advertising colleagues for a few days. Their scorn only firmed my resolve; the riverboats and trains of Monongahela were working inside me. I needed something to do that wasn't absurd more than I needed another party or a new abstract number in my bankbook.

And so I became a junior high school substitute teacher, working the beat from what's now Lincoln Center to Columbia, my alma mater, and from Harlem to the South Bronx. After three months the dismal working conditions, the ugly rooms, the torn books, the repeated instances of petty complaints from authorities, the bells, the buzzers, the drab teacher food in the cafeterias, the unpressed clothing, the inexplicable absence of conversation about children among the teachers (to this day, after twenty-six years in the business, I can honestly say I have never once heard an extended conversation about children or about teaching theory in any teachers' rooms I've been in) had just about done me in.

In fact, on the very first day I taught I was attacked by a boy waving a chair above his head. It happened in the infamous junior school Wadleigh, on 113th Street. I was given the eighth grade typing class—seventy-five students and typewriters—with this one injunction: "Under no circumstances are you to allow them to type. You lack the proper license. Is that understood?" A man named Mr. Bash said that to me.

It couldn't have taken more than sixty seconds from the time I closed the door and issued the order not to type for one hundred and fifty hands to snake under the typewriter covers and begin to type. But not all at once— that would have been too easy. First, three machines began to *clack clack* from the right rear. Quick, who were the culprits? I would race to the corner screaming *stop!*—when suddenly, from behind my back, three other machines would begin! Whirling as only a young man can do, I caught one small boy in the act. Then, to a veritable symphony of machines clicking, bells ringing, platens being thrown, I hoisted the boy from his chair and announced at the top of my foolish lungs I would make an example of this miscreant.

"Look out!" a girl shouted, and I turned toward her voice just in time to see a large brother of the little fellow I held heading toward me with a chair raised above his head. Releasing his brother, I seized a chair myself and raised it aloft. A standoff! We regarded each other at a distance of about ten feet for what seemed forever, the class jeering and howling, when the room door opened and Assistant Principal Bash, the very man who'd given the no-typing order, appeared.

"Mr. Gatto, have these children been typing?"

"No, sir," I said, lowering my chair, "but I think they want to. What do you suggest they do instead?"

He looked at me for signs of impudence or insubordination for a second, then, as if thinking better of rebuking this upstart, he said merely, "Fall back on your resources," and left the room.

Most of the kids laughed—they'd seen this drama enacted before.

The situation was defused, but silently I dubbed Wadleigh the "Death School." Stopping by the office on my way home, I told the secretary not to call me again if they needed a sub.

The very next morning my phone rang at 6:30. "Are you available for work today, Mr. Gatto?" said the voice briskly.

"Who is this?" I asked suspiciously. (Ten schools were using me for sub work in those days, and each identified itself at once.)

"The law clearly states, Mr. Gatto, that we do not have to tell you who we are until you tell us whether you are available for work."

"Never mind," I bellowed, "there's only one school who'd pull such crap! The answer is no! I am never available to work in your pigpen school!" And I slammed the receiver back onto its cradle.

But the truth was none of the sub assignments were boat rides; schools had an uncanny habit of exploiting substitutes and providing no support for their survival. It's likely I'd have returned to advertising if a little girl, desperate to free herself from an intolerable situation, hadn't drawn me into her personal school nightmare and shown me how I could find my own significance in teaching, just as those strong men in the riverboats and trains had found their own significance, a currency all of us need for our self-esteem.

It happened this way. Occasionally, I'd get a call from an elementary school. This particular day it was a third grade assignment at a school on 107th Street, which in those days was nearly one hundred percent non-Hispanic in its teaching staff and 99% Hispanic in its student body.

Like many desperate teachers, I killed most of the day listening to the kids read, one after another, and expending most of my energy trying to shut the audience up. This class had a very low ranking, and no one was able to put more than three or four words together without stumbling. All of a sudden, though, a little girl named Milagros sailed through a selection without a mistake. After class I called her over to my desk and asked why she was in this class of bad readers. She replied that "they" (the administration) wouldn't let her out because, as they explained to her mother, she was really a bad reader who had fantasies of being a better reader than she was. "But look, Mr. Gatto, my brother is in the sixth grade, and I can read every word in his English book better than he can!"

I was a little intrigued, but truthfully not much. Surely the authorities knew what they were doing. Still, the little girl seemed so frustrated I invited her to calm down and read to me from the sixth grade book. I explained that if she did well, I would take her case to the principal. I expected nothing.

Milagros, on the other hand, expected justice. Diving into "The Devil and Daniel Webster," she polished off the first two pages without a gulp. My God, I thought, this is a real reader. What is she doing here? Well, maybe it was a simple accident, easily corrected. I sent her home, promising to argue her case. Little did I suspect what a hornet's nest my request to have Milagros moved to a better class would stir up.

"You have some nerve, Mr. Gatto. I can't remember when a substitute ever told me how to run my school before. Have you taken specialized courses in reading?"

"No."

"Well then, suppose you leave these matters to the experts!"

"But the kid can read!"

"What do you suggest?"

"I suggest you test her, and if she isn't a dummy, get her out of the class she's in!"

"I don't like your tone. None of our children are dummies, Mr. Gatto. And you will find that girls like Milagros have many ways to fool amateurs like yourself. This is a matter of a child having memorized one story. You can see if I had to waste my time arguing with people like you I'd have no time left to run a school."

But, strangely, I felt self-appointed as the girl's champion, even though I'd probably never see her again.

I insisted, and the principal finally agreed to test Milagros herself the following Wednesday after school. I made it a point to tell the little girl the next day. By that time I'd come to think that the principal was probably right— she'd memorized one story—but I still warned her she'd need to know the vocabulary from the whole advanced reader and be able to read any story the principal picked, without hesitation. My responsibility was over, I told myself.

The following Wednesday after school I waited in the room for Milagros' ordeal to be over. At 3:30 she shyly opened the door of the room.

"How'd it go?" I asked.

"I don't know," she answered, "but I didn't make any mistakes. Mrs. Hefferman was very angry, I could tell."

I saw Mrs. Hefferman, the principal, early the next morning before school opened. "It seems we've made a mistake with Milagros," she said curtly. "She will be moved, Mr. Gatto. Her mother has been informed."

Several weeks later, when I got back to the school to sub, Milagros dropped by, telling me she was in the fast class now and doing very well. She also gave me a sealed card. When I got home that night, I found it, unopened, in my suitcoat pocket. I opened it and saw a gaudy birthday card with blue flowers on it. Opening the card, I read, "A teacher like you cannot be found. Signed, Your student, Milagros."

That simple sentence made me a teacher for life. It was the first praise I ever heard in my working existence that had any meaning. I never forgot it, though I never saw Milagros again and only heard of her again in 1988, twenty-four years later. Then one day I picked up a newspaper and read:

OCCUPATIONAL TEACHER AWARD

Milagros Maldonado, United Federation of Teachers, has won the Distinguished Occupational Teacher Award of the State Education Department for "demonstrated achievement and exemplary professionalism." A secretarial studies teacher at Norman Thomas High School, New York City, from which she graduated, Miss Maldonado was selected as a Manhattan Teacher of the Year in 1985 and was nominated the following year for the Woman of Conscience Award given by the National Council of Women.

Ah, Milagros, is it just possible that I was your Monongahela River? No matter, a teacher like you cannot be found.

John Taylor Gatto is an author and former New York City and New York State Teacher of the Year.

3

Death at an Early Age

The Destruction of the Hearts and Minds of Negro Children in the Boston Public Schools

Jonathan Kozol

Stephen is eight years old. A picture of him standing in front of the bulletin board on Arab bedouins shows a little light-brown person staring with unusual concentration at a chosen spot upon the floor. Stephen is tiny, desperate, unwell. Sometimes he talks to himself. He moves his mouth as if he were talking. At other times he laughs out loud in class for no apparent reason. He is also an indescribably mild and unmalicious child. He cannot do any of his school work very well. His math and reading are poor. In Third Grade he was in a class that had substitute teachers much of the year. Most of the year before that, he had a row of substitute teachers too. He is in the Fourth Grade now but his work is barely at the level of the Second. Nobody has complained about the things that have happened to Stephen because he does not have any mother or father. Stephen is a ward of the State of Massachusetts and, as such, he has been placed in the home of

NOTE: "Chapter One," from *Death at an Early Age* by Jonathan Kozol, copyright 1967, 1985, renewed 1995 by Jonathan Kozol. Used by permission of Plume, an imprint of Penguin Group (USA), Inc.

some very poor people who do not want him now that he is not a baby any more. The money that they are given to pay his expenses every week does not cover the other kind of expense—the more important kind which is the immense emotional burden that is continually at stake. Stephen often comes into school badly beaten. If I ask him about it, he is apt to deny it because he does not want us to know first-hand what a miserable time he has. Like many children, and many adults too, Stephen is far more concerned with hiding his abased condition from the view of the world than he is with escaping that condition. He lied to me first when I asked him how his eye got so battered. He said it happened from being hit by accident when somebody opened up the door. Later, because it was so bruised and because I questioned him, he admitted that it was his foster mother who had flung him out onto the porch. His eye had struck the banister and it had closed and purpled. The children in the class were frightened to see him. I thought that they also felt some real compassion, but perhaps it was just shock.

Although Stephen did poorly in his school work, there was one thing he could do well: he was a fine artist. He made delightful drawings. The thing about them that was good, however, was also the thing that got him into trouble. For they were not neat and orderly and organized but entirely random and casual, messy, somewhat unpredictable, seldom according to the instructions he had been given, and—in short—real drawings. For these drawings, Stephen received considerable embarrassment at the hands of the Art Teacher. This person was a lady no longer very young who had some rather fixed values and opinions about children and about teaching. Above all, her manner was marked by unusual confidence. She seldom would merely walk into our class but seemed always to sweep into it. Even for myself, her advent, at least in the beginning of the year, used to cause a wave of anxiety, for she came into our class generally in a mood of self-assurance and of almost punitive restlessness which never made one confident but which generally made me wonder what I had done wrong. In dealing with Stephen, I thought she could be quite overwhelming.

The Art Teacher's most common technique for art instruction was to pass out mimeographed designs and then to have the pupils fill them in according to a dictated or suggested color plan. An alternate approach was to stick up on the wall or on the blackboard some of the drawings on a particular subject that had been done in the previous years by predominantly white classes. These drawings, neat and ordered and very uniform, would be the models for our children. The art lesson, in effect, would be to copy what had been done before, and the neatest and most accurate reproductions of the original drawings would be the ones that would win the highest approval from the teacher. None of the new drawings, the Art Teacher would tell me frequently, was comparable to the work that had been done in former times, but at least the children in the class could try to copy good examples. The fact that they were being asked to copy something in which they could not believe because it was not of them and did not in any way correspond to their own interests did not occur to the Art Teacher, or if it did occur she did not say it. Like a number of other teachers at my school and in other schools of the same nature, she possessed a remarkable self-defense apparatus, and anything that seriously threatened to disturb her point of view could be effectively denied.

How did a pupil like Stephen react to a teacher of this sort? Alone almost out of the entire class, I think that he absolutely turned off his signals while she was speaking and withdrew to his own private spot. At his desk he would sit silently while the Art Teacher was talking and performing. With a pencil, frequently stubby and end-bitten, he would scribble and fiddle and cock his head and whisper to himself throughout the time that the Art Teacher was going on. At length, when the art lesson officially began, he would perhaps push aside his little drawing and try the paint and paper that he had been given, usually using the watercolors freely and the paintbrush sloppily and a little bit defiantly and he would come up with things that certainly were delightful and personal and private, and full of his own nature.

If Stephen began to fiddle around during a lesson, the Art Teacher generally would not notice him at first. When she did, both he and I and the children around him would prepare for trouble. For she would go at his desk with something truly like a vengeance and would shriek at him in a way that carried terror. "Give me that! Your paints are all muddy! You've made it a mess. Look at what he's done! He's mixed up the colors! I don't know why we waste good paper on this child!" Then: "Garbage! Junk! He gives me garbage and junk and garbage is one thing I will not have." Now I thought that that garbage and junk was very nearly the only real artwork in the class. I do not know very much about painting, but I know enough to know that the Art Teacher did not know much about it either and that, furthermore, she did not know or care anything at all about the way in which you can destroy a human being. Stephen, in many ways already dying, died a second and third and fourth and final death before her anger.

Sometimes when the Art Teacher was not present in our classroom, and when no other supervisory person happened to be there, Stephen would sneak up to me, maybe while I was sitting at my desk and going over records or totaling up the milk money or checking a paper, so that I would not see him until he was beside me. Then, hastily, secretly, with mystery, with fun, with something out of a spy movie, he would hand me one of his small drawings. The ones I liked the most, to be honest, were often not completely his own, but pictures which he had copied out of comic books and then elaborated, amended, fiddled with, and frequently added to by putting under them some kind of mock announcement ("I AM THE GREATEST AND THE STRONGEST") which might have been something he had wished. I think he must have seen something special and valuable about comic books, because another thing that he sometimes did was just cut out part of a comic book story that he liked and bring it in to me as a present. When he did this, as with his paintings and drawings, he usually would belittle his gift by crumpling it up or folding it up very tiny before he handed it to me. It was a way, perhaps, of saying that he didn't value it too much (although it was clear that he did value it a great deal) in case I didn't like it.

If the Art Teacher came upon us while he was slipping me a picture he had drawn, both he and I were apt to get an effective lashing out. Although she could be as affectionate and benevolent as she liked with other children, with Stephen she was almost always scathing in her comments and made no attempt at seeming mild. "He wants to show you his little scribbles because he wants to use you and your affection for him and make you pity him but we don't have time for that. Keep him away. If you don't, I'll do it. I don't want him getting near you during class."

For weeks after that outburst, when we had been caught in the act of friendship, he stopped coming near me. He stopped bringing me his drawings. He kept to his seat and giggled, mumbled, fiddled. Possibly he felt that he was doing this for my sake in order not to get me into further trouble. Then one day for a brief second he got up his nerve and darted forward. He crumpled up some paper in his fist and handed it to me quickly and got back into his chair. The crumpled paper turned out to be more funnies that he had painstakingly cut out. Another time he dropped a ball of crunched-up math paper on my desk. On the paper he had written out his age—eight years old—and his birthday—which I seem to remember came at Christmas. I also remember that once he either whispered to me or wrote to me on a note that he weighed sixty pounds. This information, I thought, came almost a little boastfully, even though it obviously isn't a lot to weigh if you are almost nine, and I wondered about it for a time until it occurred to me that maybe it was just one of very few things that he knew about himself, one of the half dozen measurable facts that had anything to do with him in the world, and so—like all people, using as best they can whatever they've got—he had to make the most of it.

I think that much of his life, inwardly and outwardly, must have involved a steady and, as it turned out, inwardly at least, a losing battle to survive, he battled for his existence and, like many defenseless humans, he had to use whatever odd little weapons came to hand. Acting up at school was part of it. He was granted so little attention that he must have panicked repeatedly about the possibility that, with a few slight mistakes, he might simply stop existing or being seen at all. I imagine this is one reason why he seemed so often to invite or court a tongue-lashing or a whipping. Doing anything at all that would make a teacher mad at him, scream at him, strike at him, would also have been a kind of ratification, even if it was painful, that he actually was there. Other times, outside of school, he might do things like pulling a fire alarm lever and then having the satisfaction of hearing the sirens and seeing the fire engines and knowing that it was all of his own doing and to his own credit, so that at least he would have proof in that way that his hands and his arm muscles and his mischievous imagination actually did count for something measurable in the world. Maybe the only way in which he could ever impinge upon other people's lives was by infuriating them, but that at least was something. It was better than not having any use at all.

I remember that the Art Teacher once caught him out in the back, in the hallway, in front of a big floor-length coat-closet mirror. She grabbed him by the arm and pulled him into the classroom and announced to me and to the children in the classroom that he was "just standing there and making faces at himself and staring." While she talked, he looked away and examined the floor with his eyes, as he did so often, because he was embarrassed by being exposed like that. I thought it was needlessly cruel of her to have hauled him before the children in that manner, and surely a little hesitation on her part might have given her a moment to think why he might *like* to see himself in a mirror, even if it was only to see a scratched reflection. I didn't think it was shameful for him to be doing that, even to be making funny faces. It seemed rather normal and explicable to me that he might want to check up on his existence. Possibly it was a desperate act, and certainly a curious one, but I do not think it was unnatural. What did seem to me to be unnatural was the unusual virulence of the Art Teacher's reaction.

Another time, seeing him all curled up in one of the corners, I went over to him and tried to get him to look up at me and smile and talk. He would not do that. He remained all shriveled up there and he would not cry and would not laugh. I said to him: "Stephen, if you curl up like that and will not even look up at me, it will just seem as if you wanted to make me think you were a little rat." He looked down at himself hurriedly and then he looked up at me and he chuckled grotesquely and he said, with a pitiful little laugh: "I know I couldn't be a rat, Mr. Kozol, because a rat has got to have a little tail!" I never forgot that and I told it later to a child psychiatrist, whose answer to me made it more explicit and more clear: "It is the absence of a tail which convinces him that he has not yet become a rat." Perhaps that is overly absolute and smacks a bit of the psychiatric dogmatism that seems so difficult to accept because it leaves so little room for uncertainty or doubt; yet in this one instance I do not really think that it carries the point too far. For it is the Boston schoolteachers themselves who for years have been speaking of the Negro children in their charge as "animals" and the school building that houses them as "a zoo." And it is well known by now how commonly the injustices and depredations of the Boston school system have compelled its Negro pupils to regard themselves with something less than the dignity and respect of human beings. The toll that this took was probably greater upon Stephen than it might have been upon some other children. But the price that it exacted was paid ultimately by every child, and in the long run I am convinced that the same price has been paid by every teacher too.

Jonathan Kozol is an author, winner of the National Book Award, and a former teacher.

4

Why Teach?

Herbert Kohl

There are many reasons that lead people to choose elementary and secondary school teaching. Some people choose teaching because they enjoy being with young people and watching them grow. Others need to be around young people and let their students grow for them. Teaching for some is a family tradition, a craft that one naturally masters and a world that surrounds one from childhood. For others teaching is magical because they have had magical teachers whose roles they want to assume. Teaching can be a way of sharing power, of convincing people to value what you value, or to explore the world with you or through you.

There are some cynical reasons for going into teaching which were much more prevalent when getting a job was not difficult. For example, for some people teaching becomes a matter of temporary convenience, of taking a job which seems respectable and not too demanding while going to law school, supporting a spouse through professional or graduate school, scouting around for a good business connection, or merely marking time while figuring out what one really wants to do as an adult. For others teaching is a jumping-off point into administration, research, or supervision.

Many student teachers I have known over the last five years are becoming teachers to negate the wounds they received when they were in school. They want to counter the racism, the sexual put-downs, all the other humiliations

NOTE: From *On Teaching* by Herbert R. Kohl, copyright 1976 by Herbert R. Kohl. Used by permission of Schocken Books, a division of Random House, Inc.

they experienced with new, freer ways of teaching and learning. They want to be teachers to protect and nurture people younger than they who have every likelihood of being damaged by the schools. Some of these people come from poor or oppressed communities, and their commitment to the children is a commitment to the community of their parents, brothers and sisters, and their own children as well. Others, mostly from white middle- or upper-class backgrounds, have given up dialogue with their parents and rejected the community they grew up in. Teaching for them becomes a means of searching for ways of connecting with a community they can care for and serve.

There were a number of reasons that led me to choose elementary school teaching. For one, I never wanted to put my toys away and get on with the serious business of being an adult. I enjoy playing games, building things that have no particular purpose or value beyond themselves, trying painting, sculpting, macrame without becoming obsessed by them. I enjoy moving from subject to subject, from a math problem to a design problem, from bead collecting to the classification of mollusks. Specialization does not interest me, and teaching elementary school makes it possible for me to explore many facets of the world and share what I learn. My self-justification is that the games I play and the things I explore all contribute to making a curriculum that will interest and engage my students.

I guess also I became a teacher of young children initially because I thought they were purer, more open, and less damaged than I was. They were the saviors—they could dare to be creative where I was inhibited; they could write well because they didn't know what good writing was supposed to be; they could learn with ease, whereas I was overridden with anxiety over grades and tests. I never forgot the time in high school when I was informed that I missed making Arista, the national high school honor society, by 0.1 of a point. I went into the boys' bathroom and cried, the first time I had cried since being a baby. Neither Hitler's horrors nor the deaths of relatives and friends could cause me to cry because I was a male and was too proud to show sadness and weakness. Yet 0.1 of a grade point could bring tears and self-hatred and feelings of inferiority. And what if I'd made it—would I laugh at my friends' tears because they missed by 0.1 of a point just as they did at me? There is no reward on either side of that cruel system.

When I became a teacher, some of my dreams of free development for my own students came true—they could be open and creative. But they also could be closed, destructive, nasty, manipulating—all the things I wanted to avoid in the adult world. It was important to sort out the romance of teaching from the realities of teaching and discover whether, knowing the problems, the hard work and frustration, it still made sense to teach. For me the answer has been "yes," but there are still times I wish I'd chosen some easier vocation.

Everyone who goes into teaching, even temporarily, has many reasons for choosing to spend five hours a day with young people. These reasons are often unarticulated and more complex than one imagines. Yet they have significant effects upon everyday work with students and on the satisfaction and strength the teacher gets from that work. Consequently, it makes sense, if you are thinking of becoming a teacher, to begin questioning yourself and understanding what you expect from teaching and what you are willing to give to it.

It also is of value to understand what type of children, what age, what setting is most sensible for your temperament and skills. Simple mistakes like teaching children that are too young or too old can destroy promising teachers. I had a friend who was teaching first grade and having a miserable time of it. The class was out of order, the students paid no attention to what she said, and she couldn't understand what the children were talking about. One day in anger, she blurted out to me that her major frustration was that she couldn't hold a good conversation with her class. She wanted to talk about civil rights, racism, about ways of reconstructing our society, about poverty and oppression.

She wanted to read poetry with the children, expose them to music. She prepared each class for hours, put herself into the work, cared about the children—and yet things kept on getting worse. What she wanted and needed from her six-year-olds was simply beyond them. I suggested that she try junior high if she wanted dialogue and challenge from her students. First grade was a mistake. The next year she transferred to one of the most difficult junior high schools in New York City, where she immediately felt at home. She was in the right place—what she offered could be used by the students, and therefore they could reward her with the exchange she needed.

There are a number of questions people thinking of becoming teachers might ask themselves in order to clarify their motives and focus on the type of teaching situations that could make sense for them. These questions do not have simple answers. Sometimes they cannot be answered until one has taught for a while. But I think it makes sense to keep them in mind while considering whether you actually want to teach and then, if you do, during training and the first few years of work.

1. What reasons do you give yourself for wanting to teach? Are they all negative (e.g., because the schools are oppressive, or because I was damaged, or because I need a job and working as a teacher is more respectable than working as a cab driver or salesperson)? What are the positive reasons for wanting to teach? Is there any pleasure to be gained from teaching? Knowledge? Power?

As an elaboration on this, there is another similar question:

2. Why do you want to spend so much time with young people? Are you afraid of adults? Intimidated by adult company? Fed up with the competition and coldness of business and the university? Do you feel more comfortable with children? Have you spent much time with children recently, or are you mostly fantasizing how they would behave? Before deciding to become a teacher, it makes sense to spend time with young people of different ages at camp, as a tutor, or as a playground supervisor. I have found it valuable to spend time at playgrounds and observe children playing with each other or relating to their parents or teachers. One day watch five-, ten-, fifteen-year-olds on the playground or the street, and try to see how they are alike and how they are different. The more you train your eye to observe young people's behavior, the easier it will be to pick up attitudes and feelings and relationships in your own classroom.

Elaborating on the question of why spend so much time with young people, it is important to ask . . .

3. What do you want from the children? Do you want them to do well on tests? Learn particular subject matter? Like each other? Like you? How much do you need to have students like you? Are you afraid to criticize them or set limits on their behavior because they might be angry with you? Do you consider yourself one of the kids? Is there any difference in your mind between your role and that of your prospective students?

Many young teachers are not sure of themselves as adults, feel very much like children and cover over a sense of their own powerlessness with the rhetoric of equality. They tell their students that they are all equal and then are surprised when their students walk all over them or show them no respect. If students have to go to school, if the teacher is paid and the students are not, if the young expect to learn something from the older in order to become more powerful themselves, then the teacher who pretends to be an equal of the student is both a hypocrite and a disappointment in the students' eyes. This does not mean that the teacher doesn't learn with or from the students, nor does it mean that the teacher must try to coerce the students into learning or be the source of all authority. It does mean, however, that the teacher ought to have some knowledge or skills to share, mastery of a subject that the students haven't already encountered and might be interested in. This leads to the next question:

4. What do you know that you can teach to or share with your students? Too many young people coming out of college believe that they

do not know anything worth sharing or at least feel they haven't learned anything in school worth it. Teacher training usually doesn't help since it concentrates on "teaching skills" rather than the content of what might be learned. Yet there is so much young people will respond to if the material emerges out of problems that challenge them and if the solutions can be developed without constant judging and testing. I have found that young people enjoy working hard, pushing and challenging themselves. What they hate is having their self-esteem tied up in learning and regurgitating material that bores them. Constant testing interferes with learning.

The more you know, the easier teaching becomes. A skilled teacher uses all his or her knowledge and experience in the service of building a curriculum each year for the particular individuals that are in the class. If you cannot think of any particular skills you have, but just like being with children, don't go right into teaching. Find other ways of spending time with young people while you master some skills that you believe are worth sharing.

Here is a partial list of things one could learn: printing; working with wood, plastic, fabrics, metal; how to run a store; making or repairing cars, shoes, boats, airplanes; playing and teaching cards, board, dice, ball games; playing and composing music; understanding ways of calculating and the use and construction of computers; using closed circuit TV; making films; taking pictures; understanding history, especially history that explains part of the present; knowing about animals and plants, understanding something of the chemistry of life; knowing the law; understanding how to use or care for one's body.

These subjects are intrinsically interesting to many students and can be used as well in teaching the so-called basic skills of reading, writing, and math, which are themselves no more than tools that extend people's power and make some aspects of the world more accessible. Too often these basic skills are taught in isolation from interesting content, leaving students wondering what use phonics or set theory could possibly have in their lives. It is not good enough to tell the class that what they are learning now will be of use when they are grown-ups. Six-year-olds and ten-year-olds have immediate interests, and reading and math ought to be tied to these interests, which range all the way from learning to make and build things to learning to play games and master comic books and fix bicycles and make money and cook and find out about other people's feelings and lives—the list can go on and on. The more time you spend informally with young children, the more you will learn about their interests. Listening carefully and following up on what you hear are skills a teacher has to cultivate. If students are interested in paper airplanes, it is more sensible to build a unit around flying than to ban them and assume police functions.

5. Getting more specific, a prospective teacher ought to consider what age youngster he or she feels greatest affinity toward or most comfortable with. There are some adults who are afraid of high school– or junior high school–aged people (thirteen- to seventeen-year-olds), while others are terrified at the idea of being left alone in a room with twenty-four six-year-olds. Fear of young people is neither unnatural nor uncommon in our culture. This is especially true in the schools, where undeclared warfare between the adults and the children defines much of the social climate. As long as young people feel constantly tested and judged by their teacher and have to experience the humiliation of their own or their friends' failures, they try to get even in any ways they can. Teachers who try to be kind often find themselves taken advantage of, while those who assume a strict stand are constantly tricked and mocked. It takes time and experience to win the respect of young people and not be considered their enemy in the context of a traditional American school.

It is very difficult to feel at ease in a classroom, to spend five hours with young people, and not emerge wiped out or exhausted at the end of the day. This is especially true if one is mismatched with the students.

Great patience and humor, an ease with physical contact, and an ability to work with one's hands as well as one's mouth are needed for teachers of five- and six-year-olds. A lack of sexual prudery is almost a prerequisite for junior high school teachers, while physical and personal confidence and the love of some subject make work with high school students much easier.

This does not mean that an adult shouldn't take chances working with students whose age poses a problem. I know this year has been one of the most fulfilling of my teaching years, and yet I was full of anxiety about my ability to be effective with five- and six-year-olds after working with twelve- to eighteen-year-olds for twelve years. I taught myself to be patient, learned to work with my hands, to play a lot, to expect change to develop slowly. The students' ability to express affection or dislike openly and physically moved and surprised me, and initially their energy exhausted me. I must have lost fifteen pounds the first month, just trying to keep up with them.

One way of discovering what age youngster to begin working with is to visit a lot of schools. Try to find teachers you like and respect, and spend a few days working alongside them. Don't visit for an hour or two. It is important to stay all day (or if you have time, all week) to get a sense of the flow of time and energy working with that age person involves. Of course, your rhythm as a teacher might be different, but it is important to have a sense of what it is like to be with young people all day before becoming a teacher.

6. Before becoming a teacher it is important to examine one's attitudes toward racial and class differences. Racism is part of the heritage of white Americans, and though it can be mostly unlearned, it manifests itself in many subtle ways. Some white teachers are overtly condescending toward black and brown and red children, give them crayons instead of books. Others are more subtly condescending—they congratulate themselves on caring enough to work in a ghetto, choose one or two favorite students and put the rest down as products of a bad environment. They consider themselves liberal, nonracist, and yet are repelled by most of their students while believing that they are "saving" a few. There are ways of picking up racist attitudes in one's own way of talking. When a teacher talks about his or her pupils as "them" or "these kind of children," or when a favorite pupil is described as "not like the rest of them," one is in the presence of a racist attitude. Accompanying this attitude is usually an unarticulated fear of the children. I have seen white kindergarten teachers treat poor black five-year-old boys as if they were nineteen, carried guns and knives, and had criminal intentions at all times. Needless to say, this sort of adult attitude confuses and profoundly upsets the child. It also causes the adult to ignore acts that should otherwise be prevented. Many white teachers in ghetto schools claim they are being permissive and believe in allowing their students freedom when it would be closer to the truth to say that they are afraid that their students will beat them up and that they are afraid to face the moral rage their students have from being treated in brutal and racist ways. When a student destroys a typewriter or brutalizes a smaller student, that is not an acceptable or humane use of freedom.

Young teachers have a hard time knowing how and when to be firm and when to be giving. This becomes even more complex when the teacher is white, of liberal persuasion, afraid of physical violence, and teaching a class of poor children who are not white.

However, fear is not limited to white-nonwhite situations. Many middle-class people have attitudes toward poor people in general that are manifested in the classroom in ways very close to the racist attitudes described above. Poverty is looked upon as a disease that one does not want to have contact with. Many teachers have a hard time touching poor children, as if somehow the poverty can be spread by physical contact. Then there are the condescending liberal attitudes toward "saving" a few good students from the general condition of poverty, as if the rest got what they deserve.

Prospective teachers, especially those who might choose or be assigned to work with poor or nonwhite students, have to examine their own attitudes toward class and race. If these people come from isolated white middle-class communities, I would suggest they move into a mixed urban community and live and work there before becoming teachers. Then they might be able to see their students as individuals rather than as representatives of a class or race. And they might also develop insight into the different ways people learn and teach each other and themselves. Good teaching requires an understanding and respect of the strengths of one's pupils, and this cannot develop if they and their parents are alien to one's nonschool experience.

7. Another, perhaps uncomfortable, question a prospective teacher ought to ask him- or herself is what sex-based motives he or she has for wanting to work with young people. Do you want to enable young boys or girls to become the boys or girls you could never be? To, for example, free the girls of the image of prettiness and quietness and encourage them to run and fight, and on an academic level, mess about with science and get lost in the abstractions of math? Or to encourage boys to write poetry, play with dolls, let their fantasies come out, and not feel abnormal if they enjoy reading or acting or listening to music?

Dealing with sex is one of the most difficult things teachers who care to have all their students develop fully have to learn how to manage. Often children arrive at school as early as kindergarten with clear ideas of what is proper behavior for boys and girls. The teacher has to be sensitive to parentally and culturally enforced sex roles that schools traditionally enforce, and be able to lead children to choose what they want to learn, free of those encumbrances.

There are other problems teachers have to sort out that are sexual rather than sex-based. Many male teachers enjoy flirting with female students and using flirtation as a means of controlling the girls. Similarly, some female teachers try to seduce male students into learning. All these exchanges are covert—a gesture, a look, a petulant or joking remark.

Children take adult affection very seriously, and often what is play or dalliance on the part of the adult becomes the basis of endless fantasy and expectation on the part of the child. The issue exists in the early grades, but is much more overt on the high school level, where young teachers often naively express affection and concern, which students interpret as sexual overtures (which in some cases they might actually be, however unclear to the teacher).

Entering into an open relationship with a student is another issue altogether. Obviously, love is not bound to age or status. One should be wary, however, of confusing love with conquest and manipulation, but these problems are not limited to one's life as a teacher.

A final question that should be asked with respect to sex in the classroom: do you need to get even with one sex, as a group, for real or fancied injuries you experienced? Do you dislike boys or girls as a group? Do you feel that the girls were always loved too much? That the boys brutalized you and need to learn a lesson? That somehow you have to get even in your classroom for an injury you suffered as a child? There are many good reasons for not becoming a teacher, and the need to punish others for a hurt you suffered is certainly one.

It might seem that I'm being harsh or cynical by raising questions about motives for teaching and suggesting that there are circumstances in which a person either should not become a teacher or should wait a while. If anything, these questions are too easy and can unfortunately be put aside with facile, self-deceiving answers. But teaching young people—i.e., helping them become sane, powerful, self-respecting, and loving adults—is a very serious and difficult job in a culture as oppressive and confused as ours, and needs strong and self-critical people.

There are other questions that ought to be considered. These might seem less charged, but are not less important.

8. What kind of young people do you want to work with? There are a number of children with special needs that can be assisted by adults with particular qualities. For example, there are some severely disturbed children— children whose behavior is bizarre, who are not verbal, who might not yet be toilet-trained at nine or ten, who might be engaged in dialogue for hours at a time with creatures you cannot perceive. My first experience was at a school for severely disturbed children very much like those described above. I liked the children, but lasted only six months since I didn't have the patience. I needed them to recognize and engage me, even through defiance. I couldn't bear their silence or removal, their unrelieved pain. As soon as I changed schools and began to work with normal, though angry and defiant, young people, I felt at home.

My wife, Judy, is different. She has the patience to live with small increments of change, is calm and gentle and nonthreatening to remote and scared children. She feels much more at home in silent or remote worlds than I do, and is an excellent teacher of disturbed children. It is a matter of knowing who you are and what the children need.

These same questions should be raised by people thinking of working with deaf, blind, or physically damaged people. Who are they? What is the world they live in? How can I serve them?

Let me illustrate a perverse way of going about deciding how to serve people in order to point toward a more healthy way of functioning. For a long time most schools for deaf children were controlled by nondeaf teachers, parents, and administrators who advocated the oral, rather than the manual, tradition. The oral tradition maintained that it was necessary for deaf individuals to learn to speak instead of depending on sign language. Many oralist schools prohibited their students from using sign language, and some professionals within that tradition maintained that sign language was not a "real" language at all, but some degenerate or primitive form of communication. All these prohibitions were to no avail—deaf children learned signing from each other and used it when the teachers' backs were turned. Many deaf adults trained in oralist schools ended up despising the language they were forced to learn and retreated into an all—deaf world where communication was in signs. Recently things have begun to change—sign language has been shown to be an expressive, sophisticated language with perhaps even greater potential for communication than oral language. A deaf-power movement has developed, which insists that teachers of the deaf respond to the needs of deaf adults and children. It is no longer possible to tell deaf people what they must learn from outside the community. To teach within a deaf community (and, in fact, in all communities) requires understanding the world people live in and responding to their needs as they articulate them. This does not mean that the teacher should be morally or politically neutral. Rather, it means that being a teacher does not put an individual in a position of forcing his or her values on students or community. A teacher must engage in dialogue with the students and parents if he or she hopes to change them—and be open to change as well. Many teachers have been educated in communities they initially thought they would educate.

9. Some people get along well in crowds and others function best with small groups or single individuals. Before becoming a classroom teacher, it is important to ask oneself what the effect is on one's personality of spending a lot of time with over twenty people in the same room. Some of the best teachers I know do not feel at ease or work effectively with more than a dozen students at a time. With those dozen, however, they are unusually effective. There are other people who have a gift for working on a one-to-one basis with students no one else seems to reach. There are ways to prepare oneself for individual or small-group work—as skills specialist, remedial teacher, learning disabilities specialist, and so forth. There are also schools where it is possible to work with small groups as a teacher. Once you decide how you want to begin to work in a school, then you can look around and try to discover a situation in which you can be effective.

10. A final, though complex, question is what kind of school one should teach in. This is especially difficult for people like myself, who believe that almost every school in the United States, within and without the public school system, contributes to maintaining an oppressive society based upon

an unequal distribution of wealth and a debasement of people's sense of dignity and personal worth. In the next section I will elaborate on this and suggest some ways of infiltrating the system and struggling to change it. It is my conviction that teachers who comply with the values and goals of this culture can only do so at the cost of stripping their students of self-respect and substituting violence in the form of competition in place of knowledge, curiosity, and a sense of community.

Getting a Job. There are not many teaching jobs these days. If you still care to teach, broaden your notion of where you might teach. The schools are only one possible place. Try businesses, social agencies, hospitals, parks, community service organizations. It is, for example, possible to teach literacy to hospitalized children, to use an art and recreation program as a means of teaching most anything; to become associated with a job training program or a prison program. It is possible to set up a child care operation in your home, or turn babysitting into a teaching situation, or set up an after-school tutoring program. Often there are federal or state monies available for reading or child care or delinquency prevention programs. It is important to know how to get access to that money. If necessary, go to the county board of education, to Head Start offices, to regional offices of the Department of Health, Education and Welfare and ask about the programs they sponsor. Often a few weeks of research may open up a number of unexpected possibilities. The Grantsmanship Newsletter is an excellent source of information and is worth having (for subscriptions write to Grantsmanship Center, 1015 W. Olympic Blvd., Los Angeles, CA 90015).

Also think about teaching children with problems—the severely disturbed, retarded, physically handicapped, deaf, or blind. Remember, children are children despite the way in which society labels them. Basically the same techniques and belief in the children's abilities work with all kinds of children. If there are special things one need learn, they are easy to master. The more one thinks of teaching outside the schools, the more imaginative one can be in searching for a job that will allow one to teach, or in defining a job and convincing others that it is worth supporting.

Herbert Kohl is the author of more than forty books on education. He and his wife Judy were the recipients of the National Book Award in 1978 for *The View From the Oak.*

PART II

Who Are Today's Students?

It was the end of August and Ashley Murphy was headed back to Horace Mann Elementary School for the first time since finishing the fifth grade more than 10 years ago. She was thrilled to be returning as a teacher to the very school where she had so many fond memories as a student. To think that she would be shoulder-to-shoulder with some of her former teachers and that now they would be her colleagues!

Driving up to the old brick building brought back a flood of memories: the smell of chalk dust; the neat rows of desks; Steven Parker teasing her in the third grade about her braces; and the stern and aloof principal, Mr. Dabrowski, walking into the cafeteria and immediately causing a hush to fall over the crowd of excited children's voices. Ashley couldn't wait to reunite with her old teachers, the women whose guidance and inspiration was instrumental in her decision to teach. They will be so proud of me, she thought, to see how I have changed, how I have matured.

Ashley was excited too about sharing what she had learned in her teacher education program. And, even though the principal had called this end of summer orientation meeting simply to introduce the new staff and to acquaint everyone with some new districtwide policies, Ashley came prepared with reams of beautifully prepared lessons and activities she would use to kick off the first few weeks of the year with her class of second graders. She couldn't wait to show her new colleagues what she had brought with her.

Imagine Ashley's despair then when Nancy Rush, *her* former second grade teacher, asked Ashley how she knew her carefully prepared lessons would be appropriate for the students who would soon stream into her classroom.

"But, I don't understand," Ashley said, "I've worked very hard on these lessons and each of them reflects what my professors told us about the importance of inquiry learning and engaging students in hands-on activities."

"Well," Nancy began, "how can you plan a series of lessons when you have not considered the most important question: Who are *your* students? Do you think they will look and act like your friends and you did when *you* were in second grade? Will they come from backgrounds similar to your own? Will they all speak English as a first language? Might they have disabilities or other challenges that affect their learning? Who are your students?"

Why is this such an important question? How do race, ethnicity, and income level, for example, affect the teaching and learning cycle?

5

What Should Teachers Do?

Ebonics and Culturally Responsive Instruction

Lisa Delpit

I will submit that one of the reasons [Ebonics] is a problem, if you will—a controversy—is that you cannot divorce language from its speakers. And if you have people who have been disenfranchised, are neglected, are rejected, it is very difficult for the society at large to elevate their language. And, thus, when you start to try to make a case with legitimizing Ebonics—a way of communicating by some, although not all African-Americans speak it—you, in effect, are talking about legitimizing a group of people. You are talking about bringing them to a status comparable to society at large. And that's always a difficult proposition. So, in a certain sense, we cannot talk about Ebonics

NOTE: From *The Real Ebonics Debate* by Theresa Perry. Copyright 1998 by Theresa Perry and Lisa Delpit. Reprinted by permission of Beacon Press, Boston.

separate and distinct from the state of African-American people in the United States as a neglected and as an underclass, marginalized, if you will, people.

—Orlando Taylor
Professor of Communications
at Howard University
Emerge *magazine, April 1997*

The "Ebonics Debate" has created much more heat than light for most of the country. For teachers trying to determine what implications there might be for classroom practice, enlightenment has been a completely nonexistent commodity. I have been asked often enough recently, "What do you think about Ebonics? Are you for it or against it?" My answer must be neither. I can be neither for Ebonics or against Ebonics any more than I can be for or against air. It exists. It is the language spoken by many of our African-American children. It is the language they heard as their mothers nursed them and changed their diapers and played peek-a-boo with them. It is the language through which they first encountered love, nurturance, and joy.

On the other hand, most teachers of those African-American children who have been least well-served by educational systems believe that their students' life chances will be further hampered if they do not learn Standard English. In the stratified society in which we live, they are absolutely correct. While having access to the politically mandated language form will not, by any means, guarantee economic success (witness the growing numbers of unemployed African Americans holding doctorates), not having access will almost certainly guarantee failure.

So what must teachers do? Should they spend their time relentlessly "correcting" their Ebonics-speaking children's language so that it might conform to what we have learned to refer to as Standard English? Despite good intentions, constant correction seldom has the desired effect. Such correction increases cognitive monitoring of speech, thereby making talking difficult. To illustrate, I have frequently taught a relatively simple new "dialect" to classes of preservice teachers. In this dialect, the phonetic element "iz" is added after the first consonant or consonant cluster in each syllable of a word. (Maybe becomes miz-ay-biz-ee and apple, iz-ap-piz-le.) After a bit of drill and practice, the students are asked to tell a partner in "iz" language why they decided to become teachers. Most only haltingly attempt a few words before lapsing into either silence or into Standard

English. During a follow-up discussion, all students invariably speak of the impossibility of attempting to apply rules while trying to formulate and express a thought. Forcing speakers to monitor their language typically produces silence.

Correction may also affect students' attitudes toward their teachers. In a recent research project, middle school, inner-city students were interviewed about their attitudes toward their teachers and school. One young woman complained bitterly, "Mrs. _____ always be interrupting to make you 'talk correct' and stuff. She be butting into your conversations when you not even talking to her! She need to mind her own business!" Clearly this student will be unlikely to either follow the teacher's directives or to want to imitate her speech style.

Group Identity

Issues of group identity may also affect students' oral production of a different dialect. Researcher Sharon Nelson-Barber (1982), in a study of phonologic aspects of Pima Indian language, found that, in grades 1–3, the children's English most approximated the standard dialect of their teachers. But surprisingly, by fourth grade, when one might assume growing competence in standard forms, their language moved significantly toward the local dialect. These fourth graders had the competence to express themselves in a more standard form but chose, consciously or unconsciously, to use the language of those in their local environments. The researcher believes that, by ages eight to nine, these children became aware of their group membership and its importance to their well-being, and this realization was reflected in their language. They may also have become increasingly aware of the school's negative attitude toward their community and found it necessary—through choice of linguistic form—to decide with which camp to identify.

What should teachers do about helping students acquire an additional oral form? First, they should recognize that the linguistic form a student brings to school is intimately connected with loved one's community, and personal identity. To suggest that this form is "wrong" or, even worse, ignorant, is to suggest that something is wrong with the student and his or her family. To denigrate your language is, then, in African-American terms, to "talk about your mama." Anyone who knows anything about African-American culture knows the consequences of that speech act!

On the other hand, it is equally important to understand that students who do not have access to the politically popular dialect form in this country are less likely to succeed economically than their peers who do. How can both realities be embraced in classroom instruction?

It is possible and desirable to make the actual study of language diversity a part of the curriculum for all students. For younger children, discussions about the differences in the ways TV characters from different cultural groups speak can provide a starting point. A collection of the many children's books written in the dialects of various cultural groups can also provide a wonderful basis for learning about linguistic diversity, as can audiotaped stories narrated by individuals from different cultures, including taped books read by members of the children's home communities. Mrs. Pat, a teacher chronicled by Stanford University researcher Shirley Brice Heath (1983), had her students become language "detectives," interviewing a variety of individuals and listening to the radio and TV to discover the differences and similarities in the ways people talked. Children can learn that there are many ways of saying the same thing, and that certain contexts suggest particular kinds of linguistic performances.

Some teachers have groups of students create bilingual dictionaries of their own language form and Standard English. Both the students and the teacher become engaged in identifying terms and deciding upon the best translations. This can be done as generational dictionaries, too, given the proliferation of "youth culture" terms growing out of the Ebonics-influenced tendency for the continual regeneration of vocabulary. Contrastive grammatical structures can be studied similarly but, of course, as the Oakland policy suggests, teachers must be aware of the grammatical structure of Ebonics before they can launch into this complex study.

Other teachers have had students become involved with standard forms through various kinds of role-play. For example, memorizing parts for drama productions allow students to practice and "get the feel" of speaking Standard English while not under the threat of correction. A master teacher of African-American children in Oakland, Carrie Secret, uses this technique and extends it so that students videotape their practice performances and self-critique them as to the appropriate use of Standard English. (But I must add that Carrie's use of drama and oration goes much beyond acquiring Standard English. She inspires pride and community connections that are truly wondrous to behold.) The use of self-critique of recorded forms may prove even more useful than I initially realized. California State University–Hayward professor Etta Hollins has reported that just by leaving a tape recorder on during an informal class period and playing it back with no comment, students began to code-switch—moving between Standard English and Ebonics—more effectively. It appears that they may have not realized which language form they were using until they heard themselves speak on tape.

Young students can create puppet shows or role-play cartoon characters—many "superheroes" speak almost hypercorrect Standard English. Playing a role eliminates the possibility of implying that the child's language is inadequate and suggests, instead, that different language forms are appropriate in different contexts. Some other teachers in New York City have had their students produce a news show every day for the rest of the school. The students take on the personae of famous newscasters, keeping in character as they develop and read their news reports. Discussions ensue about whether Tom Brokaw would have said it that way, again taking the focus off the child's speech.

Although most educators think of Black Language as primarily differing in grammar and syntax, there are other differences in oral language of which teachers should be aware in a multicultural context, particularly in discourse style and language use. Harvard University researcher Sarah Michaels and other researchers identified differences in children's narratives at "sharing time" (Michaels & Cazden, 1986). They found that there was a tendency among young white children to tell "topic-centered" narratives—stories focused on one event—and a tendency among Black youngsters, especially girls, to tell "episodic" narratives—stories that include shifting scenes and are typically longer. While these differences are interesting in themselves, what is of greater significance is adults' responses to the differences. C. B. Cazden (1988) reports on a subsequent project in which a white adult was taped reading the oral narratives of Black and white first graders, with all syntax dialectal markers removed. Adults were asked to listen to the stories and comment about the children's likelihood of success in school. The researchers were surprised by the differential responses given by Black and white adults.

Varying Reactions

In responding to the retelling of a Black child's story, the white adults were uniformly negative, making such comments as "terrible story, incoherent" and "[n]ot a story at all in the sense of describing something that happened." Asked to judge this child's academic competence, all of the white adults rated her below the children who told "topic-centered" stories. Most of these adults also predicted difficulties for this child's future school career, such as "This child might have trouble reading," that she exhibited "language problems that affect school achievement," and that "family problems" or "emotional problems might hamper her academic progress."

The Black adults had very different reactions. They found this child's story "well formed, easy to understand, and interesting, with lots of detail and description." Even though all five of these adults mentioned the "shifts" and "associations" or "nonlinear" quality of the story, they did not find these features distracting. Three of the Black adults selected the story as the best of the five they had heard, and all but one judged the child as exceptionally bright, highly verbal, and successful in school (Cazden, 1988).

This is not a story about racism, but one about cultural familiarity. However, when differences in narrative style produce differences in interpretation of competence, the pedagogical implications are evident. If children who produce stories based on differing discourse styles are expected to have trouble reading and viewed as having language, family, or emotional problems, as was the case with the informants quoted by Cazden, they are unlikely to be viewed as ready for the same challenging instruction awarded students whose language patterns more closely parallel the teacher's.

Most teachers are particularly concerned about how speaking Ebonics might affect learning to read. There is little evidence that speaking another mutually intelligible language form, per se, negatively affects one's ability to learn to read (Sim, 1982). For commonsensical proof, one need only reflect on nonstandard English-speaking Africans who, though enslaved, not only taught themselves to read English, but did so under threat of severe punishment or death. But children who speak Ebonics do have a more difficult time becoming proficient readers. Why? In part, appropriate instructional methodologies are frequently not adopted. There is ample evidence that children who do not come to school with knowledge about letters, sounds, and symbols need to experience some explicit instruction in these areas in order to become independent readers. Another explanation is that, where teachers' assessments of competence are influenced by the language children speak, teachers may develop low expectations for certain students and subsequently teach them less (Sims, 1982). A third explanation rests in teachers confusing the teaching of reading with the teaching of a new language form.

Reading researcher Patricia Cunningham (1976–1997) found that teachers across the United States were more likely to correct reading miscues that were "dialect"-related ("Here go a table" for "Here is a table") than those that were "nondialect"-related ("Here is a dog" for "There is a dog"). Seventy-eight percent of the former types of miscues were corrected, compared with only 27 percent of the latter. She concludes that the teachers were acting out of ignorance, not realizing that "here go" and "here is" represent the same meaning in some Black children's language.

In my observations of many classrooms, however, I have come to conclude that even when teachers recognize the similarity of meaning, they are likely to correct Ebonics-related miscues. Consider a typical example:

TEXT: Yesterday I washed my brother's clothes.
STUDENT'S
RENDITION: Yesterday I wash my bruvver close.

The subsequent exchange between student and teacher sounds something like this:

T: Wait, let's go back. What's that word again? [Points at *washed*.]
S: Wash.
T: No. Look at it again. What letters do you see at the end? You see "e-d." Do you remember what we say when we see those letters on the end of the word?
S: "ed."
T: OK, but in this case we say washed. Can you say that?
S: Wash*ed*.
T: Good. Now read it again.
S: Yesterday I wash*ed* my bruvver.
T: Wait a minute, what's that word again? [Points to *brother*.]
S: Bruvver.
T: No. Look at these letters in the middle. [Points to *brother*.] Remember to read what you see. Do you remember how we say that sound? Put your tongue between your teeth and say /th/. . . .

The lesson continues in such a fashion, the teacher proceeding to correct the student's Ebonics-influenced pronunciations and grammar while ignoring that fact that the student had to have comprehended the sentence in order to translate it into her own language. Such instruction occurs daily and blocks reading development in a number of ways. First, because children become better readers by having the opportunity to read, the overcorrection exhibited in this lesson means that this child will be less likely to become a fluent reader than other children that are not interrupted so consistently.

Second, a complete focus on code and pronunciation blocks children's understanding that reading is essentially a meaning-making process. This child, who understands the text, is led to believe that she is doing something wrong. She is encouraged to think of reading not as something you do to get a message, but something you pronounce. Third, constant corrections by the teacher are likely to cause this student and others like her to resist reading and to resent the teacher.

Language researcher Robert Berdan (1980) reports that, after observing the kind of teaching routine described above in a number of settings, he incorporated the teacher behaviors into a reading instruction exercise that he used with students in a college class. He put together sundry rules from a number of American social and regional dialects to create what he called the "language of Atlantis." Students were then called upon to read aloud in this dialect they did not know. When they made errors he interrupted them, using some of the same statements and comments he had heard elementary school teachers routinely make to their students. He concludes:

> The results were rather shocking. By the time these PhD Candidates in English or linguistics had read 10–20 words, I could make them sound totally illiterate. . . . The first thing that goes is sentence intonation: they sound like they are reading a list from the telephone book. Comment on their pronunciation a bit more, and they begin to subvocalize, rehearsing pronunciations for themselves before they dare to say them out loud. They begin to guess at pronunciations.
>
> They switch letters around for no reason. They stumble; they repeat. In short, when I attack them for their failure to conform to my demands for Atlantis English pronunciations, they sound very much like the worst of the second graders in any of the classrooms I have observed.
>
> They also begin to fidget. They wad up their papers, bite their fingernails, whisper, and some finally refuse to continue. They do all the things that children do while they are busily failing to learn to read.

The moral of this story is not to confuse learning a new language form with reading comprehension. To do so will only confuse the child, leading her away from those intuitive understandings about language that will promote reading development and toward a school career of resistance and a lifetime of avoiding reading.

Unlike unplanned oral language or public reading, writing lends itself to editing. While conversational talk is spontaneous and must be responsive to an immediate context, writing is a mediated process that may be written and rewritten any number of times before being introduced to public scrutiny. Consequently, writing is more amenable to rule application—one may first write freely to get one's thoughts down, and then edit to hone the message and apply specific spelling, syntactical, or punctuation rules. My college students who had such difficulty talking in the "iz" dialect found writing it, with the rules displayed before them, a relatively easy task.

To conclude, the teacher's job is to provide access to the national "standard" as well as to understand the language the children speak sufficiently to celebrate its beauty. The verbal adroitness, the cogent and quick wit, the brilliant use of metaphor, the facility in rhythm and rhyme, evident in the language of Jesse Jackson, Whoopi Goldberg, Toni Morrison, Henry Louis Gates, Jr., Tupac Shakur, and Maya Angelou, as well as in that of many inner-city Black students, may all be drawn upon to facilitate school learning. The teacher must know how to effectively teach reading and writing to students whose culture and language differ from that of the school, and must understand how and why students decide to add another language form to their repertoire. All we can do is provide students with access to additional language forms. Inevitably, each speaker will make his or her own decision about what to say in any context.

But I must end with a caveat that we keep in mind a simple truth: Despite our necessary efforts to provide access to Standard English, such access will not make any of our students more intelligent. It will not teach them math or science or geography—or, for that matter, compassion, courage, or responsibility. Let us not become so overly concerned with the language form that we ignore academic and moral content. Access to the standard language may be necessary, but it is definitely not sufficient to produce intelligent, competent caretakers of the future.

Lisa Delpit is Eminent Scholar and Executive Director of the Center for Urban Education and Innovation at Florida International University.

6

Racism, Discrimination, and Expectations of Students' Achievement

Sonia Nieto

[Racists have power] only if you let them! We'll stick with (the example of striped shirts): If I go where everyone is wearing solids, and I'm wearing a stripe, and someone comes up to me and tells me, "You don't belong here; you're wearing stripes," I'll say, "I belong anywhere I want to belong." And I'll stand right there! But there are some people who just say, "Oh, okay," and will turn around and leave. Then the racist has the power.

—Linda Howard
Interviewee

L inda Howard is a young woman who has been directly harmed by racism in and out of school, and she has a highly evolved understanding of it on

NOTE: From Sonia Nieto. *Affirming Diversity: The Sociopolitical Context of Multicultural Education*, 4e. Published by Allyn and Bacon Merrill Education, Boston, MA. Copyright 2004 by Pearson Education. Adapted by permission of the publisher.

both an individual and an institutional level. As you will see in her case study, Linda has thought very deeply about racism. Many teachers and other educators, however, have not. In this chapter, we will explore the impact that racism, other biases, and expectations of student abilities may have on achievement. We will focus on racism as an example of bias, but I will also point out other kinds of personal and situational discrimination when appropriate. These include discrimination on the basis of gender (sexism), ethnic group (ethnocentrism), social class (classism), language (linguicism), or other perceived differences. I will also mention anti-Semitism, discrimination against Jews; anti-Arab discrimination, directed against Arabs; ageism, discrimination based on age; heterosexism, discrimination against gay men and lesbians; and ableism, discrimination against people with disabilities.

Definitions of Racism and Discrimination

Discussions of prejudice and discrimination tend to focus on the biases and negative perceptions of individuals toward members of other groups. For example, Gordon Allport, in his groundbreaking work on the nature of prejudice, quotes a United Nations document defining discrimination as "any conduct based on a distinction made on grounds of natural or social categories, which have no relation either to individual capacities or merits, or to the concrete behavior of the individual person." This definition is helpful but incomplete because it fails to describe the harmful effects of such conduct. More broadly speaking, discrimination denotes negative or destructive behaviors that can result in denying some groups' life necessities as well as the privileges, rights, and opportunities enjoyed by other groups. Discrimination is usually based on prejudice, that is, the attitudes and beliefs of individuals about entire groups of people. These attitudes and beliefs are generally, but not always, negative.

Our society, among many others, categorizes people according to both visible and invisible traits, uses such classifications to deduce fixed behavioral and mental traits, and then applies policies and practices that jeopardize some and benefit others. Classifications based on race, ethnicity, gender, social class, and other physical or social differences are all around us. Frequently, they result in gross exaggerations and stereotypes: Girls are not as smart as boys; African Americans have rhythm; Asians are studious; Poles are simple-minded; Jews are smart; and poor people need instant gratification. Although some of these may appear to be "positive" stereotypes, both "negative" and "positive" stereotypes have negative results because they limit our perspective of an entire group of people. There are two major problems with categorizing people in this way: First, people of all groups begin to believe the stereotypes; and second, both material and psychological resources are doled out accordingly.

We see a clear example of the implications of such categorizations in the case study of Rich Miller. Rich was quite severe in his criticism of other African Americans, whom he characterized as "settling for the easiest way out," "lazy," and "tacky." He had internalized the myth of success based completely on individual endeavor rather than as also influenced by structural issues such as institutional racism and lack of opportunity. It is easy to understand how this happens: In our society, the metaphor of "pulling yourself up by your bootstraps" is powerful indeed; it allows little room for alternative explanations based on structural inequality.

Racism and other forms of discrimination are based on the perception that one ethnic group, class, gender, or language is superior to all others. In the United States, the conventional norm used to measure all other groups is European-American, upper-middle class, English-speaking, and male. Discrimination based on perceptions of superiority is part of the structure of schools, the curriculum, the education most teachers receive, and the interactions among teachers, students, and the community. But discrimination is not simply an individual bias; it is above all an institutional practice.

Most definitions of racism and discrimination obscure the institutional nature of oppression. Although the beliefs and behaviors of individuals may be hurtful, far greater damage is done through institutional discrimination, that is, the systematic use of economic and political power in institutions (such as schools) that leads to detrimental policies and practices. These policies and practices have a harmful effect on groups that share a particular identity (be it racial, ethnic, gender, or other). The major difference between individual and institutional discrimination is the wielding of power, because it is primarily through the power of the people who control institutions such as schools that oppressive policies and practices are reinforced and legitimated. Linda Howard, one of our young interviewees, already understood this distinction. In her case study, she distinguished between prejudice and racism in this way: "We all have some type of person that we don't like, whether it's from a different race, or from a different background, or they have different habits." But she went on to explain, as we saw in the quote at the beginning of this chapter, that a racist is someone who has power to carry out his or her prejudices.

Let me give another example: Let's say that I am prejudiced against tall people. Although my bias may hurt individual tall people because I refuse to befriend them or because I make fun of them, I can do very little to limit their options in life. If, however, I belonged to a group of powerful "non-talls" and we limited the access of tall persons to certain neighbor-hoods, prohibited them from receiving quality health care, discouraged intermarriage with people of short or average height, developed policies against their employment in high-status professions, and placed all children who were the offspring of "talls" (or who showed early signs of becoming above average in height) in the lowest ability tracks in schools, then my bias would have teeth and its institutional power would be clear. In the discussion that follows, we will be concerned primarily with institutional discrimination.

Institutional discrimination generally refers to how people are excluded or deprived of rights or opportunities as a result of the normal operations of the institution. Although the individuals involved in the institution may not be prejudiced or have any racist intentions or even awareness of how others may be harmed, the result may nevertheless be racist. In this sense, intentional and unintentional racism are different. But because they both result in negative outcomes, in the end it does not really matter whether racism and other forms of discrimination are intentional. Rather than trying to figure out whether the intent was to do harm or not, educators would do better to spend their time addressing the effects of racism.

When we understand racism and other forms of discrimination as a systemic problem, not simply as an individual dislike for a particular group of people, we can better understand the negative and destructive effects it can have. Vanessa Mattison provides a good example of a young person struggling to reconcile our country's lofty ideals of equality and fair play with the reality of the injustice she saw around her. Vanessa was committed to social justice, but she saw it primarily as working to change the attitudes and behaviors of individuals. She had not yet made the connection between racism and institutional oppression, and she did not grasp that institutional racism was far more harmful than individual biases or acts of meanness. But she was beginning to see that certain norms existed that were unfair to Blacks, women, and gays and lesbians. In her words: "There's all these underlying rules that if you're not this, you can't do that."

This is meant neither to minimize the powerful effects of individual prejudice and discrimination, which can be personally painful, nor to suggest that discrimination occurs only in one direction, for example, from Whites toward Blacks. There is no monopoly on prejudice and individual discrim-ination; they happen in all directions, and even within groups. However, interethnic and intraethnic biases and personal prejudices, while negative and hurtful, simply do not have the long-range and life-limiting effects of institutional racism and other kinds of institutional discrimination.

As an illustration of institutional racism, let us look at how testing practices are sometimes used in schools: Students from dominated groups may be stigmatized and labeled because of their performance on standardized tests. What places these students at a disadvantage is not that particular teachers have prejudiced attitudes about them; teachers may, in fact, like the students very much. What places the students at jeopardy is the fact that they may be labeled, grouped, and tracked, sometimes for the length of their schooling, because of their score on an ethnocentric and biased test. In this case, it is institutions—schools and the testing industry—that have the major negative impact on students from culturally dominated groups.

Prejudice and discrimination, then, are not just personality traits or psychological phenomena; they are also a manifestation of economic, political, and social power. The institutional definition of racism is not always easy to accept because it goes against deeply held notions of equality and justice in our nation. According to Beverly Tatum, "An understanding of racism as a system of advantage presents a serious challenge to the notion of the United States as a just society where rewards are based solely on one's merits." Racism as an institutional system implies that some people and groups benefit and others lose. Whites, whether they want to or not, benefit in a racist society; males benefit in a sexist society. Discrimination always helps somebody—those with the most power—which explains why racism, sexism, and other forms of discrimination continue.

According to Meyer Weinberg, racism is a system of privilege and penalty. That is, one is rewarded or punished in housing, education, employment, health, and so on, by the simple fact of belonging to a particular group, regardless of one's individual merits or faults. He goes on to explain, "Racism consists centrally of two facets: First, a belief in the inherent superiority of some people and the inherent inferiority of others; and second, the acceptance of distributing goods and services—let alone respect—in accordance with such judgments of unequal worth." In addressing the institutional nature of racism, he adds, " . . . racism is always collective. Prejudiced individuals may join the large movement, but they do not cause it." According to this conception, the "silence of institutional racism" and the "ruckus of individual racism" are mutually supportive. It is sometimes difficult to separate one level of racism from the others, as they feed on and inform one another. What is crucial, according to Weinberg, is understanding that the doctrine of White supremacy is at the root of racism.

The History and Persistence of Racism in U.S. Schools

As institutions, schools respond to and reflect the larger society. It therefore is not surprising that racism finds its way into schools in much the same way that it finds its way into other institutions such as housing, employment, and the criminal justice system. Overt expressions of racism may be less frequent in schools today than in the past, but racism does not just exist when schools are legally segregated or racial epithets are used against Black students. Racism is also manifested in rigid ability tracking, low expectations of students based on their identity, and inequitably funded schools.

Racism and other forms of discrimination—particularly sexism, classism, ethnocentrism, and linguicism—have a long history in our schools and their effects are widespread and long lasting. The most blatant form of discrimination is the actual withholding of education, as was the case with African Americans and sometimes with American Indians during the nineteenth century. To teach enslaved Africans to read was a crime punishable under the law and it became a subversive activity that was practiced by Blacks in ingenious ways. Other overt forms of discrimination include segregating students, by law, according to their race, ethnicity, or gender, as was done at one time or another with African American, Mexican American, Japanese, and Chinese students, as well as with females; or forcing them into boarding schools, as was done with American Indian students. In such groups, children have been encouraged to adopt the ways of the dominant culture in sundry ways, from subtle persuasion to physical punishment for speaking their native language. This, too, is a bitter reminder of the inequities of U.S. educational history.

Unfortunately, the discrimination that children face in schools is not a thing of the past. School practices and policies continue to discriminate against some children in very concrete ways. Recent studies have found that most students of color are still in schools that are segregated by race and social class, and the situation is worsening rather than improving. At the impetus of the civil rights movement, many school systems throughout the United States were indeed desegregated. But less than rigorous implementation of desegregation plans, "White flight," and housing patterns have succeeded in resegregating many schools. Segregation invariably results in school systems that are "separate and unequal" because segregated schools are differently funded, with fewer resources provided to schools in poor communities and vastly superior resources provided to schools in wealthier communities.

Segregation often results in students receiving differential schooling on the basis of their social class, race, and ethnicity. In addition, schools that serve students of color tend to provide curricula that are watered down and at a lower level than schools that serve primarily White students. Also, teachers in poor urban schools tend to have less experience and less education than colleagues who teach in schools that serve primarily European American and middle-class students. Even when they are desegregated, many schools resegregate students through practices such as rigid ability tracking. Consequently, desegregating schools in and of itself does not guarantee educational equity.

Manifestations of Racism and Discrimination in Schools

Racism and discrimination are manifested in numerous school practices and policies. Policies most likely to jeopardize students at risk of educational failure are most common precisely in the institutions in which those students are found. For example, many studies have found that rigid tracking is most evident in poor communities with large numbers of African American, Latino, and American Indian students.

It is sometimes difficult to separate what is racist or discriminatory from what appear to be neutral school policies and practices or behaviors of individual teachers. An early study cited by Ray McDermott can help illustrate this point. Through filmed classroom observations, he found that a White teacher tended to have much more frequent eye contact with her White students than with her Black students. Was this behavior the result of racism? Was it because of cultural and communication differences? Or was poor teacher preparation responsible for her behavior?

David and Myra Sadker cite many anecdotes in their powerful report on sexism in schools that bring up similar questions. They found that well-intentioned and otherwise excellent teachers often treat their female students far differently from their male students, interacting with them less frequently, asking them fewer questions, and giving them less feedback than they give male students. Because boys are expected to be more verbal and active and are both praised and reproached more often by their teachers, girls become invisible in the classroom. Girls are singled out neither for praise nor for disciplinary action. They are simply expected, as a group, to be quiet, attentive, and passive. Is this because of inherent sexism? Are teachers simply unaware of how such practices may jeopardize girls and, in a different way, boys as well?

In another example of how difficult it is to separate racism from individual teachers' behaviors or seemingly neutral policies, Patricia Gandara found, in a study of 50 low-income and high-achieving Mexican Americans, that most were either light-skinned or European-looking. Few of the sample, according to Gandara, looked "classically Mexican in both skin color and features." Does this mean that teachers intentionally favored them because of their light skin? Did teachers assume that their light-skinned students were smarter?

These questions are impossible to answer in any conclusive way; it is probable that institutional racism and teachers' biases both play a role in negative outcomes such as those described in the studies. The results, however, are very clear: In the study by McDermott, the Black children had to strain three times as hard to catch the teacher's eye, looking for approval, affection, and encouragement. In the Sadker and Sadker report, the researchers concluded that girls are frequently denied an equal education simply because of their gender, rather than because of any personal talents or deficits. In Gandara's study, the light-skinned students were able to derive more benefits from their schooling than their darker-skinned peers.

Thus students' educational success or failure cannot be explained solely by family circumstance, social class, race, gender, or language ability. Racism and other forms of institutional discrimination also play a part. African American, Latino, American Indian, and poor children in general continue to achieve below grade level, drop out in much greater numbers, and go to college in much lower proportion than their middle-class and European American peers. Two concrete examples illustrate this point: Black students are chronically underrepresented in programs for the gifted and talented, being only half as likely to be placed in a class for the gifted as are White students, even though they may be equally gifted. Latino students drop out of school at a rate higher than any other major ethnic group; and in some places, the rate has been as high as 80 percent. If educational failure were caused only by students' background and other social characteristics, it would be difficult to explain why similar students are successful in some classrooms and schools and not in others. For instance, students at Central Park East High School in East Harlem, one of the most economically impoverished communities in New York City, have reached unparalleled levels of success compared to their peers in other neighborhood schools who are similar to them in every way.

School structures have also proved to be sexist in organization, orientation, and goals. Most schools are organized to meet best the needs of White males; that is, the policy and instruction in schools generally reflect what is most effective for the needs of their male students, not the needs of either females or students of color. This organization includes everything from the curriculum, which follows the developmental level of males more closely than that of females, to instructional techniques, which favor competition as a preferred learning style, although it is not necessarily the best learning environment for either females or most students of color. The effect of such discrimination on female students is to reinforce the persistent message that they are inferior. In fact, high-achieving female students tend to receive the least attention of all from their teachers.

Discrimination based on social class is also prevalent in our public schools. In a study of affluent and low-income youth in a secondary school, Ellen Brantlinger found that students' social class was highly correlated with their academic placement, with most low-income students in special education or low tracks and all the high-income students in college preparatory classes. This was the case in spite of the fact that two of the high-income students were classified as "learning disabled." Using data from 1993, the National Center for Education Statistics also found a significant correlation between social class and dropping out of school. While only 6 percent of high-income students dropped out, over 40 percent of low-income students did so.

The hidden curriculum, that is, subtle and not-so-subtle messages that are not part of the intended curriculum, may also have an impact on students. These messages may be positive (e.g., the expectation that all students are capable of high quality work) or negative (e.g., that children of working-class backgrounds are not capable of aspiring to professional jobs), although the term is generally used to refer to negative messages. These frequently unintentional messages may contradict schools' stated policies and objectives. For instance, Carolyn Persell found that, in spite of schools' and teachers' stated commitment to equal education, social class is repeatedly related to how well students do in school. In fact, she found that students are more different from one another when they leave school than when they enter it, thus putting to rest the myth of school as the "great equalizer." Persell found that differences in academic achievement experienced by students of different economic and cultural backgrounds are due primarily to a number of specific factors: the kinds of schools the students attend, the length of time they stay in school, the curriculum and pedagogy to which they are exposed, and societal beliefs concerning intelligence and ability.

Rather than eradicate social class differences, then, it appears that schooling reflects and even duplicates them. This finding was confirmed by Samuel Bowl and Herbert Gintis in their ground-breaking class analysis of schooling. They compared the number of years of schooling of students with the socioeconomic status of their parents and found that students whose parents were in the highest socioeconomic group tended to complete the most years of schooling. They concluded that schooling in and of itself does not necessarily move poor children out of their parents' low economic class. More often, schooling maintains and solidifies class divisions.

Intentional or not, racism, classism, and other forms of discrimination are apparent in the quality of education that students receive. A graphic example of discrimination based on both race and class is found in the differential resources given to schools. As is evident in Jonathan Kozol's searing indictment of the funding of public education, the actual money spent on schools is very often directly correlated with the social class and race of the student body. Furthermore, a review of relevant literature by Carol Ascher and Gary Burnett reported that disparities in funding between rich and poor states, and between rich and poor districts in the same state, has actually grown in the recent past.

In the case of African American youth, Angela Taylor found that to the extent that teachers harbor negative stereotypes about them, African American children's race alone is probably sufficient to place them at risk for negative school outcomes. Of course, many teachers and other educators prefer to think that students' lack of academic achievement is due solely to conditions inside their homes or inherent in their cultures. But the occurrence of racism in schools has been widely documented. In a report about immigrant students in California, more than half of the students interviewed indicated that they had been the victims of teachers' biases, citing instances where they were punished, publicly embarrassed, or ridiculed because of improper use of English. They also reported that teachers had made derogatory comments about immigrant groups in front of the class. Most of the middle and high school students interviewed in a study by Mary Poplin and Joseph Weeres also had witnessed incidents of racism in school. And in a study in an urban high school in the Northeast, Karen Donaldson found that an astounding 80 percent of students surveyed said they had experienced or witnessed racism or other forms of discrimination in school.

Studies focusing specifically on Latino youth have reported similar results. Marietta Saravia-Shore and Herminio Martinez interviewed Puerto Rican youths who had dropped out of school and were currently participating in an alternative high school program. These youths keenly felt the discrimination of their former teachers, who they said were "against Puerto Ricans and Blacks." One young woman said that a former teacher had commented, "Do you want to be like the other Puerto Rican women who never got an education? Do you want to be like the rest of your family and never go to school?" In Virginia Zanger's study of high-achieving Latino and Latina high school students in Boston, one young man described his shock when his teacher called him "spic" right in class. Although the teacher was later suspended, the incident had clearly affected how this young man perceived school and his teachers. If we keep in mind that these are successful students, who are apt to hear far fewer of such damaging comments than other students, we can begin to grasp the enormity of the problem confronted by young people who are not as successful in school.

The effect of discrimination on students is most painfully apparent when students themselves have the opportunity to speak. Their thoughts concerning their education are revealing. In her study, Karen Donaldson found that students were affected by racism in three major ways: White students experienced guilt and embarrassment when they became aware of the racism to which their peers were subjected; students of color sometimes felt they needed to compensate and overachieve to prove they were equal to their White classmates; and at other times, students of color said that their self-esteem was badly damaged. However, self-esteem is a complicated issue that includes many variables. It does not come fully formed out of the blue, but is created in particular contexts and responds to conditions that vary from situation to situation. Teachers' and schools' complicity in creating negative self-esteem cannot be discounted. This point was illustrated by Lillian, a young woman in a study of an urban high school by Nitza Hidalgo. Lillian commented, "That's another problem I have, teachers, they are always talking about how we have no type of self-esteem or anything like that. . . . But they're the people that's putting us down. That's why our self-esteem is so low."

Racism, Discrimination, and Silence

Many times, unintentional discrimination is practiced by well-meaning teachers who fear that talking about race will only exacerbate the problem. As a consequence, most schools are characterized by a curious absence of talk about differences, particularly about race. The process begins with the preparation of teachers. In one study, Alice Mcintyre interviewed a group of White female student teachers working in urban schools in order to understand how they made meaning of their Whiteness in relation to teaching. She found that these pre-service teachers were reluctant to discuss racism or to consider their individual or collective role in perpetuating it. Because they saw their students primarily as victims of poverty and parental neglect, these student teachers preferred to place themselves in relationship to their students as protective "White Knights." This patronizing stance facilitated their denial of racism.

Silence and denial about racism are still quite prevalent when student teachers become teachers. In a follow-up study to her initial research concerning students' experiences with racism, Karen Donaldson had a hard time recruiting White teachers to take part in an antiracist education teacher study because most White teachers were not aware (or claimed not to be aware) of racial biases in schools and of how these biases could influence students' achievement. In another study, Julie Wollman-Bonilla found that a sizable proportion of the teachers in her children's literature courses explicitly rejected children's books about race and racism or use with their students. Whether it was to shield their students from unpleasant realities, or to uphold particular societal myths, Wollman-Bonilla concluded that many teachers lack the courage to present views that differ from the mainstream perspective. As a result, their role becomes one of maintaining the status quo rather than helping children question social inequality and injustice. That this attitude can be taken to an extreme is evident in research by Ellen Bigler: When she asked a middle school librarian in a town with a sizable Puerto Rican community if there were any books on the Hispanic experience, the librarian answered that carrying such books was inadvisable because it would interfere with the children's identification of themselves as "American"!

Silence pervades even schools committed to equity and diversity. This was a major finding in a study by Kathe Jervis of the first year of a New York City middle school consciously designed to be based on these principles. Although she had not originally intended to focus her study on race, Jervis found that there was an odd silence on the part of most teachers to address it. Their reluctance to discuss race resulted in their overlooking or denying issues of power that are imbedded in race. Jervis concluded that "even in the 'best' schools, where faculty try hard to pay attention to individuals, Whites' blindness to race clouds their ability to notice what children are really saying about themselves and their identities."

Failure to discuss racism, unfortunately, will not make it go away. Linda Howard's close relationship with Mr. Benson, her English teacher, was no doubt partly due to the fact that they were able to talk openly about racism and other biases. Racism, classism, and other forms of discrimination play a key role in setting up and maintaining inappropriate learning environments for many students. A related phenomenon concerns the possible impact of teachers' expectations on student achievement.

Expectations of Students' Achievement

Much research has focused on teachers' interactions with their students, specifically teacher expectations. The term *self-fulfilling prophecy,* coined by Robert Merton in 1948, means that students perform in ways that teachers expect. Student performance is based on both overt and covert messages from teachers about students' worth, intelligence, and capability. The term did not come into wide use until 1968, when a classic study by Robert Rosenthal and Lenore Jacobson provided the impetus for subsequent extensive research on the subject. In this study, several classes of children in grades one through six were given a nonverbal intelligence test (the researchers called it the "Harvard Test of Influenced Acquisition"), which researchers claimed would measure the students' potential for intellectual growth. Twenty percent of the students were randomly selected by the researchers as "intellectual bloomers," and their names were given to the teachers. Although the students' test scores actually had nothing at all to do with their potential, the teachers were told to be on the alert for signs of intellectual growth among these particular children. Overall these children, particularly in the lower grades, showed considerably greater gains in IQ during the school year than did the other students. They were also rated by their teachers as being more interesting, curious, and happy, and thought to be more likely to succeed later in life.

Rosenthal and Jacobson's research on teacher expectations caused a sensation in the education community, and controversy surrounding it continues to be present. From the beginning, the reception to this line of research has been mixed, with both supporters and detractors. But one outcome was that the effect of teachers' expectations on the academic achievement of their students was taken seriously for the first time. Before this research, students' failure in school was usually ascribed wholly to individual or family circumstances. Now, the possible influence of teachers' attitudes and behaviors and the school's complicity in the process had to be considered as well. The most compelling implications were for the education of those students most seriously disadvantaged by schooling, that is, for students of color and the poor.

Early research by Ray Rist on teachers' expectations is also worth mentioning here. In a groundbreaking study, he found that a kindergarten teacher had grouped her class by the eighth day of class. In reviewing how she had done so, Rist noted that the teacher had already roughly constructed an "ideal type" of student, most of whose characteristics were related to social class. By the end of the school year, the teacher's differential treatment of children based on who were "fast" and "slow" learners became evident.

The "fast" learners received more teaching time, more reward-directed behavior, and more attention. The interactional patterns between the teacher and her students then took on a "castelike" appearance. The result after three years of similar behavior by other teachers was that teachers' behavior toward the different groups influenced the children's achievement. In other words, the teachers themselves contributed to the creation of the "slow" learners in their classrooms.

In the research by Rist, all the children and teachers were African American but represented different social classes. But similar results have been found with poor and working-class children of any race. Persell, in a review of relevant research, found that expectations for poor children were lower than for middle-class children even when their IQ and achievement scores were similar. Teachers' beliefs that their students are "dumb" can become a rationale for providing low-level work in the form of elementary facts, simple drills, and rote memorization. Students are not immune to these messages. On the other hand, a study by Diane Pollard found that the academic performance of African American students is enhanced when they perceive their teachers and other school staff to be supportive and helpful.

Some of the research on teacher expectations is quite old. Although it is reasonable to expect that, with the increasing diversity in our schools, it no longer holds true, there are still numerous examples of teachers' low expectations of students. A recent study by Francisco Rios underscores the problem. Rios studied teachers in an urban city in the Midwest to determine what principles of practice they used for teaching in culturally diverse classrooms. Among the 16 teachers he studied, he found that most of the comments they made about their students were negative; further, none of the teaching principles that they identified focused on academic achievement and only one teacher said that her students wanted to learn.

These findings are particularly problematic when we consider the impact that such beliefs can have on students. Given the increasing diversity in our public schools, the problem is even more acute because many teachers know little or nothing about the background of their students. Consequently, teachers may consider their students' identity to be at fault. This was the result found by Bram Hamovitch in an ethnographic study of an urban after-school program for adolescents at risk of dropping out of school. In his study, Hamovitch concluded that the program failed to meet its objective of motivating students to continue their education because "it allegorically asks them to dislike themselves and their own culture."

Teachers' attitudes about the diversity of their students develop long before they become teachers, however. In a review of recent literature,

Kenneth Zeichner found that teacher education students, who are mostly White and monolingual, by and large view diversity of student backgrounds as a problem. He also found that the most common characteristics of effective teachers in urban schools are a belief that their students are capable learners, and an ability to communicate this belief to the students. Martin Haberman reached a similar conclusion, identifying a number of functions of successful teachers of the urban poor. Most significant, he found that successful teachers did not blame students for failure and they had consistently high expectations of their students. Rich Miller offers compelling evidence of this reality. According to Rich, standards would be higher in his high school if there were more White students. But the reason was not because White students are smarter, but because White teachers don't push the Black students as much as they push White students. On the other hand, Black teachers, Rich said, have "expectations that are higher than White teachers . . . because they know how it was for them."

What happens when teachers develop high expectations of their students? In a wonderful example of how changing the expectations of students can influence achievement in a positive direction, Rosa Hernandez Sheets recounted her own experience with five Spanish-speaking students who had failed her Spanish class. Just one semester after placing them in what she labeled her "advanced" class, the very same students who had previously failed, passed the AP Spanish language exam, earning college credits while just sophomores and juniors. A year later, they passed the AP Spanish Literature exam. As a result of the change in her pedagogy, over a three-year period, Latino and Latina students who had been labeled "at risk" were performing at a level commonly expected of honors students.

The issue of labeling is key in this situation. In a similar case, Ruben Rumbaut found that the self-esteem of immigrant students is linked to how they are labeled by their schools. Specifically, he found that students' self-esteem is diminished when they are labeled "Limited English Proficient." If this is the case with a seemingly neutral term, more loaded labels no doubt have a much greater impact. But explicit labeling may not even be needed. According to Claude Steele, the basic problem that causes low student achievement is what he terms "stigma vulnerability" based on the constant devaluation faced by Blacks and other people of color in society and schools. In schools, this devaluation occurs primarily through the harmful attitudes and beliefs that teachers communicate, knowingly or not, to their students. Steele maintains, "Deep in the psyche of American educators is a presumption that black students need academic remediation, or extra time with elemental curricula to overcome background deficits."

Although disadvantage may contribute to the problem, Steele contends that Blacks underachieve even when they have sufficient material resources, adequate academic preparation, and a strong value orientation toward education. To prove his point, he reviewed a number of programs that have had substantial success in improving the academic achievement of Black students without specifically addressing either their culturally specific learning orientations or socioeconomic disadvantage. What made the difference? In these programs, student achievement was improved simply by treating students as if they were talented and capable. Steele concludes, "That erasing stigma improves black achievement is perhaps the strongest evidence that stigma is what depresses it in the first place."

Research on teachers' expectations is not without controversy. First, it has been criticized as unnecessarily reductionist because, in the long run, what teachers expect matters less than what teachers do. Second, the term itself and the research on which it is based imply that teachers have the sole responsibility for students' achievement or lack of it. This is both an unrealistic and an incomplete explanation for student success or failure. The study by Rosenthal and Jacobson, for example, is a glaring indication of the disrespect with which teachers have frequently been treated and raises serious ethical issues in research. Blaming teachers, or "teacher bashing," provides a convenient outlet for complex problems, but it fails to take into account the fact that teachers function within contexts in which they usually have little power.

There are, of course, teachers who have low expectations of students from particular backgrounds and who are, in the worst cases, insensitive and racist. But placing teachers at the center of expectations of student achievement shifts the blame to some of those who care most deeply about students and who struggle every day to help them learn. The use of the term *teachers' expectations* distances the school and society from their responsibility and complicity in student failure. That is, teachers, schools, communities, and society interact to produce failure.

Low expectations mirror the expectations of society. It is not simply teachers who expect little from poor, working-class, and culturally dominated groups. Garfield High School in East Los Angeles, a school made famous by the extraordinary efforts of Jaime Escalante and other teachers in propelling an unprecedented number of students to college in spite of poverty and discrimination, was visited by George Bush when he was running for U.S. president. Rather than build on the message that college was both possible and desirable for its students, Bush focused instead on the idea that a college education is not needed for success. He told the largely Mexican American student body that "we need people to build our buildings . . . people who do the hard physical work of our society." It is doubtful that he would even have considered uttering these same words at Beverly Hills High School, a short distance away. The message of low expectations to students who should have heard precisely the opposite is thus replicated even by those at the highest levels of a government claiming to be equitable to all students.

The Complex Connections Between Diversity and Discrimination

Because societal inequities are frequently reflected in schools, institutional racism and other biases are apparent in inequitable school policies and practices in complex ways. Let us take the example of language. The fact that some children do not enter school speaking English cannot be separated from how their native language is viewed by the larger society or from the kinds of programs available for them in schools. Each of these programs—whether ESL, immersion, or two-way bilingual education—has an underlying philosophy with broad implications for students' achievement or failure. As a consequence, each approach may have a profound influence on the quality of education that language minority children receive. But linguistic and other differences do not exist independently of how they are perceived in the general society or by teachers; there is a complex relationship between students' race, culture, native language, and other differences with institutional discrimination, school practices, and teachers' expectations.

Social class provides another example of the complex links between difference and discrimination. In spite of the firm belief in our society that social class mobility is available to all, classism is a grim reality because economic inequality is now greater in the United States than in any other industrial or postindustrial country in the world; in fact, social class inequality has actually increased in the past 20 years. Related to this reality is the widely accepted classist view among many educators that poverty causes academic failure. Yet although poverty may have an adverse effect on student achievement, the belief that poverty and failure go hand-in-hand is questionable. Research by Denny Taylor and Catherine Dorsey-Gaines provides evidence that by itself poverty is not an adequate explanation for the failure to learn. In their work with Black families living in urban poverty, they found inspiring cases of academically successful students. They discovered children who consistently did their homework, made the honor roll, and had positive attitudes about school. The parents of these children motivated them to learn and study, had high hopes for their education, were optimistic about the future, and considered literacy an integral part of their lives—this in spite of such devastating conditions as family deaths; no food, heat, or hot water; and a host of other hostile situations.

Similarly, an in-depth study by David Hartle-Schutte of four Navajo students, who might be identified as "at risk" by their teachers because of poverty and culture, found that these students came from homes where literacy was valued. But their school failed to recognize and build on the many literacy experiences they had in their homes to help them become successful readers. These cases point out that home background can no longer be accepted as the sole or primary excuse for the school failure of large numbers of students.

Examples such as these demonstrate that although poverty is certainly a disadvantage, it is not an insurmountable obstacle to learning. The economic condition of African American and other poor students has often been used as an explanation for academic failure, but as Kofi Lomotey, in a review of the education of African American youths, states: ". . . there are clear examples of environments that have, over long periods of time, been successful in educating large numbers of African-American students. These models can be replicated; the situation is not hopeless." In fact, one major explanation for students' lack of academic achievement lies in the lack of equitable resources given to students of different social classes and cultural backgrounds. For instance, one of the most disturbing patterns found in the 1997 National Condition of Education report was that, compared with middle-class White children, children of color and low-income students were much more likely to be taught by teachers who had little academic preparation for their teaching field. Furthermore, the skills differentials that result from this inequity will lead to earnings differentials as adults to a much greater extent than was the case even 20 years ago.

In the ideal sense, education in the United States is based on the lofty values of democracy, freedom, and equal access. Historically, our educational system proposed to tear down the rigid systems of class and caste on which education in most of the world was (and still is) based and to provide all students with an equal education. Education was to be, as Horace Mann claimed, "the great equalizer." On the other hand, some educational historians have demonstrated that the common school's primal purposes were to replicate inequality and to control the unruly masses. Thus, the original goals of public school education were often at cross purposes.

Mass public education began in earnest in the nineteenth century through the legislation of compulsory education and its most eloquent democratic expression is found in the early-twentieth-century philosophy of John Dewey. The commitment that Dewey articulated for educational equity continues today through policies such as desegregation and nonsexist education and through legislation and policies aimed at eradicating many existing inequalities. But the legacy of inequality also continues through policies and practices that favor some students over others, including unequal funding, rigid tracking, and unfair tests. As a result, schools have often been sites of bitter conflict.

Race is another pivotal way in which privilege has been granted on an unequal basis. Based on his research, the historian David Tyack asserts that the struggle to achieve equality in education is nothing new, and that race has often been at the center of this struggle. He adds: "Attempts to preserve white supremacy and to achieve racial justice have fueled the politics of education for more than a century." But resistance on the part of parents, students, and teachers has been crucial in challenging the schools to live up to their promise of equality. That is, schools were not racially desegregated simply because the courts ordered it, and gender-fair education was not legislated only because Congress thought it was a good idea. In both cases, as in many others, educational opportunity was expanded because many people and communities engaged in struggle, legal or otherwise, to bring about change.

Although in theory education is no longer meant to replicate societal inequities but rather to reflect the ideals of democracy, we know that such is not always the reality. Our schools have consistently failed to provide an equitable education for all students. The complex interplay of student differences, institutional racism and discrimination, teachers' biases that lead to low expectations, and unfair school policies and practices all play a role in keeping it this way.

Conclusion

Focusing on the persistence of racism and discrimination and low expectations is meant in no way to deny the difficult family and economic situation of many poor children and children of color, or its impact on their school experiences and achievement. Drug abuse, violence, and other social ills, as well as poor medical care, deficient nutrition, and a struggle for the bare necessities for survival harm children's lives, including their school experiences. The fact that poor children and their parents do not have at their disposal the resources and experiences that economic privilege would give them is also detrimental.

But blaming poor people and people from dominated racial or cultural groups for their educational problems is not the answer to solving societal inequities. Teachers can do nothing to change the conditions in which their students may live, but they can work to change their own biases as well as the institutional structures that act as obstacles to student learning. As we have seen, racism and other forms of discrimination play a central role in educational failure, as does the related phenomenon of low expectations.

Sonia Nieto is a professor of Teacher Education at the University of Massachusetts.

7

Challenging Deficit Thinking

Lois Weiner

*Urban teachers must question unspoken assumptions about the
sources of their students' struggles.*

—Lois Weiner

Although my research and expertise are in urban teaching, I am now
regularly asked to assist schools that are a far cry from the typical
urban school. Clearly, teachers and school leaders in suburbs are now grap-
pling with many of the challenges traditionally associated with urban
schools, including growing demographic diversity and financial stress. In
addition, suburban educators increasingly work in the kind of regulatory
environment that has long characterized urban schools operations and
influenced their culture.

We know from research on urban schools that an impersonal, bureaucratic school culture undercuts many of the teaching attitudes and behaviors
that draw on student strengths (Weiner, 2000). This bureaucratic culture fos-
ters the pervasive assumption that when students misbehave or achieve

NOTE: "Challenging Deficit Thinking," by Lois Weiner. In the September, 2006 issue of
Educational Leadership, 64(1), pp. 42–45. Copyright 2006 by ASCD. Used with permission.
Learn more about ASCD at www.ascd.org.

poorly, they must be "fixed" because the problem inheres in the students or their families, not in the social ecology of the school, grade, or classroom.

The deficit paradigm that is so deeply embedded in urban schools mirrors a proclivity in national debates about a range of problems. For example, in response to the epidemic of obesity in our youth, public debate and proposed solutions frequently focus on individual behavior and character: If individuals would just say no to french fries or make healthy meals for their children, we could solve the crisis. Of course, many of us would do well to spurn the temptations that await us in supermarket aisles and restaurants. But the social causes of childhood obesity are at least as important as individual failings and choices. Advertising aimed at children, the abundance of cheap fast food, and such school policies as eliminating recess to make time for more literacy and math instruction are powerful influences. A narrow focus on individual weaknesses obscures the importance of these other, more potent, factors.

School practices and assumptions emerging from the deficit paradigm often hide student and teacher abilities. These assumptions are especially powerful because they are unspoken. We overlook our taken-for-granted ideas and practices to an extraordinary degree.

Uncovering Tacit Assumptions and Practices

The graduate program that I coordinate at New Jersey City University provides university-based professional development focusing on teaching and learning in urban schools. The program guides teachers in uncovering, contextualizing, and challenging tacit assumptions about students' weaknesses. Most of the younger teachers are stunned when we question the pervasive diagnoses of student problems. They assume that a "hyperactive" 1st grader requires medication and placement in special education. We challenge them to think about how this explanation makes the teacher a mere referral agent and locates responsibility for student achievement beyond the teacher's reach.

In our discussions, I describe the racially segregated elementary school I attended in Wilmington, Delaware, where as a 1st grader I had recess three times a day (10:00 a.m., after lunch, and 2:00 p.m.) and a nap after lunch. Back then, "heterogeneity" consisted of mixing children of upwardly-mobile Jewish, Protestant, and Catholic European-American families. None of the children had disabilities. My blind sister could not attend the school that her siblings attended, and neither could the African American children who lived 10 blocks away.

Looking at this historical context, teachers in our graduate program can readily identify some outdated assumptions and practices, such as legal segregation and the exclusion of students with disabilities. Other changes in assumptions are more difficult for them to see at first. For example, could the definition of "hyperactivity" that their schools take for granted have something to do with today's decreased opportunities for physical activity and rest during the school day?

In one of our online courses, teachers read and analyze research about critical issues in urban education. Most of the teachers work in small suburban or rural districts far away from the university's urban campus. As a result of our readings and discussions they see, often for the first time, that problems they have considered "urban" are present—but hidden—in their communities and schools. For example, one reading helps teachers examine the disproportionate placement of African American males in special education (Civil Rights Project, 2002), and the teachers look at data for their own schools. Almost without exception, the teachers are surprised to discover that their school's special education placements conform to the skewed demographics we see across the United States.

Disrupting the Deficit Paradigm

Educators may become discouraged when they come face-to-face with hitherto unquestioned practices and conditions because they know that they cannot eliminate these practices on their own. What we can all do, however, is acknowledge deficit explanations and examine them critically. Invariably this illuminates possibilities that have eluded us, including strategies that focus on student strengths. In our graduate program, teachers have designed and carried out interventions in their classrooms that have proven remarkably effective in disrupting the deficit paradigm.

Reframing Hyperactivity

One project required teachers to address chronic behavior problems that they had been unable to solve. Using a strategy I have found effective in unearthing and challenging deficit paradigm explanations (Weiner, 2003), I guided the teachers in working to reframe the problem behavior of a student or colleague. As Molnar and Lindquist (1989) explain, the reframing process has four steps:

1. Describe the problem behavior in neutral, observable terms.

2. Identify positive characteristics or contributions the individual makes. This part of the process is often challenging because we are so frustrated and angry that we cannot see the individual's strengths.

3. Create a new, positive perspective on the individual—a frame that you can articulate in a short sentence.

4. State the new frame to the person and act on it. Do not refer back to the previous frame.

Deven, a young white teacher working in a predominantly black school, chose to apply the reframing strategy with April, a student in her kindergarten class. April would not sit still and frequently wandered around during whole-class instruction, disturbing other students. Deven considered April a strong candidate for medication for hyperactivity and referral to special education. In her report, Deven described her original frame—her understanding of April's behavior:

> I spoke with her and modeled the correct way to act. . . . When her misbehavior continued, I believed April was looking for attention. I attempted to ignore her behavior, which made the situation worse. . . . As I became more and more frustrated, I felt April was directly disobeying my instructions, distracting the class, and undermining my lessons.

With support from other teachers in the course, Deven developed and acted on a new explanation of April's behavior:

> I told April that I understood that she had a lot of energy, and that was great! I let her know that lots of people need to move around in order to learn. It was just another thing that made her special. . . . I asked that April please do her exercises on the carpet or by the classroom library. I let her know that whenever she felt she was ready, she could return to the group. I also predicted a relapse. I said that I knew she might forget to move to the carpet or library to do her exercises, but that was OK and I would remind her with our special sign—touching the tip of my nose. She seemed a little surprised, but she said she understood.

Reporting on the results of her intervention, Deven commented,

> The retraining changed my negative, critical altitude toward April's behavior to a positive, supportive outlook. As a result, the exercises and movement no longer upset or distracted me. Once I became comfortable with the retraining, April's behavior really improved. Now, April automatically moves to the carpet or library to exercise. The other students don't seem to mind at all, and there is no more tattling. April is happier and more relaxed during whole-group instruction. My teaching assistant thought that this was a crazy idea. Neither one of us can get over the change. We are already planning to reframe several other behaviors.

Deven's new way of understanding April's behavior—that "lots of people need to move around in order to learn"—drew on Deven's previous knowledge of multiple intelligences. Although Deven had been able to access this previous knowledge in earlier conversations about April, she was unable to apply it without the push, from the assignment and her class-mates, to reject her negative explanation for April's behavior.

Reframing Incivility

In another project, teachers applied ideas from Courtney Cazden's classic book *Classroom Discourse* (2001). Teachers identified a problem in achievement connected to discourse practices in their classrooms and designed instructional changes to address the problem. Their analysis of the problem and the changes they planned to make in their instruction were grounded in data they had collected about students' use of language, either through videotaping or audiotaping.

Veronica taught in one of New Jersey's poorest communities. For her project, she chose to address the problems she encountered with the class of 5th graders she met for homeroom and math. She wanted to alter the students' discourse to build a sense of community that would support aca-demic work.

Hired to take over this class in March after the (unsuccessful) teacher had deserted it, Veronica felt overwhelmed. She could not implement her excellent ideas for lessons because students treated one another so disre-spectfully, cursing and jeering at any perceived error. A student who answered a question incorrectly or stumbled over a word would be taunted as a "stupid ass." Those who followed instructions and did their work were ridiculed for behaving well.

Although Veronica is the daughter of Hispanic immigrants and is alert to the ways in which deficit paradigms can obscure student strengths, she was dismayed at her students' behavior. When she observed videotapes of her lessons, she was equally stunned at her own unfriendly tone of voice and her incessant nagging. She observed students' increasingly glazed looks as one scolding followed another. Veronica had taught a kindergarten lit-eracy pull-out class in the same school, and in watching the videotape she became aware of her previously unrecognized assumption that older children should already know acceptable norms of behavior and speech.

The other teachers in our class reminded Veronica that her 5th graders had been miseducated about acceptable norms of conduct by the previous teacher's failure to clarify, support, and enforce appropriate behavior. I suggested that Veronica include role-playing exercises to help students expe-rience and practice their new language skills. In a subsequent class meeting,

Veronica reported delightedly that role-playing had become a highlight of homeroom, especially when normally polite students assumed the role of the person using inappropriate discourse and the usual offenders suddenly became well-mannered.

Changing the class ecology brought out the creativity and leadership of Veronica's most troublesome student, Tyrone. Tyrone proposed, created, and led his classmates in using a remarkably effective tool, which he called the Helping Hand—an illustration on a wall chart of a large hand whose fingers contained reminders of words and phrases that students should use. Tyrone foresaw, correctly, that students would need a helping hand when tempted to use familiar but inappropriate language. At this point, they could turn to the chart and find an acceptable substitute. For instance, instead of saying "you stupid," the Helping Hand reminded students to say "I see it differently." Tyrone's role in this venture helped him earn a new reputation, as a class leader and star student.

Teacher Strengths, Student Strengths

Although this discussion has focused so far on deficit thinking as it relates to students, the deficit paradigm actually takes two contradictory forms. The first variation casts student and family deficits as the cause of poor achievement. Teachers often find this version seductive because it locates responsibility outside their classrooms. The second variation presents teacher characteristics and deficits as the only factor that really counts in undermining student learning. Legislators and parents often find this explanation persuasive because it implies an uncomplicated solution: Fix the teachers we have or hire new and better individuals.

Unfortunately, most professional development, even when the training is aimed to arrest deficit thinking about students, is based on the teacher deficits variant. Like remedial programs for students, professional development programs "fix" teachers by identifying what they don't know or do and telling them how to do it. In my work with teachers in the New Jersey City University graduate program, I have found that both experienced and new teachers already know enough—after learning to challenge their deficit frameworks, scrutinizing qualitative data about their own practice, and working with other teachers who provide support as critical friends—to significantly improve student achievement.

Deven and April, Veronica and Tyrone taught one another. Their learning and growth were synergistic. Assumptions reinforced by school practices, traditions, and political and social conditions initially obscured both teacher and student strengths. Deven and Veronica are urban teachers, but their success in altering their classrooms to capitalize on these strengths has implications far beyond schools that serve primarily poor, minority, or urban students.

As social and political changes alter the face of public education, it becomes increasingly important that all educators scrutinize and challenge tacit assumptions. We can make powerful changes when we break through the pervasive influence of the deficit paradigm and recognize the untapped strengths of students and teachers.

School practices and assumptions emerging from the deficit paradigm often hide student and teacher abilities.

An impersonal, bureaucratic school culture undercuts many of the teaching attitudes and behaviors that draw on student strengths.

References

Cazden, C. B. (2001). *Classroom discourse: The language of teaching and learning* (2nd ed.). Portsmouth, NH: Heinemann.

Civil Rights Project, Harvard University. (2002, June). Racial inequity in special education. Executive summary for federal policy makers. Available at www.civil rightsproject.ucla.edu/research/specialed/IDEA_paper02.php.

Molnar, A., & Lindquist, B. (1989). *Changing problem behavior in schools*. San Francisco: Jossey-Bass.

Weiner, L. (2000). Research in the '90s: Implications for urban teacher preparation. *Review of Educational Research, 70,* 369–406.

———. (2003). Why is classroom management so vexing to urban teachers? *Theory Into Practice, 42,* 305–312.

Lois Weiner is Professor of Elementary and Secondary Education at New Jersey City University in Jersey City, New Jersey; lweiner@njcu.edu. She is author of *Urban Teaching: The Essentials* (Teachers College Press, 2006) and a consultant to schools and districts on teacher development.

8

Inclusion

Rejecting Instruction That Disables

Bruce A. Marlowe

Marilyn Page

In 1997, when her world was still fresh and ripe with possibility, Bruce's six-year-old daughter Rachel ran off the school bus one windy October afternoon waving a single sheet of paper high over her head. "I have homework! I have homework!" she shouted excitedly. Now, seven years later, her delight in school learning has been replaced with ennui, languor, and a precocious world-weariness about formal education. Rachel's school narrative lumbers forward, plodding predictably to its tedious, anticlimactic finish. But, she will survive. Unfortunately for students with disabilities, their school stories are considerably less sanguine, even for the fewer than half that finish high school. And, what of students who are gifted and talented? Students who don't fit the mold, for whatever reasons, need good teachers who understand that the *questions students ask* are the most central issue to knowledge construction and active engagement. You already know that teachers who simply deliver information, or provide all of the questions without ever turning to student-developed inquiries (even if the teacher-created questions are interesting), will invariably face students

NOTE: From *Creating and Sustaining the Constructivist Classroom* by Bruce A. Marlowe and Marilyn Page, copyright 2005. Reprinted with permission from Corwin.

who are unmotivated, disengaged, and perhaps even hostile. For students with disabilities and other learning differences, the stakes are even higher and the need more urgent.

Sham Inquiry

As noted in previous chapters, in spite of the avalanche of both anecdotal and empirical reports (Capraro, 2001; Cole & McGuire, 2004; Fraser & Spinner, 2002; Thomason, 2003; Marlowe & Page, 1998) concerning the positive results of progressive, inquiry-based learning, passive traditional practices appear firmly entrenched (Goodlad, 1984; Cuban, 1990, 2001; Apple, 2001). In fact, the repertoire of most teachers continues to be limited strictly to the familiar cycle of information transmission and evaluation.

More chillingly, there is a relatively new trend taking place in our schools, one that arose, ostensibly, to counter the perception of teacher over-reliance on *talk and chalk*. And it is this trend that, perhaps more than any other reason, accounts for the scarcity of constructivist pedagogy in our classrooms. For lack of a better term, we refer to it simply as *sham inquiry*—that is, teaching practices that look like inquiry, sound like inquiry, but on closer inspection are revealed to be just as unhealthy to student learning as a steady, uniform diet of teacher telling. In its various guises, sham inquiry gives no one solace but the teacher, who, thinking she has refined her practice, continues to ignore, discount, or put aside the questions *students ask* in favor of those she believes are more valuable.

At the root of sham inquiry is the fundamental misunderstanding that constructivism is largely about what teachers do, as opposed to what their students do. From at least the time of Dewey, progressive educational movements have always been co-opted by a large set of players who, historically, have viewed teachers simply as technicians. In an effort to codify good practice, school administrators, teacher education programs, state licensing agencies, professional developers, and textbook publishers have become overly preoccupied with the *how to*, often producing scripted materials, teacher prompts, protocols, and other programmed forms of instruction—what Ohanian refers to as "Stir and Serve Recipes for Teaching." Such approaches are based on the erroneous assumption that all students can learn from the same materials, classroom instructional techniques, and modes of evaluation. Nowhere is this sort of sham inquiry more prevalent than in its use with students with disabilities and other learning differences. This appears to be true for two separate but related reasons: first, the predominance of low expectations by teachers of low-achieving students (particularly those who are African-American and Latino); and second, a fix which is worse than the problem: "teaching styles that stress drill, practice, and other mind-numbing strategies" based on the mistaken belief that "such children lack ability" (Berliner & Biddle in Kohn, 1999, p. 99).

Tough Question

• Why are students with disabilities less likely to have constructivist learning experiences than nondisabled students? Is this justifiable?

Sham Inquiry in Practice

. . . inquiry is the way people learn when they're left alone. (Suchman, 1966, p. 2)

Consider Jonah, a highly gifted fifth-grade student in a mixed-ability classroom. His school story captures the need for constructivist classrooms, as well as the seduction and danger of sham inquiry. Jonah's teacher, Mr. Stevens—young, energetic, charismatic—began his review of fractions and their relationships one Friday by passing out a variety of materials to each of the cooperative groups he had previously established: poster board, empty egg cartons, calculators, construction paper, markers, scissors. He asked simply, "Using the strategies we have talked about all week, please demonstrate that three-fourths is greater than two-thirds." As Mr. Stevens circled the room, checking for understanding and periodically asking probing questions to individual groups about their work, the students attacked the problem with vigor, applying what they had been taught during the last four days. They divided the fractions (in order to compare the decimal amounts), filled the egg cartons, drew pie charts, and found common denominators. Mr. Stevens was thrilled that the students seemed to remember everything he had *covered* and as he made the rounds, he expressed his pride in them with great enthusiasm.

Jonah sat pensively, immobile.

While his group was busy pasting their work onto the poster board, he seemed to just stare at the numbers. And then, 15 minutes after the activity had begun, he said to Mr. Stevens, "I just noticed something. . . . That's *so* cool. Look, Mr. Stevens, if you multiply from the bottom-up and across like this:

$$\frac{3}{4} \diagup\!\!\!\!\diagdown \frac{2}{3}$$

You get 9 on the left side and 8 on the right side. That's *really* cool. Is that a way to show that three-fourths is greater than two-thirds? I mean will this always work? I think it will, but I'm not sure I really get it yet. Why does this work? I think I can figure it out. Can I work on this instead? Can I?" Uncertain of where Jonah was going, and nervous about his taking of such a divergent path, Mr. Stevens reminded Jonah that he was to use the strategies he had taught the class during the week. Mr. Stevens pointed out that there was no evidence that Jonah had done any work at all. Besides, Mr. Stevens had no idea if Jonah was on to something or not.

In the span of 15 minutes, Mr. Stevens communicated several potent lessons to Jonah; lessons that distinguish sham inquiry from a true constructivist classroom and underscore the need for real inquiry for students with learning differences. Mr. Stevens believes, mistakenly, that his classroom provides opportunities for all students to engage in constructivist activities.

But, here is what Jonah learned:

1. It is more important that I answer my teacher's questions than my own.

2. Independent thinking and problem solving is not to be pursued, unless my teacher understands it and/or it conforms to teacher-approved methods and strategies.

3. It is very important that I move at the same pace and produce the same products as my peers.

4. And, my understanding can only be demonstrated by repeating back what has been transmitted and nothing more.

There is another, subtler message often embedded in practices that masquerade as constructivism as well, a message to which Mr. Stevens probably does not ascribe. The message, delivered inadvertently, but powerfully through his words and actions, is that memorization is more important than deep understanding; that activity, simply for the sake of activity, leads to greater comprehension than deep reflection and inquiry. To wit, teacher-directed activities often sabotage real inquiry. As Sewall (2000) has noted:

> Activity based learning is vain. . . . At rock bottom, projects and activities provide mere entertainment. Teachers . . . seek to fill dead time in the classroom. Projects and activities keep kids occupied and unmutinous.

Clearly, Jonah is a remarkably bright and unusually perceptive student. Yet, there is something all too familiar about his developing school story, a story that most of us remember from our own school experiences, or see in our children, or, worse, watch unfold on the faces of our students.

Many students are essentially teacher-proof; they will survive years of bad schooling relatively unscathed. Students like Jonah, however, and those with a myriad of other learning differences, often get trampled in school. As noted above, although constructivist educational practices clearly benefit all students, its implementation is considerably more urgent for our students who learn differently than their peers. That is, while the implications of poor instruction for most students' learning is relatively benign, the relationship between such traditional notions of teaching and learning and the outcomes for students with exceptionalities is much more dire. And, because special education law now requires that students with disabilities be educated with their nondisabled peers to the maximum extent appropriate (i.e., in the least restrictive environment), all teachers, regardless of their politics about inclusion, must assume responsibility for the learning of all students.

Full Inclusion Is Changing Classrooms

For the last 20 years, most special education students received a large part of their education in public schools—but on a *pull-out* basis. Most still do. That is, students leave their regular classrooms for part or all of the day to work with a special education teacher or aide in a resource room on individual academic skills or behavioral goals; however, including students with disabilities in regular classrooms for most or all of their day (regardless of the severity of their disability) has become increasingly popular around the nation and about 80% of students with disabilities spend at least some of their day in a regular classroom. (That means they are in *your* classroom.) This change in thinking has been variously described as the *full inclusion* or *mainstreaming* movement. Several persuasive arguments have driven this change. For example, special education is prohibitively expensive, stigmatizes students, fragments instruction, and contributes to a high drop-out rate.

Although research shows (Henley, Ramsey, & Algozzine, 1993; Giangreco et al., 2004) that special-needs students appear to do better in regular classrooms than in special education settings, recent surveys indicate that most teachers are still uncomfortable with special education students in their classrooms because they feel that they do not have the proper training to work with students with disabilities. Are these fears justified? Perhaps, but in some sense, this appears irrelevant because virtually every public school classroom (K–12) has at least one student with a disability; teachers must learn to adjust to mainstrearning, regardless of their politics. Still, legitimate questions remain.

Tough Questions

- Do students with disabilities require something regular education teachers cannot provide?
- What is it that special education teachers provide that is so critical to the needs of students with disabilities?
- What additional training do regular education teachers need to ensure that students with disabilities receive an appropriate education in their classrooms?

What's So Special About Special Education?

As it turns out, very little. There is some good news about what works (and what does not) for students with disabilities. What we can say with certainty about what students with disabilities need is contrary to what many regular (and special) educators believe. For example, many classroom teachers operate under the assumption that only specialized training in fields like learning disabilities, mental retardation, and speech and language disorders will allow them to work effectively with disabled students in their classrooms. Similarly, many special educators believe that they are somehow uniquely qualified (by virtue of their training) to work with children with disabilities. Many assume that the magic bullet for working with students with disabilities is finding the right placements and particular academic or behavioral curricula that match the disability in question. We now know, from a variety of research, that all these assumptions are false. In fact, Ysseldyke and Algozzine (1995) have summarized these findings by noting that research in special education has been unable to demonstrate that:

- specific instructional practices and techniques match or work better with specific learner characteristics;
- children with mental retardation need X, whereas children with learning disabilities need Y;
- certain placements result in improved academic achievement; or that
- special educators are more effective in working with students with disabilities than are regular educators.

A Closer Look at Today's Classrooms

On average, public school districts formally identify between 10%–12% of their students with disabilities, and about 2%–5% of their students as gifted and talented if IQ scores are used as the sole criterion, and

15%–20% if a talent pool model is employed (Renzulli, 1999; Turnbull A. P., Turnbull, H. R., Shank, & Smith, 2004). At the national level, Table 8.1 provides a brief overview of who these students are and how their learning differences manifest themselves in today's classrooms.

Table 8.1   Brief Overview of Categories of Disabilities

Term	Definitions	*% of All Students with Disabilities*
Specific Learning Disabilities	Students of average intellectual ability or higher with significant difficulty in one or more academic domain (e.g., reading).	50.5
Speech or Language Impairment	Students with significant difficulty in either producing language (e.g., articulation difficulty) or understanding language (e.g., following directions).	19
Mental Retardation	Students with significantly below average measured intellectual ability and age-appropriate social skills (e.g., communication, independent living, etc.).	10.8
Emotional Disabilities	Students with chronic emotional, behavioral, or interpersonal difficulties extreme enough to interfere with learning.	8.2
Other Health Impairments	Students with chronic conditions that limit strength, vitality, alertness (e.g., epilepsy, arthritis, asthma).	4.5
Multiple Disabilities	Students with more than one disability.	2
Orthopedic Impairments	Students who have limited functional use of legs, feet, arms, hands, or other body parts.	1.3
Hearing Impairments	Students with significant hearing loss in one or both ears.	1.3
Visual Impairments	Students with low vision, even when corrected.	0.46
Traumatic Brain Injury	Students who have had brain injury as the result of external force (e.g., car accident) or internal occurrence (e.g., stroke).	0.24
Deaf-blindness	Students with both significant hearing loss and low vision.	0.03
Giftedness	(% of total population)	15–20

Despite the progressive nature of special education legislation, individuals with identified disabilities, as a group, continue, as noted above, to fare quite poorly both in our schools and in their transition to adulthood. Here is some of what we know:

- Although the overall national graduation rate is approximately 88%, only about 27% of all students with disabilities leave high school with a diploma (Turnbull et al., 2004).
- The employment rates of people with disabilities is only about 32%, compared to an 81% employment rate for people without disabilities; the employment rate either full or part time for individuals with severe disabilities is only 19% (National Center on Education Statistics, 2003).
- Approximately two-thirds of individuals without disabilities report that they are *very satisfied* with life; only one-third of individuals with disabilities report the same level of satisfaction (Turnbull et al., 2004).
- One in five school-aged children is estimated to have reading disabilities. Eighty percent of these students who fail to make significant reading progress by the age of nine will continue to be unskilled readers in the 12th grade, if they even stay in school that long (Shaywitz, 1995).
- Juel (1988) found that about 40% of unskilled readers in the fourth grade would prefer cleaning their rooms to reading.
- Seventy-five to eighty percent of the prison population is estimated to have specific learning disabilities and/or serious emotional disturbance.

Although clearly beyond the scope of this chapter, the most recent data on independent living, wage earning, and rates of incarceration are equally bleak for individuals with disabilities. We must ask to what extent teaching approaches that focus on the transmission of information contribute to student failure, disengagement, and disenfranchisement.

Tough Questions

- Why is the dropout rate so high for students with disabilities?
- Why is academic underachievement so prevalent?
- Why have behavioral problems increased so dramatically?
- Why do students prefer cleaning their rooms to reading?

Is it plausible in all (or even most) cases of student failure that students and/or their families are to blame for weak academic skills and/or behavioral problems? Goodlad (1984) and Cuban (1990) found that students spend a little more than 10% of their time in school asking questions, reading, writing, or engaged in some other form of active learning. Is there something wrong with our children, or are schools and teachers contributing to this state of affairs?

> **Consider:** Could 5,000 reports be right in finding that no student difficulty was related to shortcomings in school practice? Or would Carnine's (1994) question about this finding ring more true:
> "If 5,000 medical files of patients who failed to respond to treatment were analyzed, would there be an absence of professional shortcomings in all 5,000 cases?" (Carnine, 1994, p. 341).

Consider how this plays out for Sam, a 10th-grade student who was described simply as a behavior problem when we met him some years ago. Sam's school struggles began in the first grade. Since that time, he had been labeled as learning disabled, mentally retarded, emotionally disturbed, and language impaired, depending on the year he was tested and the person who did the testing. By the time Sam had reached the 10th grade, he refused to go to school and began receiving home tutoring from a man named Mr. Smith.

Mr. Smith reported that Sam was able to do a great deal more than he was led to believe by school personnel. He spoke at length about Sam's knack for fixing virtually anything mechanical (including car engines, grandfather clocks, and electric kitchen ranges), his strong ability to draw, and his memory for exactly how things looked long after he had seen them. Mr. Smith noted that Sam had difficulty expressing himself, read and wrote at about the sixth-grade level, and was extremely anxious and self-conscious about his weak academic skills. Although the primary focus of Mr. Smith's work was on helping Sam to obtain his driver's license, he indicated that he had successfully introduced academics through the back door. For example, Mr. Smith had structured math and physics lessons around ice fishing trips and other outdoor activities, brought car manuals to Sam's house that they read together, and communicated in writing on the computer, frequently sending e-mail messages to one another about interesting engineering and mechanically oriented Web sites.

When we met Sam at one of our homes for an evaluation, we found him to be an extremely polite, personable, and engaging adolescent. Although Sam was somewhat slow to warm up, after a brief walk outdoors and some tinkering with an old car, Sam initiated conversation easily, and rapport was established quickly. Sam struggled markedly on tests of reading and writing and on virtually all the evaluation measures that required fluent speaking skill, but he performed extremely well on measures that demanded mechanical problem solving, such as jigsaw puzzles and block designs. Sam shared with us his love of cars, information about his collection of small engines, and a small portfolio of sketches he had made of various sorts of machinery. When asked about school, Sam became sullen. He noted that teachers only asked him to do "stuff I can't." He said that students frequently teased him; that he often became so frustrated that he got involved in fights; and that he hated school and would never return.

The teachers at school were happy that Sam was receiving home tutoring—they were happy that he was no longer their problem. Most believed he was headed for the criminal justice system; others noted that it was just as well. Sam, after all, was not bright, and he had an attitude problem to boot.

Do you know Sam? What is so sad about this story is that it is not fiction, not for Sam and not for others like him whose gifts lie outside what we for too long have considered to be intelligence. What is most striking about Sam, and about so many students in our schools, is what powerful learners they can be and what enormous talents they possess. To recognize these talents, we must look beyond our limited conception that to be intelligent and to learn, one must have strong verbal and/or logical mathematical ability. Let's look more closely at an alternative way of thinking about intelligence, then return to Sam at the end of this section.

A Table: Expanding Our Cognitive Horizons

Howard Gardner's *Frames of Mind: The Theory of Multiple Intelligences* (1983) indicates that there are at least seven, perhaps more, distinct types of human intelligences. Although he was not the first to theorize that intelligence comes in many forms, Gardner has written extensively on the ways in which an understanding of multiple intelligences, or MI, can be applied in educational settings. See Table 8.2 below.

Extending Your Learning

Since 1983 Gardner has proposed additional types of human intelligence. What are they? How can they be explored in your classroom?

When we think of students who are doing poorly in our classrooms, we typically focus on the things they cannot do, or we speculate about the kinds of difficulty we believe may account for their weak school performance. The MI theory allows us to reframe our thinking about student performance. It calls on us to consider what our students do well, how they learn, and what they find intrinsically interesting so that we may label their strengths, as opposed to their weaknesses.

Table 8.2   Types of Human Intelligences

Intelligence	Learner's Strengths
Intrapersonal	Ability to know self; ability to understand one's own strengths/weaknesses and motivations
Interpersonal	Ability to know others; ability to "read" social and /or political situations; ability to influence others; ability to lead and/or care for others—to be sensitive to needs of others
Bodily-kinesthetic	Ability to control the movement of one's body; ability to move in a graceful, highly coordinated fashion
Musical	Ability to produce, write, and/or appreciate music
Spatial	Ability to shape, perceive, design, and/or conceive visual-spatial information; ability to remember visual information
Logical-mathematical	Ability to manipulate numbers and symbolic information; ability to draw logical conclusions; ability to think abstractly
Verbal-linguistic	Ability to manipulate, create, and appreciate the rhythms of language; ability to speak, read, and/or write fluently

Let's return for a minute to Sam, who has always done poorly in school. Given what we know about him, would you say it is because he lacks intelligence? Are there things Sam does well? Could you think of a way that Sam could shine in your classroom? Or do you think simply that school should not be for kids like Sam? How do we want to label students like Sam—by what they can do or what they cannot do?

Why Students With Disabilities Need Constructivist Classrooms

Clearly, disabilities make learning and classrooms more challenging. Some disabilities may even make the learning of some things impossible. As teachers, we must create opportunities for learning that are more exciting, more enriching, and more rewarding—in short, more appealing—than the desire to clean one's room, leave school, get involved in criminal activity, or become a ward of the state.

Tough Questions

- How do students with disabilities learn? Is it really different from the learning of other students?
- Shouldn't we instead be asking how can we spark their curiosity, facilitate their learning, and, perhaps most important, get out of their way as Suchman suggests above?

These questions are extremely important for students with disabilities, as they are at increased risk of school failure, and difficult transitions to adulthood. As noted above, the high school dropout rate for students with disabilities is unacceptably high. Without a compelling reason to stay, and with little academic success and a great deal of frustration, this should come as no surprise. For many students with disabilities, school is deadly boring; it is irrelevant to their lives, needs, and interests; and for many others, it is extremely punishing as well. But the tough questions posed above are virtually never asked. Instead, teachers often assume that students with disabilities are so different, so impaired, so damaged that it is a waste of time to pursue inquiry with them. As Golfus remarks in "When Billy Broke His Head and Other Tales of Wonder" (Simpson & Golfus, 1995), many believe individuals with disabilities are just " . . . too gimped out to work."

In fact, students with disabilities, although in much more urgent need of constructivist approaches, are far less likely to receive them. The most recent research indicates that students with disabilities spend much of their day on tasks requiring little more cognitive energy than rote memorization. Worse still, many advocate for just such an approach. Consider the following, which neatly summarizes not only a very popular view of inclusion, but one about constructivism as well:

There are several reasons for opposing a policy of full inclusion. One reason is because full inclusion . . . makes direct, systematic instruction nearly impossible. In addition, once full inclusion is implemented, teachers are forced to change their teaching methods to more child-directed, discovery-oriented, project-based learning activities in which every student works at his or her own pace. (Crawford, 2001)

What is shocking about Crawford's position is only his candor.

Assuming, as we do, that there is nothing wrong, and everything right, with changing one's teaching so that it *is* "more child-centered, discovery-oriented, project based," how does one begin to develop an inquiry-based learning environment knowing that students with an enormous range of abilities and interests may populate a single classroom? With earlier caveats about following a lock-step, prescribed sequence of instructional activities in mind, we propose instead a series of *infrequently* asked questions, or IAQs, as a point of departure for setting up constructivist approaches in mixed ability classrooms. These IAQs are not simply designed to be provocative; rather, it is our hope that they will lead to careful teacher self-reflection about the importance of constructivist approaches, about the pitfalls of sham inquiry, and about the true conditions necessary for students to get excited about learning.

IAQs

1. How are constructivism and rigid, lock-step, standards-based education incompatible for students with learning differences?

The short answer to this IAQ is that rigid application of standards and constructivism can be incompatible in many, many ways—particularly for students with disabilities. Students with disabilities and/or giftedness are, by definition, different academically, emotionally, physically, or cognitively than their age peers. Thus, in some sense, they are the paradigmatic case of how standards and inquiry are often incompatible, as such students are in a nonstandard place at a nonstandard time, and will by necessity have questions that may differ from those of their peers. But this raises an even larger question: Does it make sense to assume that there is a *standard* time and place in which students are ready (to say nothing of eager) for particular kinds of content learning? Despite overwhelming evidence to the contrary, an increasing number of states seem to be making precisely this assumption as an ever-growing number of them prepare to roll out detailed sets of grade-level expectations. Yet, in a recent study by Peterson and colleagues (2002) when teachers were asked about the range of abilities of students in their class *every* teacher in the sample stated that students crossed at least five grade levels, with some teachers assessing even larger grade-level differences. Clearly, student difference is not merely a special education issue. In a very succinct summary of this problem Tomlinson (2000) notes that:

> Students who are the same age differ in their readiness to learn, their interests, their styles of learning, their experiences, and their life circumstances. The differences in students are significant enough to make a major impact on what students need to learn, the pace at which they need to learn it, and the support they need from teachers and others to learn it well. (p. 6)

As every alert teacher knows, what Tomlinson says is true whether one's classroom contains students with disabilities or not. What is important is that teachers think flexibly about standards and avoid the same rigid expectations for all of their students.

2. Don't students with learning differences need to learn basic skills before they engage in real inquiry?

The value of special education can be summed up as follows: What's good for the goose is necessary for the gander. That is, although all students benefit from good teachers, students with a history of academic and/or behavioral challenges (for whatever reason) need good teachers and the kind of classroom experiences supported and driven by constructivist propositions, including the proposition that student talent and ability can be key to developing knowledge. If a teacher is simply delivering information, he cannot ever deal with the infinite variety of ways of knowing and learning that students with disabilities present. To remain interested and engaged in learning, students need opportunities to discover, create, and problem solve. But, what if problem-solving skill is precisely what they lack?

Many teachers treat students with disabilities as if they have a defect that needs correcting. To fix the disability, some professionals believe that students need high levels of teacher-directed information transmission. At the other extreme, some advocate fostering student strengths (wherever they may be), following the students' leads in learning, and letting students choose whether or not to attempt to improve the academic skill areas in which they may struggle. The first approach often results in the temporary memorization of increased content knowledge. The second approach is also inappropriate because most students with disabilities demonstrate weak ability to approach tasks strategically and often have difficulty carefully monitoring their own progress. The majority of students with disabilities also do not spontaneously initiate problem-solving behaviors, and they demonstrate difficulty sustaining attention (even in areas of their interest), inhibiting impulsive responding, and remaining cognitively flexible. Many students with disabilities, therefore, need a bridge from traditional special education to inquiry-based learning experiences.

Learning in constructivist terms is simply not possible until students possess some fundamental skills; however, this does not mean students need to earn the right to engage in inquiry by demonstrating minimum competencies in reading, writing, or mathematics. The skills referred to here are not academic skills, per se. Rather, they are thinking tools based largely on the work of Meichenbaum's (1977) cognitive behavioral approach to problem solving. These tools were initially developed to help students initiate their own learning; sustain attention for complex, multistep tasks; form hypotheses; and evaluate their own performance. Although there are many kinds of learning strategy models that have grown from this work, perhaps the easiest and most practical of these approaches is Bonnie Camp's *Think Aloud Program* (1987; 1996). The *Think Aloud Program* is designed to increase student self-control by the explicit teaching of self-talk strategies for solving a range of problems. Because many students with disabilities lack verbal mediation skills, teaching them to *think aloud* provides a bridge to help them move toward self-directed, inquiry-based learning. You can also easily incorporate this into whole-class instruction. Camp (1996) suggests that teachers introduce specific questions students can ask themselves as they set about to learn. They involve:

- identifying problems ("What am I to do? How can I find out?");
- choosing a plan or strategy ("How can I do it? What are some plans?");
- self-monitoring ("Am I using my plan?"); and
- self-evaluating ("Is my plan working? How did I do? Do I need a new plan?").

When students use these questions in the context of the curriculum (and not separate from it), together with a menu of problem-solving strategies (such as brainstorming, means/ends analysis, mnemonic memory strategies, and so on), they quickly acquire a wide repertoire of powerful learning tools that can be used for real inquiry.

3. Isn't "I differentiate my instruction for students with disabilities" just a more politically palatable way to say "I use tracking within my classroom"?

In practice this is, unfortunately, almost always the case. As Peterson, Hittie, and Tamor (2002b) have noted, most of what is referred to as differentiated instruction is simply tracking within a classroom under a different name. Even well-intentioned teachers traditionally think of differentiation this way and will often group students by a single, global measure of their perceived ability; require less of students they view as below average; and create more challenging assignments for those who are facile verbally and/or mathematically. What distinguishes true differentiation from such ability grouping is largely dispositional. That is, in classrooms where instruction is truly differentiated so that all learners may engage in real inquiry, teachers believe that all learners have strengths, that a uniform lesson format for the whole class is doomed to fail, that flexible grouping strategies (see, for example, Aronson's Jigsaw Model [Aronson & Bridgeman, 1979]) are critical for every student to succeed, and that the collaborative problem solving of authentic (i.e., student created) problems is essential to learning. Such teachers believe further that there are many ways students might obtain information and demonstrate their learning.

Gardner's (1983; 1993) MI theory is one way in which teachers can adapt and modify their instruction for heterogeneous grouping. Gardner reminds us that to recognize student talents and interests, to give value to *their questions,* we must look beyond our limited conception that to be intelligent and to learn, one must have strong verbal and/or logical-mathematical ability. Indeed, failure to perform well in one of these two ways is how virtually all students with disabilities come to be identified, labeled, and ultimately thought of as *not able.* When we think of students who are doing poorly in our classrooms, we typically focus on the things they cannot do, or we speculate about the kinds of difficulty we believe may account for their weak school performance. The MI theory allows us to reframe our thinking about student performance. It calls on us to consider what our students do well, how they learn, and what they find intrinsically interesting so that we can label their strengths, as opposed to their weaknesses, and validate the types of inquiry they are most likely to pursue.

4. How can I demonstrate to my students, colleagues, and administrators that having different behavioral and academic expectations is not only necessary but also fair?

For most students who are eligible for special education service, disabilities are life-span issues. The ways in which they approach material, the challenges they face, and the compensatory strategies they use—all these things are unlikely to change over time. Many years ago, one of us was involved in a consultation with a 10th-grade chemistry teacher who complained that a hyperactive student in her class continually tapped his pencil on the lab table, disrupting her and other students. The teacher shared with us that most days ended with arguments (because the student would continue tapping moments after he was asked to stop) and an occasional angry exchange. From the teacher's point of view, it was unclear whether the tapping was a willful attempt to continually disrupt the classroom or a manifestation of a behavior out of the boy's control. Either way, the behavior had to stop. Thinking about this behavior as something that must be changed (i.e., thinking that the student must be changed) is a mindset that guarantees teacher frustration and anger, student resentment, and often feelings of inferiority and impotence in both. One way to frame this dilemma is the following: The student needs to tap, and the teacher needs a distraction-free environment. Accepting for a moment that both are in fact true needs (and that the student is not simply trying to be difficult), are these needs mutually exclusive? Of course not. Readers who already have begun to think about how we can change the environment and not the student already know this. For the rest of you, one solution to this dilemma can be found at the end of the chapter.

Unfortunately, many teachers believe that accommodating an individual student need is somehow unfair to other students.

Consider: As Richard Lavoie has elegantly pointed out on his well-known video about the F.A.T. city workshop (1989), it is not about the other students! Lavoie points out that a teacher who fails to accommodate a student with a disability (because she feels this is unfair to others students) uses the same logic as a teacher skilled in CPR who refuses to resuscitate a student who collapses after heart failure because there isn't time to administer CPR to all the students in her room. Obviously, all the students do not need CPR. Fairness is about need, not about ensuring all students receive the same things at the same time.

In practical terms, this may mean that some students will need note-takers, others will need books on tape, and still others will need extended time to take tests, complete assignments, and so on. Some students will need to demonstrate their learning in writing, whereas others may demonstrate comprehension orally, in song, or through some other form of creative expression. What is important is that we remember our goal: to facilitate real learning. For some students getting out of their way is not enough; they will need support.

---

5. How can students with disabilities teach each other?

Ironically, perhaps one of the most powerful learning approaches for students with disabilities is to prepare, and encourage, them to teach others. We observed this (and it was dramatic) in Jan Carpenter's classroom, a teacher in a multi-age elementary school. Steve, a student with severe attentional and organizational difficulties, typically arrived unprepared for school—he rarely arrived with his books or writing utensils, had difficulty settling down for class work, and often appeared confused shortly after directions had been given. Many special educators and proponents of collaborative groups emphasize the importance of pairing students like Steve with academically advanced students who can model appropriate classroom and social behaviors. Jan chose a seemingly counterintuitive approach and paired Steve with a student whose organizational skills were weaker than his own. After a variety of interventions that often resulted in Steve becoming upset and Jan becoming frustrated, she asked Steve if he could help a student with mild autism named Maria to get organized in the morning, to keep her materials tidy, and to remember to bring her books home for homework assignments. On the first day of Steve's teaching, Steve approached Maria at the end of the school day and asked the following questions: "Maria, what do you need to do to make sure you have everything you need? How can you remember to bring these materials home? What will you do tomorrow morning to remember to bring your homework to school?" Jan's strategy worked brilliantly. Steve began to rehearse verbally the strategies and questions he needed to ask himself to become more focused, responsible, and engaged with school assignments. For the first time, Steve began to feel empowered, as if learning was something within his control. For the first time, Steve saw at first hand the value of self-questioning, of teaching, and of collaborating with another. Finally, Steve became a model for Maria, and slowly she began to learn. Who might she teach next?

More Tough Questions

- Should all students, regardless of the severity of disability, be educated in regular classrooms? Why? Why not?
- At what age, if ever, should a decision be made that a student should pursue vocational preparation instead of a more academically based education? Who should be involved in such a decision?
- Is there a value to labeling students? Why? Why not?
- Are certain intelligences more important for students to develop than others?

THE PEN-TAPPING DILEMMA

A rubber pad was placed on the lab table, allowing the student to tap to his heart's content without disturbing his classmates or the teacher.

PART III

What Makes a Good Teacher?

Vignette 1

Cathy Johnson is charged with teaching her tenth-grade biology class about the digestive system of sheep, their eating habits, and their grazing preferences. Here is her plan: From Monday to Wednesday, she will present a forty-minute lecture, fielding questions as they arise; Thursday is scheduled for review; and on Friday she'll give a multiple-choice test based on the information that she covered during the week.

Let's take a glimpse at a typical exchange between Cathy and her students.

On Tuesday, after twenty-five minutes of lecture, Billy raises his hand and, after being acknowledged by Ms. Johnson, says, "I still don't understand. How come sheep can digest grass but people can't?"

"We covered this yesterday. Can someone help Billy out? Who knows why sheep can digest grass. Come on, people. Anyone? Anyone?"

Jessica dutifully raises her hand. When called on, she says, "Sheep are ruminants. They have three extra specialized stomach sections and humans have one stomach section."

"Thank you, Jessica. At least I know one person is listening."

On Friday, Cathy administers her multiple-choice test. A few students fail, but most earn passing grades. Even though she will not return to the subject of sheep for the remainder of the year, Cathy feels confident that the generally strong test scores indicate that she has adequately covered the content and that her students have learned the material.

Vignette 2

Monday through Thursday, Frankie Stevens, an elder Navajo sheep herder, spends forty minutes each afternoon with tribal children, listening to their questions about sheep's eating habits and grazing preferences. When a child asks a question, the elder often replies, "What do *you* think?" and continues to encourage further observation and inquiry. On Friday, Mr. Stevens asks the students to herd the sheep without him, to rely on one another, and to return prepared to demonstrate what they have learned.

Is Cathy Johnson a good teacher? Is Frankie Stevens teaching? How might Mr. Stevens answer Billy's question to Ms. Johnson in the first vignette?

9

The Banking
Concept of Education

Paulo Freire

A careful analysis of the teacher-student relationship at any level, inside or outside the school, reveals its fundamentally *narrative* character. This relationship involves a narrating Subject (the teacher) and patient listening objects (the students). The contents, whether values or empirical dimensions of reality, tend in the process of being narrated to become lifeless and petrified. Education is suffering from narration sickness.

The teacher talks about reality as if it were motionless, static, compartmentalized, and predictable. Or else he expounds on a topic completely alien to the existential experience of the students. His task is to "fill" the students with the contents of his narration—contents which are detached from reality, disconnected from the totality that engendered them and could give them significance. Words are emptied of their concreteness and become a hollow, alienated, and alienating verbosity.

The outstanding characteristic of this narrative education, then, is the sonority of words, not their transforming power. "Four times four is sixteen; the capital of Para is Belem." The student records, memorizes, and repeats these phrases without perceiving what four times four really means,

NOTE: From *Pedagogy of the Oppressed* by Paulo Freire. Copyright 1970, 1993 by the author. Reprinted by permission of The Continuum International Publishing Group. For additional information, please e-mail kgallof@continuum-books.com.

or realizing the true significance of "capital" in the affirmation "the capital of Para is Belem," that is, what Belem means for Para and what Para means for Brazil.

Narration (with the teacher as narrator) leads the students to memorize mechanically the narrated account. Worse yet, it turns them into "containers," into "receptacles" to be "filled" by the teachers. The more completely she fills the receptacles, the better a teacher she is. The more meekly the receptacles permit themselves to be filled, the better students they are.

Education thus becomes an act of depositing, in which the students are the depositories and the teacher is the depositor. Instead of communicating, the teacher issues communiques and makes deposits which the students patiently receive, memorize, and repeat. This is the "banking" concept of education, in which the scope of action allowed to the students extends only as far as receiving, filing, and storing the deposits. They do, it is true, have the opportunity to become collectors or cataloguers of the things they store. But in the last analysis, it is the people themselves who are filed away through the lack of creativity, transformation, and knowledge in this (at best) misguided system. For apart from inquiry, apart from the praxis, individuals cannot be truly human. Knowledge emerges only through invention and re-invention, through the restless, impatient continuing, hopeful inquiry human beings pursue in the world, with the world, and with each other.

In the banking concept of education, knowledge is a gift bestowed by those who consider themselves knowledgeable upon those whom they consider to know nothing. Projecting an absolute ignorance onto others, a characteristic of the ideology of oppression, negates education and knowledge as processes of inquiry. The teacher presents himself to his students as their necessary opposite; by considering their ignorance absolute, he justifies his own existence. The students, alienated like the slave in the Hegelian dialectic, accept their ignorance as justifying the teacher's existence—but unlike the slave, they never discover that they educate the teacher.

The *raison d'etre* of libertarian education, on the other hand, lies in its drive towards reconciliation. Education must begin with the solution of the teacher-student contradiction, by reconciling the poles of the contradiction so that both are simultaneously teachers *and* students.

This solution is not (nor can it be) found in the banking concept. On the contrary, banking education maintains and even stimulates the contradiction through the following attitudes and practices, which mirror oppressive society as a whole:

a. the teacher teaches and the students are taught;

b. the teacher knows everything and the students know nothing;

c. the teacher thinks and the students are thought about;

d. the teacher talks and the students listen—meekly;

e. the teacher disciplines and the students are disciplined;

f. the teacher chooses and enforces his choice, and the students comply;

g. the teacher acts and the students have the illusion of acting through the action of the teacher;

h. the teacher chooses the program content, and the students (who were not consulted) adapt to it;

i. the teacher confuses the authority of knowledge with his or her own professional authority, which she and he sets in opposition to the freedom of the students;

j. the teacher is the Subject of the learning process, while the pupils are mere objects.

It is not surprising that the banking concept of education regards men as adaptable, manageable beings. The more students work at storing the deposits entrusted to them, the less they develop the critical consciousness which would result from their intervention in the world as transformers of that world. The more completely they accept the passive role imposed on them, the more they tend simply to adapt to the world as it is and to the fragmented view of reality deposited in them.

The capability of banking education to minimize or annul the student's creative power and to stimulate their credulity serves the interests of the oppressors, who care neither to have the world revealed nor to see it transformed. The oppressors use their "humanitarianism" to preserve a profitable situation. Thus they react almost instinctively against any experiment in education which stimulates the critical faculties and is not content with a partial view of reality but always seeks out the ties which link one point to another and one problem to another.

Indeed, the interests of the oppressors lie in "changing the consciousness of the oppressed, not the situation which oppresses them,"[1] for the more the oppressed can be led to adapt to that situation, the more easily they can be dominated. To achieve this, the oppressors use the banking concept of education in conjunction with a paternalistic social action apparatus, within which the oppressed receive the euphemistic title of "welfare recipients."

They are treated as individual cases, as marginal persons who deviate from the general configuration of a "good, organized and just" society. The oppressed are regarded as the pathology of the healthy society which must therefore adjust these "incompetent and lazy" folk to its own patterns by changing their mentality. These marginals need to be "integrated," "incorporated" into the healthy society that they have "forsaken."

The truth is, however, that the oppressed are not "marginals," are not living "outside" society. They have always been "inside" the structure which made them "beings for others." The solution is not to "integrate" them into the structure of oppression, but to transform that structure so that they can become "beings for themselves." Such transformation, of course, would undermine the oppressors' purposes; hence their utilization of the banking concept of education to avoid the threat of student *conscientização*.

The banking approach to adult education, for example, will never propose to students that they critically consider reality. It will deal instead with such vital questions as whether Roger gave green grass to the goat, and insist upon the importance of learning that, on the contrary, Roger gave green grass to the rabbit. The "humanism" of the banking approach masks the effort to turn women and men into automatons—the very negation of their ontological vocation to be more fully human.

Those who use the banking approach, knowingly or unknowingly (for there are innumerable well-intentioned bank-clerk teachers who do not realize that they are serving only to dehumanize), fail to perceive that the deposits themselves contain contradictions about reality. But sooner or later, these contradictions may lead formerly passive students to turn against their domestication and the attempt to domesticate reality. They may discover through existential experience that their present way of life is irreconcilable with their vocation to become fully human. They may perceive through their relations with reality that reality is really a *process*, undergoing constant transformation. If men and women are searchers and their ontological vocation is humanization, sooner or later they may perceive the contradiction in which banking education seeks to maintain them, and then engage themselves in the struggle for their liberation.

But the humanist revolutionary educator cannot wait for this possibility to materialize. From the outset, her efforts must coincide with those of the students to engage in critical thinking and the quest for mutual humanization. His efforts must be imbued with a profound trust in people and their creative power. To achieve this, they must be partners of the students in their relations with them.

The banking concept does not admit to such partnership—and necessarily so. To resolve the teacher-student contradiction, to exchange the role of depositor, prescriber, domesticator, for the role of student among students would be to undermine the power of oppression and serve the cause of liberation.

Implicit in the banking concept is the assumption of a dichotomy between human beings and the world: a person is merely *in* the world, not *with* the world or with others; the individual is spectator, not re-creator. In this view, the person is not a conscious being (*corpo consciente*); he or she is rather the possessor of *a* consciousness: an empty "mind" passively open to the reception of deposits of reality from the world outside. For example, my desk, my books, my coffee cup, all the objects before me—as bits of the world which surround me—would be "inside" me, exactly as I am inside my study right now. This view makes no distinction between being accessible to consciousness and entering consciousness. The distinction, however, is essential: the objects which surround me are simply accessible to my consciousness, not located within it. I am aware of them, but they are not inside me.

It follows logically from the banking notion of consciousness that the educator's role is to regulate the way the world "enters into" the students. The teacher's task is to organize a process which already occurs spontaneously, to "fill" the students by making deposits of information which he or she considers to constitute true knowledge.[2] And since people "receive" the world as passive entities, education should make them more passive still, and adapt them to the world. The educated individual is the adapted person, because she or he is better "fit" for the world. Translated into practice, this concept is well suited for the purposes of the oppressors, whose tranquility rests on how well people fit the world the oppressors have created and how little they question it.

The more completely the majority adapt to the purposes which the dominant majority prescribe for them (thereby depriving them of the right to their own purposes), the more easily the minority can continue to prescribe. The theory and practice of banking education serve this end quite efficiently. Verbalistic lessons, reading requirements,[3] the methods for evaluating "knowledge," the distance between the teacher and the taught, the criteria for promotion: everything in this ready-to-wear approach serves to obviate thinking.

The bank-clerk educator does not realize that there is no true security in his hypertrophied role, that one must seek to live *with* others in solidarity. One cannot impose oneself, nor even merely co-exist with one's students. Solidarity requires true communication, and the concept by which such an educator is guided fears and proscribes communication.

Yet only through communication can human life hold meaning. The teacher's thinking is authenticated only by the authenticity of the students' thinking. The teacher cannot think for her students, nor can she impose her thought on them. Authentic thinking, thinking that is concerned about *reality*, does not take place in ivory tower isolation, but only in communication. If it is true that thought has meaning only when generated by action upon the world, the subordination of students to teachers becomes impossible.

Because banking education begins with a false understanding of men and women as objects, it cannot promote the development of what Fromm calls "biophily," but instead produces its opposite: "necrophily."

> While life is characterized by growth in a structured functional manner, the necrophilous person loves all that does not grow, all that is mechanical. The necrophilous person is driven by the desire to transform the organic into the inorganic, to approach life mechanically, as if all living persons were things. . . . Memory, rather than experience; having, rather than being, is what counts. The necrophilous person can relate to an object—a flower or a person—only if he possesses it; hence a threat to his possession is a threat to himself, if he loses possession he loses contact with the world . . . He loves control, and in the act of controlling he kills life.[4]

Oppression—overwhelming control—is necrophilic; it is nourished by love of death, not life. The banking concept of education, which serves the interests of oppression, is also necrophilic. Based on a mechanistic, static, naturalistic, spatialized view of consciousness, it transforms students into receiving objects. It attempts to control thinking and action, leads women and men to adjust to the world, and inhibits their creative power.

When their efforts to act responsibly are frustrated, when they find themselves unable to use their faculties, people suffer. "This suffering due to impotence is rooted in the very fact that the human has been disturbed."[5] But the inability to act which causes men's anguish also causes them to reject their impotence, by attempting

> . . . to restore [their] capacity to act. But can [they], and how? One way is to submit to and identify with a person or group having power. By this symbolic participation in another person's life, [men have] the illusion of acting, when in reality [they] only submit to and become a part of those who act.[6]

Populist manifestations perhaps best exemplify this type of behavior by the oppressed, who, by identifying with charismatic leaders, come to feel that they themselves are active and effective. The rebellion they express as they emerge in the historical process is motivated by that desire to act effectively. The dominant elites consider the remedy to be more domination and repression, carried out in the name of freedom, order, and social peace (that is, the peace of the elites). Thus they can condemn—logically, from their point of view—"the violence of a strike by workers and [can] call upon the state in the same breath to use violence in putting down the strike."[7]

Education as the exercise of domination stimulates the credulity of students, with the ideological intent (often not perceived by educators) of indoctrinating them to adapt to the world of oppression. This accusation is not made in the naive hope that the dominant elites will thereby simply abandon the practice. Its objective is to call the attention of true humanists to the fact that they cannot use banking educational methods in the pursuit of liberation, for they would only negate that very pursuit. Nor may a revolutionary society inherit these methods from an oppressor society. The revolutionary society which practices banking education is either misguided or mistrusting of people. In either event, it is threatened by the specter of reaction.

Unfortunately, those who espouse the cause of liberation are themselves surrounded and influenced by the climate which generates the banking concept, and often do not perceive its true significance or its dehumanizing power. Paradoxically, then, they utilize this same instrument of alienation in what they consider an effort to liberate. Indeed, some "revolutionaries" brand as "innocents," "dreamers," or even "reactionaries" those who would challenge this educational practice. But one does not liberate people by alienating them. Authentic liberation—the process of humanization—is not another deposit to be made in men. Liberation is a praxis: the action and reflection of men and women upon their world in order to transform it.

Those truly committed to liberation must reject the banking concept in its entirety, adopting instead a concept of women and men as conscious beings, and consciousness as consciousness intent upon the world. They must abandon the educational goal of deposit-making and replace it with the posing of the problems of human beings in their relations with the world. "Problem-posing" education, responding to the essence of consciousness—*intentionality*—rejects communiques and embodies communication. It epitomizes the special characteristic of consciousness: being *conscious* of, not only as intent on objects but as turned in upon itself in a "Jasperian split"—consciousness as consciousness *of* consciousness.

Liberating education consists in acts of cognition, not transferals of information. It is a learning situation in which the cognizable object (far from being the end of the cognitive act) intermediates the cognitive actors—teacher on the one hand and students on the other. Accordingly, the practice of problem-posing education entails at the outset that the teacher-student contradiction be resolved. Dialogical relations—indispensable to the capacity of cognitive actors to cooperate in perceiving the same cognizable object—are otherwise impossible.

Indeed, problem-posing education, which breaks with the vertical characteristic of banking education, can fulfill its function of freedom only if it can overcome the above contradiction. Through dialogue, the teacher-of-the-students and the students-of-the-teacher cease to exist and a new term emerges: teacher-student with students-teachers. The teacher is no longer merely the-one-who-teaches, but one who is himself taught in dialogue with the students, who in turn while being taught also teach. They become jointly responsible for a process in which all grow. In this process, arguments based on "authority" are no longer valid; in order to function authority must be *on the side* of freedom, not *against* it. Here, no one teaches another, nor is anyone self-taught. People teach each other, mediated by the world, by the cognizable objects which in banking education are "owned" by the teacher.

The banking concept (with its tendency to dichotomize everything) distinguishes two stages in the action of the educator. During the first he cognizes a cognizable object while he prepares his lessons in his study or his laboratory; during the second, he expounds to his students about that object. The students are not called upon to know, but to memorize the contents narrated by the teacher. Nor do the students practice any act of cognition, since the object towards which that act should be directed is the property of the teacher rather than a medium evoking the critical reflection of both teacher and students. Hence in the name of the "preservation of culture and knowledge" we have a system which achieves neither true knowledge nor true culture.

The problem-posing method does not dichotomize the activity of teacher-student: she is not "cognitive" at one point and "narrative" at another. He is always "cognitive," whether preparing a projector or engaging in dialogue with the students. He does not regard objects as his private property, but as the object of reflection by himself and his students. In this way, the problem-posing educator constantly re-forms his reflections in the reflection of the students. The students—no longer docile listeners— are now critical co-investigators in dialogue with the teacher. The teacher presents the material to the students for their consideration, and re-considers her earlier considerations as the students express their own. The role of the problem-posing educator is to create, together with the students, the conditions under which knowledge at the level of the *doxa* is superseded by true knowledge at the level of the *logos*.

Whereas banking education anesthetizes and inhibits creative power, problem-posing education involves a constant unveiling of reality. The former attempts to maintain the *submersion* of consciousness; the latter strives for the *emergence* of consciousness and *critical intervention* in reality. Students, as they are increasingly posed with problems relating to themselves in the world and with the world, will feel increasingly challenged and obliged to respond to that challenge. Because they apprehend the challenge as interrelated to other problems within a total context not as a theoretical question, the resulting comprehension tends to be increasingly critical and thus constantly less alienated. Their response to the challenge evokes new challenges, followed by new understandings; and gradually the students come to regard themselves as committed.

Education as the practice of freedom—as opposed to education as the practice of domination—denies that man is abstract, isolated, independent and unattached to the world; it also denies that the world exists as a reality apart from people. Authentic reflection considers neither abstract man nor the world without people, but people in their relations with the world. In these relations consciousness and world are simultaneous: consciousness neither precedes the world nor follows it.

> La conscience et le monde sont dormes d'un meme coup: exterieur par essence a la conscience, le monde est, par essence relatif a elle.[8]

In one of our culture circles in Chile, the group was discussing (based on a codification) the anthropological concept of culture. In the midst of the discussion, a peasant who by banking standards was completely ignorant said: "Now I see that without man there is no world." When the educator responded: "Let's say, for the sake of argument, that all the men on earth were to die, but that the earth remained, together with trees, birds, animals, rivers, seas, the stars . . . wouldn't all this be a world?" "Oh no," the peasant replied. "There would be no one to say: 'This is a world.'"

The peasant wished to express the idea that there would be lacking the consciousness of the world which necessarily implies the world of consciousness. I cannot exist without a *non-I*. In turn, the *non-I* depends on that existence. The world which brings consciousness into existence becomes the world of that consciousness. Hence, the previously cited affirmation of Sartre: "*La conscience et le monde sont dormes dun meme coup.*"

As men, simultaneously reflecting on themselves and on the world, increase the scope of their perception, they begin to direct their observations towards previously inconspicuous phenomena:

> In perception properly so-called, as an explicit awareness [*Gewahren*], I am turned towards the object, to the paper, for instance. I apprehend it as being

this here and now. The apprehension is a singling out, every object having a background inexperience. Around and about the paper lie books, pencils, inkwell and so forth, and these in a certain sense are also "perceived" perceptually there, in the "field of intuition"; but whilst I was turned towards the paper there was no turning in their direction, nor any apprehending of them, not even in a secondary sense. They appeared and yet were not singled out, were posited on their own account. Every perception of a thing has such a zone of background intuitions or background awareness, if "intuiting" already includes the state of being turned towards, and this also is a "conscious experience," or more briefly a "consciousness of" all indeed that in point of fact lies in the co-perceived objective background.[9]

That which had existed objectively but had not been perceived in its deeper implications (if indeed it was perceived at all) begins to "stand out," assuming the character of a problem and therefore of challenge. Thus, men and women begin to single out elements from their "background awareness" and to reflect upon them. These elements are now objects of their consideration, and, as such, objects of their action and cognition.

In problem-posing education, people develop their power to perceive critically *the way they exist* in the world *with which* and *in which* they find themselves; they come to see the world not as a static reality, but as a reality in process, in transformation. Although the dialectical relations of women and men with the world exist independently of how these relations are perceived (or whether or not they are perceived at all), it is also true that the form of action they adopt is to a large extent a function of how they perceive themselves in the world. Hence, the teacher-student and the students-teachers reflect simultaneously on themselves and the world without dichotomizing this reflection from action, and thus establish an authentic form of thought and action.

Once again, the two educational concepts and practices under analysis come into conflict. Banking education (for obvious reasons) attempts, by mythicizing reality, to conceal certain facts which explain the way human beings exist in the world; problem-posing education sets itself the task of demythologizing. Banking education resists dialogue; problem-posing education regards dialogue as indispensable to the act of cognition which unveils reality. Banking education treats students as objects of assistance; problem-posing education makes them critical thinkers. Banking education inhibits creativity and domesticates (although it cannot completely destroy) the *intentionality* of consciousness by isolating consciousness from the world, thereby denying people their ontological and historical vocation of becoming more fully human. Problem-posing education bases itself on creativity and stimulates true reflection and action upon reality, thereby responding to the vocation of persons as beings only when engaged in inquiry and creative transformation. In sum: banking theory and practice, as immobilizing and fixating forces, fail to acknowledge men and women as historical beings; problem-posing theory and practice take the people's historicity as their starting point.

Problem-posing education affirms men as beings in the process of *becoming*—as unfinished, uncompleted beings in and with a likewise unfinished reality. Indeed, in contrast to other animals who are unfinished, but not historical, people know themselves to be unfinished; they are aware of their incompletion. In this incompletion and this awareness lie the very roots of education as an exclusively human manifestation. The unfinished character of human beings and the transformational character of reality necessitate that education be an ongoing activity.

Education is thus constantly remade in the praxis. In order to be, it must *become*. Its "duration" (in the Bergsonian meaning of the word) is found in the interplay of the opposites *permanence* and *change*. The banking method emphasizes permanence and becomes reactionary; problem-posing education— which accepts neither a "well-behaved" present nor a predetermined future— roots itself in the dynamic present and becomes revolutionary.

Problem-posing education is revolutionary futurity. Hence it is prophetic (and as such, hopeful). Hence, it corresponds to the historical nature of humankind. Hence, it affirms men as beings who transcend themselves, who move forward and look ahead, for whom immobility represents a fatal threat for whom looking at the past must only be a means of understanding more clearly what and who they are so that they can more wisely build the future. Hence, it identifies with the movement which engages people as beings aware of their incompletion—an historical movement which has its point of departure, its Subjects and its objective.

The point of departure of the movement lies in the men themselves. But since men do not exist apart from the world, apart from reality, the movement must begin with the men-world relationship. Accordingly, the point of departure must always be with men and women in the "here and now," which constitutes the situation within which they are submerged, from which they emerge, and in which they intervene. Only by starting from this situation—which determines their perception of it—can they begin to move. To do this authentically they must perceive their state not as fated and unalterable, but merely as limiting—and therefore challenging.

Whereas the banking method directly or indirectly reinforces men's fatalistic perception of their situation, the problem-posing method presents this very situation to them as a problem. As the situation becomes the object of their cognition, the naive or magical perception which produced their fatalism gives way to perception which is able to perceive itself even as it perceives reality, and can thus be critically objective about that reality.

A deepened consciousness of their situation leads people to apprehend that situation as an historical reality susceptible of transformation. Resignation gives way to the drive for transformation and inquiry, over which men feel themselves to be in control. If people, as historical beings necessarily engaged with other people in a movement of inquiry, did not control that movement, it would be (and is) a violation of their humanity. Any situation in which some individuals prevent others from engaging in the process of inquiry is one of violence. The means used are not important; to alienate human beings from their own decision-making is to change them into objects.

This movement of inquiry must be directed towards humanization—the people's historical vocation. The pursuit of full humanity, however, cannot be carried out in isolation or individualism, but only in fellowship and solidarity; therefore it cannot unfold in the antagonistic relations between oppressors and oppressed. No one can be authentically human while he prevents others from being so. Attempting *to be more* human, individualistically, leads to *having more,* egotistically, a form of dehumanization. Not that it is not fundamental to *have* in order *to be* human. Precisely because it *is* necessary, some men's *having* must not be allowed to constitute an obstacle to others' *having,* must not consolidate the power of the former to crush the latter.

Problem-posing education, as a humanist and liberating praxis, posits as fundamental that the people subjected to domination must fight for their emancipation. To that end, it enables teachers and students to become Subjects of the educational process by overcoming authoritarianism and an alienating intellectualism; it also enables people to overcome their false perception of reality. The world—no longer something to be described with deceptive words—becomes the object of that transforming action by men and women which results in their humanization.

Problem-posing education does not and cannot serve the interests of the oppressor. No oppressive order could permit the oppressed to begin to question: Why? While only a revolutionary society can carry out this education in systematic terms, the revolutionary leaders need not take full power before they can employ the method. In the revolutionary process, the leaders cannot utilize the banking method as an interim measure, justified on grounds of expediency, with intention of *later* behaving in a genuinely revolutionary fashion. They must be revolutionary—that is to say, dialogical—from the outset.

Notes

1. Simon de Beauvoir. *La Pensee de Droite, Aujord'hui* (Paris); ST, *El Pensamiento politico de la Derecha* (Buenos Aires, 1963), p. 34.

2. This concept corresponds to what Sartre calls the "digestive" or "nutritive" in which knowledge is "fed" by the teacher to the students to "fill them out." See Jean-Paul Sartre, "Une idee fundamentals de la phenomenologie de Husserl: L'intentionalite," *Situations I* (Paris, 1947).

3. For example, some professors specify in their reading lists that a book should be read from pages 10 to 15—and do this to "help" their students!

4. Fromm, op. cit. p. 41.

5. Ibid. p. 31.

6. Ibid. p. 7.

7. Reinhold Niebuhr, *Moral Man and Immoral Society* (New York, 1960), p. 130.

8. Sartre, op. cit., p. 32.

9. Edmund Husserl, *Ideas: General Introduction to Pure Phenomenology* (London, 1969), pp. 105–106.

Paulo Freire (deceased) was an author and social activist.

10

On Stir-and-Serve Recipes for Teaching

Susan Ohanian

The notion that just about any Joe Blow can walk in off the street and take over a classroom is gaining ground. It makes me nervous. No, more than that: it infuriates me. We should squash once and for all the idea that schools can be adequately staffed by 32 bookkeepers and a plumber. The right teacher-proof curriculum is not sufficient; children need real teachers, and real teachers must be trained.

Nor am I charmed by the idea of signing up out-of-work computer programmers and retired professors to teach math and science. The mass media like to scoff that current certification requirements would keep Albert Einstein from teaching in the public schools. That news is not all bad. Is there any evidence that Einstein worked particularly well with young children? A Nobel Prize does not guarantee excellence in the classroom.

Having sat through more stupid education courses than I wish to recall, I am not altogether comfortable defending schools of education. But I suspect that the blame for worthless courses lies as much with the teachers who take them as with the professors who teach them. As a group, we teachers are intransigently anti-intellectual. We demand from our professors carry-out

---

NOTE: Reprinted with kind permission from the author.

formulae, materials with the immediate applicability of scratch-and-sniff stickers. We are indignant when they try instead to offer ideas to grow on, seeds that we have to nurture in our own gardens.

We teachers frequently complain that education courses do not prepare us for the rigorous, confusing work ahead—that they do not show us how to run our classrooms. We refuse to admit that no course or manual can give us all the help we crave. We should not expect professors to set up our classroom systems, as though each of us were heading out to operate a fast-food franchise. There is no instant, stir-and-serve recipe for running a classroom.

Too often, teachers judge the success of education courses by the weight of the materials they cart away—cute cutouts or "story starters," all ready for immediate use. One popular journal for teachers promises 100 new ideas in every issue. "You can use them on Monday" is the promise. No one gets rich admitting that genuinely good ideas are hard to come by.

I understand only too well this yearning for the tangible, the usable. We are, after all, members of a profession ruled by pragmatism. People who sit in judgment on us don't ask about our students, "Are they happy? Are they creative? Are they helpful, sensitive, loving? Will they want to read a book next year?" Instead, these people demand, "What are their test scores?" as if those numbers, though they passeth understanding, will somehow prove that we're doing a good job.

During my first 12 years of teaching I was desperate for new ideas, constantly foraging for schemes with which to engage the children. My frenetic activity was due, in part, to the fact that I was given a different teaching assignment every two years. I figured, "Different children require different methods, different materials." So I would race off to the library or to the arts-and-crafts store. I'd buy another filing cabinet and join another book club for teachers.

But even when I settled in with the same assignment for a six-year stretch, my frenzy did not abate. My classroom became a veritable curriculum warehouse, stuffed with every innovative whiz-bang gizmo I could buy, borrow, or invent. I spent hundreds of hours reading, constructing, laminating. My husband gave up reminding me that I had promised to put the cut-and-paste factory in our living room out of business, once I figured out what to teach. When I wasn't inventing projects, I was taking courses: cardboard carpentry, architectural awareness, science process, Cuisenaire rods, Chinese art, test construction and evaluation, curriculum development, and so on. I even took two courses in the computer language, BASIC. (I thought maybe I'd missed the point in the first course, so I took another—just to be sure.)

I didn't take those courses on whim, any more than I invented curriculum because I had nothing better to do. I chose my courses deliberately, tying to inform my work as a reading teacher. Although I now look back on much of my frenzied search for methods and media as rather naïve, I don't see it as time wasted. I learned a lot. Mostly I learned to simplify. And then to simplify some more.

But the path to simplicity is littered with complexities. And I suspect that it is hard to figure out how to simplify our lives if we haven't cluttered them in the first place. Sure, we teachers clutter up our classrooms with too much claptrap. The fribble is often alluring at first, and it is hard to recognize that the more gadgets we rely on, the poorer we are—at home as well as at school.

People probably always yearn for gadgets, especially if they haven't had much chance to fool around with them. A university research project makes this point rather nicely. The researcher decided to investigate the effects of computer-assisted instruction in English-as-a-second-language (ESL) classes. He set up a computer-taught group and a control group. Both were instructed in ESL for one year. And guess which group had the more positive attitude about computer-assisted instruction at the end of that year? The youngsters who didn't get to use the computers.

Not surprisingly, we teachers are compulsive pack rats. Fearing the vagaries of future school budgets, we hoard construction paper until it is old and brittle and unusable. We worry that we may need that paper more next year than we need it today. Have you ever known a teacher who could throw away a set of ditto masters? Or half a game of Scrabble? For years I had a gross of tiny, childproof, left-handed scissors. Childproof scissors are a horror in the first place. Those designed for left-handers are beyond description. Why did I keep them? Hey, they were mine, weren't they?

Most of us never use 80% of the materials jammed into our classrooms, but we cling to them "just in case." Because our job is hectic, pressured, stressful, we seldom have a reflective moment to clear our minds, let alone our cupboards. Maybe every teacher should change schools every three years and be allowed to take along only what he or she can carry. However, I must add to this suggestion my own statement of full disclosure: the last time I changed classrooms, after 13 years in the district, it took six strong men and a truck to transfer my belongings. And that was after I had filled two dumpsters.

The good professors must stop yielding to our acquisitive pressures; they must refuse to hand out their 100—or even 10—snazzy new ideas for the well-stocked classroom. They must offer fewer methods, fewer recipes. We teachers need less practicality, not more. We need to have our lives informed by Tolstoy, Jane Addams, Suzanne Langer, Rudolf Arnheim, and their ilk—not by folks who promise the keys to classroom control and creative bulletin boards, along with 100 steps to reading success.

We need a sense of purpose from our professors, not a timetable. Better that they show us a way to find our own ways than that they hand out their own detailed maps of the territory. A map isn't of much use to people who don't know where they're headed. The only way to become familiar with the terrain is to explore a little. I nominate the professors to scout ahead, chart the waters, post the quicksand. I know that I still have to climb my own mountain, but I would welcome scholarly advice about the climbing conditions.

Critics of schools of education insist that prospective teachers would profit more from observing good teachers at work than from taking impractical courses on pedagogy. Maybe so, but what are those novices going to see? Is one observation as good as another? After all, a person can look at "Guernica" and not see it, listen to the "Eroica" and not hear it. E. H. Gombrich says that every observation we make is the result of the questions we ask. And where do novices get the questions? How can they ask intelligent questions without knowing something about the subject? Can anyone really see a classroom without some theoretical, historical, developmental savvy?

No one enters a classroom as a *tabula rasa,* of course. We all know something about schools because we have, for better or for worse, been there. We know how schools are supposed to be. At least we think we do. So we judge schools, as we judge anything, with a notion—or schema—of reality in our heads. Most of us don't just look *at* something; we look *for* something, because we have a hypothesis, a hidden agenda. We observe and evaluate with our minds, our memories, our experiences, our linguistic habits. Obviously, the more we know, the more we see.

But teachers cannot walk into classrooms and simply teach what they know. First, they don't know enough. Second, even this seemingly restrictive world—constrained by bells, desks, and textbooks—contains a rich stock of themes from which teachers must choose their own motifs. They must be flexible and inventive enough to modify the schema they carried into their classrooms.

I was one of those people almost literally picked up off a street corner and allowed to teach in New York City under an emergency credential. I walked into the middle of someone else's lesson plan, and, though it didn't take me 10 minutes to realize that a round-robin reading of "Paul Revere's Ride" was not going to work, it took me quite a while to come up with something much better.

All I could manage at first was to teach as I had been taught. But as I learned more about the students and about ways to get around the assigned curriculum, a more ideal classroom began to emerge in my head. It remains a shadowy image—one I glimpse and even touch occasionally, but one I have long since stopped trying to file neatly in my planbook. That's okay. The bird seen through the window is more provocative than the one in the cage.

Teaching, like art, is born of a schema. That's why we need the professors with their satchels of theory, as well as our own observations and practice. Those who hope to be effective teachers must recognize that teaching is a craft of careful artifice; the profession requires more than a spontaneous overflow of good intentions or the simple cataloguing and distribution of information. It is possible, I suppose, to have an inborn talent for teaching, but I am sure that those teachers who endure and triumph are *made*—rigorously trained—and not born.

Much of the training must be self-initiated. People who have some nagging notion of the ideal classroom tickling their psyches probably look more for patterns that appeal than for practices that are guaranteed to produce higher standardized test scores. Such teachers probably have a capacity for ambiguity; they look for snippets of familiarity but do not insist on sameness. Such teachers have a greater need for aesthetic and psychological satisfaction than for a neat and tidy cupboard. But they also have a willingness to practice the craft, to try out new brushstrokes, to discard dried-out palettes.

Most of us, children and adults alike, have a strong need to make sense of the disparate elements in our lives, to bring them together, to find patterns, to make meaning. This desire for meaning is so strong that some teachers, tired and defeated by the system, rely on ritual to get them through the day, the week, the year. External order and ritual are the only things they have left to give. And these things usually satisfy the casual observer, who believes that teachers who provide clean and orderly classrooms are providing enough.

This is one reason I want the professors in on the act—out of their ivory towers and into our dusty school corridors. Maybe well-informed people, good observers who are not bogged down by school minutiae, could convince us that a tidy desk is far from enough. The professors need to promote the search for a different order, a subtler pattern—one that lies not in behavioral checklists but rather, to use Chia Yi's words, in constant "combining, scattering, waning, waxing."

It was my own search for pattern that led me to try using science as a way to inform, enhance, and give order to my work as a reading teacher. The children and I were far too familiar with the rituals of remedial reading for those routines to fall much short of torture. I've never understood why students who have trouble with a certain system of decoding should be made to rehearse that system over and over again. A few times over the course of a few years, maybe. But surely there comes a time to try a different approach. Reading had already been ruined for my students by the time they came to me. I needed to see how they approached pedagogic puzzlement, and such puzzlement would never occur if I persisted in making them circle blends on worksheets. That's why I learned how to mess around in science.

Tell a poor reader that it's time to read, and watch the impenetrable curtain of defeat and despair descend. So my students and I spent our time on science. All year. We made cottage cheese, explored surface tension, built bridges, figured out optical illusions. And not once did my students associate experiment cards, books on the theory of sound, or my insistence that observations be recorded in writing with the onerous task that they knew reading to be. Children told me that my room was a good place. Too bad, they added, that I wasn't a real teacher.

That reading room, where children were busily measuring, making—and reading—received full parental support and had its moment in the limelight. There were a lot of visitors. The teachers among them invariably asked, "How did you get this job?" Clearly, they intended to apply for one like it.

Get the job? Only in the first year of my teaching career was I ever handed a job. Ever after, I've made my own. No job of any value can be given out, like a box of chalk. We get the jobs we deserve. Maybe that's why so many teachers are disappointed. They believe all those promises that someone else can do the thinking for them.

I held seven different jobs in my school district, and I earned the right to love every one of them. That's not to say that I didn't have plenty of moments of anger, frustration, rage. But I also experienced deep satisfaction.

Because my seven jobs required some pretty dramatic shifts in grade level, people were always asking me, "Where is it better—high school or the primary grades?" It's a question I have never been able to answer, mainly because the more grade levels I taught, the more similarities I saw. Sure, high school dropouts enrolled in an alternative program are harder to tune in to the beauty of a poem than are seventh-graders. Third-graders cry more, talk more; seventh-graders scale more heights and sink into deeper pits. But a common thread runs throughout, and it was that thread I clung to.

Maybe I see this sameness because my teaching is dominated less by skill than by idea—the secret, elusive form. I have a hard time reading other people's prescriptions, let alone writing my own. I always figure that, if you can get the idea right, the specific skill will come. Teaching is too personal, even too metaphysical, to be charted like the daily temperature. Teaching is like a Chinese lyric painting, not a bus schedule.

We need to look very closely at just who is calling for "the upgrading of teacher skills," lest this turn out to be the clarion call of those folks with something to sell. The world does not come to us in neat little packages. Even if we could identify just what a *skill* is, does *more* definitely denote *better?* What profiteth a child whose teacher has gathered up an immense pile of pishposh? We must take care, lest the examiners who claim they can dissect and label the educational process leave us holding a bag of gizzards.

We teachers must recognize that we do not need the behaviorist-competency thugs to chart our course. For us, reality is a feeling state, details of daily routine fade, and what remains is atmosphere, tone, emotion. The ages and the talents of the children become irrelevant. What counts is attitude and endeavor. That's why, even when we try, we often can't pass on a terrific lesson plan to a friend; we probably can't even save it for ourselves to use again next year. It's virtually impossible to teach the same lesson twice.

I'm afraid that all of this sounds rather dim, maybe even dubious. But this is where the professors might step in. There are so many outrageous examples of bad pedagogy that it's easy to overlook the good—easy, but not excusable. The professors need to shape up their own schools of education first—getting rid of Papercutting 306, even if it's the most profitable course in the summer school catalogue. Then they need to get out in the field to work with student teachers, principals, and children.

Is it outrageous to think that the professors might even pop into the classrooms of veteran teachers now and then? Wouldn't it be something if their research occasionally involved real children and real teachers (and if they had to face bells, mandated tests, bake sales, and field trips to mess up their carefully laid plans), instead of four children in a lab staffed by 63 graduate students? That's probably a scary thought for some professors.

I know of one school of education that relegates the observation and direction of student teachers to the local school district. The district, in turn, passes this responsibility on to an administrator who has never taught. In such a situation, pedagogy gets turned upside down and inside out. The outcome is empty platitudes, not effective classroom practice. The student teacher, who is paying for expert training, is being defrauded. The children are being cheated. The system is stupid and immoral. We need teacher trainers who know educational theory and who are savvy about children. Those professors who won't help us should be replaced by ones who will.

But aspiring teachers have a responsibility, too. They must heed the advice of Confucius:

If a man won't try, I will teach him; if a man makes no effort, I will not help him. I show one corner, and if a man cannot find the other three, I am not going to repeat myself.

We teachers must stop asking the education professors for the whole house. I know plenty of teachers who are disappointed, indignant, and eventually destroyed by the fact that nobody has handed them all four corners. But the best we can expect from any program of courses or training is the jagged edge of one corner. Then it is up to us to read the research and to collaborate with the children to find the other three corners. And, because teaching must be a renewable contract, if we don't keep seeking new understanding, we'll find that the corners we thought we knew very well will keep slipping away. There are constant, subtle shifts in the schoolroom. One can never be sure of knowing the floorplan forever and ever.

In trying to renew my faith in myself as a teacher, I find little help in the "how to" books, those nasty little tomes that define learning in 87 steps. I like to think of learning as a wave that washes over the learner, rather than as a series of incremental hurdles to be pre- and posttested. I reject *How to Teach Reading in 100 Lessons,* relying instead on *The Mustard Seed Garden Manual of Painting,* which advises that "neither complexity in itself nor simplicity is enough"—nor dexterity alone nor conscientiousness. "To be without method is worse."

What can we do? What is the solution? In painting, there is an answer: "Study 10,000 volumes and walk 10,000 miles." One more thing is required of teachers. We must also work with 10,000 children.

Susan Ohanian is a freelance writer and former teacher.

11

Psst . . . It Ain't About the Tests

It's Still About Great Teaching

Robert DiGiulio

If you are planning to become a teacher, welcome, and prepare to be overwhelmed. If you are already teaching, you know this already. After a seminar I gave for teachers recently, we were standing by the coffee: "My head is spinning! There's too much to think about: Portfolios, standards-based lessons, differentiated instruction, IEPs, ESTs, continuous assessment, making sure the kids pass those standardized tests, fundraisers, getting the computers to work, inclusion, trying to keep discipline in a classroom where some can't even sit still for a minute!" As I drove home from that seminar, I thought about how right they were. There seemed to be two huge but connected problems here: First, teachers today have been swamped by tasks—often, trivial and unconnected to students—that demand compliance, to the point where it is difficult for teachers to balance or to discern what was really important. Second, teachers have a vague (or all-too-clear) uneasiness, based on a hazy sense of how well they were

NOTE: Parts of this essay first appeared in the book *Great Teaching Is Still Great Teaching*, by Robert DiGiulio, copyright 2003. Reprinted with permission from Corwin.

doing. There was a lack of useful information that ought to help teachers connect what they were doing to how well students were learning. A common form of data—students' standardized test scores, now all the rage—provide little guidance for teachers, and are among the most useless (and harmful) pieces of data, in terms of helping teachers and future teachers, to say nothing of useless in helping students actually be successful.

Since I began teaching in the inner-city public schools of New York City in 1970, I have been absorbed by the question of good teaching. Along with the New York State and City teacher licensing boards, Al Shanker and the teachers' union defined good teaching in terms of qualifications, years teaching, seniority, number of advanced degrees, and so on. But my first-hand observation of some great teachers contradicted that—I saw no connection between these paper qualifications and how excellent teachers actually were in the classroom. The skills and qualities of great teachers seemed to be increasingly marginalized; crowded out by administrative, compliance paperwork (I call it "ditto worksheets for teachers"), somebody's Great New Idea, and other time killers imposed on teachers. Later, as a school principal, my awareness grew of even darker reasons for the downplaying of good teaching, and I suppose money has a lot to do with it. Simply stated, when one acknowledges someone as being good (or great), there is a corresponding expectation to pay those people well. So while I have heard a lot over thirty years about teacher competency and merit pay, I have yet to hear a sincere effort to acknowledge what is the essence of great teaching. For once that is done, it forces the question of how we should expect it, recognize it, and maybe, pay great teachers well for what they do. I am still waiting for that discussion.

In a sense, I am writing this piece as an historical document. Great teaching has existed since one of the first humans—generously and competently—showed another how to make a fire and how to cook food. Great teaching has been great because it placed the learner's needs and interests first. Today, however, I see a tendency to marginalize great teaching by redefining it as teaching that emphasizes interests other than the needs of students. These other interests include those of special interest groups that often hide their interests behind the cloak of reform and of school improvement. They address alleged defects of teachers and/or public schools, and provide solutions to problems that only they have identified, and narrowly so at that. In these cases, neither the public's best interests nor students' best interests are at the heart of their "solutions." Some groups insist, for example, that standardized testing is essential to accountability. I am not opposed to accountability, and I can agree that under some circumstances standardized tests can provide useful information. But they don't inform teaching; standardized tests are beside the point of great teaching because they are too narrow in scope. While data from well-designed tests can help inform teachers as to their students' mastery of content, those tests cannot provide help for teachers seeking to improve their teaching skills and qualities. No standardized test for students can ever inform us of a teacher's enthusiasm, caring, or belief that students can be successful—three factors that have an enormous effect on student achievement and self-esteem. We simply have to use other means to focus on these important traits.

And focus we must. We see great teachers, and we see the undeniably powerful effect great teachers have on students. Yet, I worry that special-interest agendas are distorting (or submerging) the traditional, common sense notion of what great teaching is. As proof, think about what we know works in schools. After thousands of studies (some better than others), we know a lot about high-quality teaching. We know that there are good and better things that teachers do with and for students, and we know there are not-so-good things that teachers do. Yet despite the research data, and despite our common sense perceptions, how often do we hear about teachers who do the right things? How often do we see what and how they do those good things? I am not simply calling for mere praise for the great, even heroic teacher, although that is long overdue. I am calling for simply naming, noting, identifying what these teachers do, teachers whose students are succeeding—academically and socially—despite unfortunate conditions in their schools and communities. How often do we hear about students who do not bring weapons to school, students who are not violent? Students who don't hurt others; students who have learned how civilized human beings behave, learning much of this, in large part, from a good teacher? I am only asking for "the facts," not for a massive public relations campaign promoting teachers and schools.

When well-organized and well-funded anti-public education voices and special interest group voices have reached a fever pitch so that the acts of great teachers and great teaching are marginalized or disregarded, it is time to speak out. When the elements comprising great teaching are minimized, it is time to speak out. Again, I am concerned not so much that great teachers and their successes are being ignored (which they are), but that the qualities and skills that great teachers bring to great teaching are in danger of vanishing, disappearing from both the public eye and from the curriculum of teacher preparation. I speak out not as a cheerleader of great teachers, but as a curator who seeks to keep alive the awareness of the qualities and skills that comprise great teaching. These qualities and skills apply to all levels of education, from preschool through graduate school, private school as well as public school. They apply to teaching throughout the world, because they go directly to the heart of how teachers teach so that students learn most effectively.

As we get to the heart of what really matters in fostering student achievement, we realize more and more how important the individual teacher is. We know this; we have known this since the time of the wise Buddha, but we still seem to dance around focusing on the essence of the great teacher. Teacher education college programs are just as guilty as corporate interests: When was the last time you heard an education professor talk about great teaching? Is there anything in any syllabus that refers to great teaching? Yet we know—or *should know*—that this issue should not be summarily ignored. Probably the strongest voice is that of University of Tennessee professor William Sanders (2003), whose research shows how the effective teacher is more important—as a predictor of student success—than any of the other traditional social indicators usually blamed for student failure:

> . . . we've been able to get a very fair measure of the school district, the school, and the individual classroom. And we've been able to demonstrate that ethnicity, poverty, and affluence can no longer be used as justifications for the failure [of students] to make academic progress. The single biggest factor affecting academic growth of any population of youngsters is the effectiveness of the individual classroom teacher. [Furthermore,] [t]he teacher's effect on academic growth dwarfs and nearly renders trivial all these other factors that people have historically worried about.

Fine. But the devil is in the details, and how we define the "effectiveness" of that teacher is the heart of the problem. Shall we use standardized test scores? I think not. What shall we do instead? Richard B. Traina, former President of Clark University, is a research historian who asked, "What makes a good teacher?" (1999, 34). He looked through the biographies and autobiographies of prominent 19th and 20th century Americans, focusing on what they had to say about the traits their best teachers possessed. Traina saw a thread that ran through their stories: The best teachers—the memorable ones—were remembered as being skillful and enthusiastic, having such a solid command of the subject matter that students could "pick up on their excitement" for the subject. Second, these teachers were *caring*—they cared "deeply about each student and about that student's accomplishment and growth." Third, Traina said that these teachers had "distinctive character . . . there was a palpable energy that suffused the competent and caring teacher, some mark-making quality." In short, the memorable teachers were skillful, enthusiastic, caring, and perhaps even idiosyncratic. Dr. Traina's third trait—"distinctive character"—is indeed the most elusive category. Although we can't *teach* teachers to "acquire distinctive character," we certainly can work to not destroy it, by demanding conformity and narrow definitions of what successful teachers are. Distinctive character is a fragile naturally occurring resource. Like a gemstone, the distinctive character of each teacher is revealed as she or he teaches. Our job is to guard it, and not allow it to be shattered.

Aside from this *je ne sais qua* of distinctive character, what else do great teachers do that helps kids learn? Knowledge and "distinctive character" are part of it, but it is also about efficacy, a teacher's belief that she or he will be successful, because his or her students will be successful. And, to achieve student success, great teachers help move their students via three paths: producing, empowering, and connecting.

Great teachers know that to actually be successful, a student must first do something of value. Simply telling kids they are good won't wash. Student success is fostered by the work students do, by what they produce. This can include participating, performing, creating, practicing, designing, producing, carrying out an experiment, finishing an assignment, or any of hundreds of other activities. Worksheets, on the other hand, are all too often mindless, and require little thinking (input). The quality and value of the output, then, is quite low. Some worksheets may be okay for practicing, or passing time with puzzles, but not for producing. In the final analysis, what the student does will have a greater impact on how successful the student is (and feels he or she is) than what the teacher knows, says, or believes.

Student success is also fostered by empowering students (and students are automatically empowered when they are producing!). Empowering means actively teaching students how to help themselves, how to take responsibility for their work; how to get help: How to ask for help, whom to ask for help, and when to seek help. This is a real-world skill that starts and grows in class and in school. Students must also be weaned from depending on the teachers to provide direction at every step.

The third path to student success lies in helping students make connections. Success is fostered by activities/assignments that draw on—connect with—what students already know, and/or what they do well. Perhaps it is too obvious to state that what I learn best and fastest is that which is closest to what I already know; I learn best what builds on what I already know. What I do not learn well is when I try to make sense of material that is alien to what I presently know. Making connections is a core tenet of constructivism, and classrooms with a constructivist orientation are not only the most productive, but are happier places than classrooms with reward-and-punishment teachers, and far, far better than classrooms with laissez-faire (uninvolved) teachers.

Among its other provisions, the "No Child Left Behind" Act includes a provision that all public schools have a highly qualified teacher in each classroom. Unfortunately, there is nothing promising in that goal, especially when we have created so many alternative routes to licensure that even a measurable pulse may not any longer be a consistent requirement to teach (the poorest school districts in America tend to qualify almost anyone to teach).

Every classroom should have not merely a qualified teacher, but a great teacher. But for this to happen, we must move the definition of "qualified" back from *quantity indicators* (test scores, teachers' college degrees, number of years teaching, and other items easily tallied) and onto *quality,* by teaching teachers about efficacy and caring, about the ways one can empower and engage students, while allowing teachers to retain their "distinctive character." What matters at every turn is the teacher, and all kids deserve great teachers. This need has never before been so pressing.

Robert DiGiulio (deceased) was an author and a professor of Education at Johnson State College in Johnson, Vermont.

12

So What Do You Do Now?

Neil Postman and Charles Weingartner

Y ou are a teacher in an ordinary school, and the ideas in this book make sense to you. . . . What can you do about it, say tomorrow?

1. Your first act of subversion might be conducted in the following way: write on a scrap of paper these questions:

- What am I going to have my students do today?
- What's it good for?
- How do I know?

Tape the paper to the mirror in your bathroom or some other place where you are likely to see it every morning. If nothing else, the questions will begin to make you uneasy about shilling for someone else and might weaken your interest in "following the syllabus." You may even, after a while, become nauseous at the prospect of teaching things which have a specious value or for which there is no evidence that your anticipated outcomes do, in fact, occur. At their best, the questions will drive you to reconsider almost everything you are doing, with the result that you will

NOTE: From *Teaching as a Subversive Activity* by Neil Postman and Charles Weingartner, copyright 1969 by Neil Postman and Charles Weingartner. Used by permission of Dell Publishing, a division of Random House, Inc.

challenge your principal, your textbooks, the syllabus, the grading system, your own education, and so on. In the end, it all may cost you your job, or lead you to seek another position, or drive you out of teaching altogether. Subversion is a risky business—as risky for its agent as for its target.

2. In class, try to avoid *telling* your students any answers, if only for a few lessons or days. Do not prepare a lesson plan. Instead, confront your students with some sort of problem which might interest them. Then, allow them to work the problem through without your advice or counsel. Your talk should consist of questions directed to particular students, based on remarks made by those students. If a student asks you a question, tell him that you don't know the answer, even if you do. Don't be frightened by the long stretches of silence that might occur. Silence may mean that the students are thinking. Or it may mean that they are growing hostile. The hostility signifies that the students resent the fact that you have shifted the burden of intellectual activity from you to them. Thought is often painful even if you are accustomed to it. If you are not, it can be unbearable.

There are at least two good accounts of what happens when a teacher refrains from telling students answers. One of them appears in Nathaniel Cantor's *The Dynamics of Learning;* the other, in Carl Rogers' *On Becoming a Person.* You may want to read these accounts before trying your experiment. If you have any success at all, you ought to make your experiment a regular feature of your weekly lessons: one hour every day for independent problem solving, or one hour every week. However much you can do will be worth the effort.

3. Try listening to your students for a day or two. We do not mean reacting to what they say. We mean listening. This may require that you do some role playing. Imagine, for example, that you are not their teacher but a psychiatrist (or some such person who is not primarily trying to teach but who is trying to understand). Any questions you ask or remarks you make would, therefore, not be designed to instruct or judge. They would be attempts to clarify what someone has said. If you are like most teachers, your training has probably not included learning how to listen. Therefore, we would recommend that you obtain a copy of *On Becoming a Person* by Carl Rogers. The book is a collection of Rogers' best articles and speeches. Rogers is generally thought of as the leading exponent of non-directive counseling, and he is a rich source of ideas about listening to and understanding other people. You probably will not want to read every article in the book, but do not overlook "Communication: Its Blocking and Facilitation." In this article, Rogers describes a particularly effective

technique for teaching listening: the students engage in a discussion of some issue about which they have strong feelings. But their discussion has an unusual rule applied to it. A student may say anything he wishes but only after he has restated what the previous speaker has said *to that speaker's satisfaction*. Astounding things happen to students when they go through this experience. They find themselves concentrating on what others are saying to the point, sometimes, of forgetting what they themselves were going to say. In some cases, students have a unique experience. They find that they have projected themselves into the frame of mind of another person. You might wish to make this special listening game a permanent part of your weekly lessons. But, of course, you ought to try it yourself first. An additional aid to you in your efforts at listening will be "Do You Know How to Listen?" by Wendell Johnson. The article appeared in *ETC* in autumn 1949. This publication is edited by S. I. Hayakawa, and we enthusiastically suggest that you become a permanent subscriber.

It is important for us to say that the principal reason for your learning how to listen to students is that you may increase your understanding of what the students perceive as relevant. The only way to know where a kid is "at" is to listen to what he is saying. You can't do this if you are talking.

Invite another teacher to observe your class when you are experimenting with listening. After the lesson, ask your colleague this question: On the basis of what you heard these students say, what would you have them do tomorrow, or next week? Perhaps your colleague will then invite you to observe her class while she experiments with listening. After a while, both of you may find that you are becoming increasingly more effective at designing activities based on what students actually know, feel, and care about.

4. If you feel it is important for your students to learn how to ask questions, try this:

Announce to the class that for the next two days, you will not permit them to make any utterances that are not in the form of questions. Then, present the class with some problem. Tell them that their task is to compile a list of questions, the answers to which might help in solving the problem. If your students require an inducement, tell them you will reward (with A's, gold stars, or whatever sugar cubes you conventionally use) those students who produce the most questions. At this point, you need only be concerned with the quantity of questions, not their quality. Your students probably have had very little experience with question-asking behavior (at least in school), and the primary problem is to get them to begin formulating questions. Later, you can have them examine their questions in an effort to determine if there are certain criteria by which the quality of a question can be evaluated. (For example: Does the question contain unwarranted assumptions? Does it leave important terms undefined? Does it suggest some procedure for obtaining an answer?)

You might use some such problems as the following, depending on the age of your students:

Suppose we wanted to make the school the best possible school we can imagine, what would you need to know in order to proceed?

Read the following speech (for example by the President). What would you need to know in order to evaluate the validity of the speech?

Suppose our job was to make recommendations to improve the traffic problem (or pollution problem or population problem or whatever), what would you need to know in order to suggest a solution?

5. In order to help yourself become more aware of the subjectivity of your judgments, try this experiment:

The next time you grade your students, write down your reasons for whatever grade you assigned to a student. Then, imagine that you are the student. Study the reasons that your teacher gave to explain your grade. Ask yourself if you can accept these reasons and reflect on what you think of a teacher who would offer them. You might discover that your basis for assigning grades is prejudicial to some students, or lacks generosity, or is too vague. You might also discover, as some teachers have, that the conventional grading system is totally inadequate to evaluate the learning process. Some teachers have grown to resent it bitterly and have been driven to invent another system to complement the one they are forced to use.

Another experiment that might be helpful: Each time you give a grade to a student, grade your own perception of that student. The following questions might be useful:

1. To what extent does my own background block me from understanding the behavior of this student?

2. Are my own values greatly different from those of the student?

3. To what extent have I made an effort to understand how things look from this student's point of view?

4. To what extent am I rewarding or penalizing the student for his acceptance or rejection of my interests?

5. To what extent am I rewarding a student for merely saying what I want to hear, whether or not he believes or understands what he is saying?

You may discover that your answers to these questions are deeply disturbing. For example, you may find that you give the lowest grades mostly to those students you least understand, in which case, the problem is yours—isn't it?—not theirs. What we are driving at is this: too many teachers seem to believe that the evaluations they make of their students reflect only the "characteristics," "ability," and "behavior" of the students. The teacher merely records the grade that the student "deserves." This is complete nonsense, of course. A grade is as much a product of the teacher's characteristics, ability, and behavior as of the student's. Any procedure you can imagine that would increase your awareness of the role you play in "making" the student what you think he is will be helpful, even something like the following:

Keep track of the judgments you make about students. Every time you say words such as right, wrong, good, bad, correct, incorrect, smart, stupid, nice, annoying, polite, impertinent, neat, sloppy, etc., keep a record. Do it yourself or have a student do it. You can simply make a check on a sheet of paper that has been divided in two, with one column marked "+" and the other marked "–." Beyond the verbal judgments, you might keep track of the judgments you make that are made visible nonverbally, through facial expression, gesture, or general demeanor. Negative judgments are, not surprisingly, impediments to good learning, particularly if they have the effect of causing the learner to judge himself negatively.

Positive judgments, perhaps surprisingly, can also produce undesirable results. For example, if a learner becomes totally dependent upon the positive judgments of an authority (teacher) for both motivation and reward, what you have is an intellectual paraplegic incapable of any independent activity, intellectual or otherwise.

The point to all of this is to help you become conscious of the degree to which your language and thought is judgmental. You cannot avoid making judgments but you can become more conscious of the way in which you make them. This is critically important because once we judge someone or something we tend to stop thinking about them or it. Which means, among other things, that we behave in response to our judgments rather than to that which is being judged. People and things are processes. Judgments convert them into fixed states. This is one reason that judgments are commonly self-fulfilling. If a boy, for example, is judged as being "dumb" and a "nonreader" early in his school career, that judgment sets into motion a series of teacher behaviors that cause the judgment to become self-fulfilling.

What we need to do then, if we are seriously interested in helping students to become good learners, is to suspend or delay judgments about them. One manifestation of this is the ungraded elementary school. But you can practice suspending judgment yourself tomorrow. It doesn't require any major changes in anything in the school except your own behavior.

For example, the following incident—in this case outside of a classroom—is representative of the difference between a stereotypic and a suspended judgment.

A man and his seventeen-year-old son on Monday evening had a "discussion" about the need for the son to defer his social activities on week nights until he has finished doing all of the home work he has for school the next day.

It is now Wednesday evening, 48 hours later, about 7:30 P.M. Father is watching TV. Son emerges from his room and begins to put on a jacket.

FATHER: Where are you going?

SON: Out.

FATHER: Out where?

SON: Just out.

FATHER: Have you finished your homework?

SON: Not yet.

FATHER: I thought we decided [*that's the way parents talk*] that you wouldn't go out on week nights until you finished your home work.

SON: But I have to go out.

FATHER: What do you mean you "have to?"

SON: I just do.

FATHER: Well, you're not going out. You just have to learn to live up to the terms of the agreements you make.

SON: But. . . .

FATHER: That's all. I want no back talk.

MOTHER: Please. Let him go out. He'll be back soon.

FATHER: I don't want you butting in.

MOTHER: [*to son*] Go ahead. It will be all right.
[Son exits.]

FATHER: [*in a rage*] What the hell do you mean by encouraging his impertinence. How do you expect him to learn responsibility if you side with him in an argument with me? How . . .

MOTHER: [*interrupting*] Do you know what tomorrow is?
FATHER: What the hell has that got to do with it? Tomorrow's Thursday.
MOTHER: Yes, and it's your birthday.
FATHER: [*silence*]
MOTHER: Your son has been making a birthday gift for you at Jack's house. He wanted it to be a surprise for you tomorrow morning. A nice start for the day. He has just a bit more work to do on it to finish it. He wanted to get it done as early as possible tonight so he could bring it home and wrap it up for tomorrow. And then he'd still have time to do his homework.

Well, you see how easy it is to judge someone as something on the basis of *x* amount of data perceived in one way while simultaneously they are not only not that, but are something quite different.

Judgments are relative to the data upon which they are based and to the emotional state of the judge.

Learning to suspend judgment can be most liberating. Yon might find that it makes you a better learner (meaning maker) too.

6. Along the lines of the above, we would suggest an experiment that requires only imagination, but plenty of it. Suppose you could convince yourself that your students are the smartest children in the school; or, if that seems unrealistic, that they have the greatest potential of any class in the school. (After all, who can say for certain how much potential anyone has?) What do you imagine would happen? What would you do differently if you *acted* as if your students were capable of great achievements? And if you acted differently, what are the chances that many of your students would begin to act as if they *were* great achievers? We believe that the chances are quite good. There is, as we have noted, considerable evidence to indicate that people can become what others think they are. In fact, if you reflect on how anyone becomes anything, you are likely to conclude that becoming is almost always a product of expectations—one's own or someone else's. We are talking here about the concept of the "self-fulfilling prophecy." This refers to the fact that often when we predict that something will happen, the prediction itself contributes to making it happen. Nowhere is this idea more usable than in education, which is, or ought to be, concerned with the processes of becoming.

A *warning:* You will have great difficulty in imagining that your students are smart if you hold on to the belief that the stuff you know about, or would like to know about, constitutes the only ingredients of "smartness."

Once you abandon that idea, you may find that your students do, in fact, know a great deal of stuff, and that it is easier than you supposed to imagine they are the brightest children you ever had.

7. The extent to which you can try the following experiment depends on the degree to which the administration and the school community are rigid. In its most effective form, the experiment involves telling your students that all of them will get A's for the term and, of course, making good on your promise. At first, the students will not believe you, and it has sometimes taken as long as four weeks before all the students accept the situation. Once such acceptance is achieved, the students can begin to concentrate on learning, not their grades. There is no need for them to ask, "When is the midterm?" "Do we have to do a paper?" "How much weight is given to classwork?" and so on. If such questions do arise, you can reply, honestly, by saying that the questions are not necessary since the grades have already been given and each student will receive the highest possible grade the system allows. (We can assure you that such questions will come up because students have been conditioned to think of education as being indistinguishable from grades.) The next step is to help the students discover what kind of knowledge they think is worth knowing and to help them decide what procedures can most profitably be used to find out what they want to know. You will have to remind your students that there is no need for them to make suggestions that they think will please *you*. Neither is there any need for them to accept your suggestions out of fear of reprisal. Once they internalize this idea, they will pursue vigorously whatever course their sense of relevance dictates. Incidentally, they are likely to view your proposals not as threats, but as possibilities. In fact, you may be astonished at how seriously your own suggestions are regarded once the coercive dimension is removed.

If you are thinking that students, given such conditions, will not do any work, you are wrong. Most will. But, of course, not all. There are always a few who will view the situation as an opportunity to "goof off." So what? It is a small price to pay for providing the others with perhaps the only decent intellectual experience they will ever have in school. Beyond that, the number of students who do "goof off" is relatively small when compared with those who, in conventional school environments, tune out.

There is no way of our predicting what "syllabus" your students will evolve. It depends. Especially on them, but also on you and how willing you are to permit students to take control of the direction of their own studies. If you, or your administration and community, could not bear this possibility, perhaps you could try the experiment on a limited basis: for example, for a "unit" or even a specific assignment.

8. Perhaps you have noticed that most examinations and, indeed, syllabi and curricula deal almost exclusively with the past. The future hardly exists in school. Can you remember ever asking or being asked in school a question like "If such and such occurs, what do you think will happen"? A question of this type is usually not regarded as "serious" and would rarely play a central role in any "serious" examination. When a future-oriented question is introduced in school, its purpose is usually to "motivate" or to find out how "creative" the students can be. But the point is that the world we live in is changing so rapidly that a future-orientation is essential for everybody. Its development in schools is our best insurance against a generation of "future shock" sufferers.

You can help by including in all of your class discussions and examinations some questions that deal with the future. For example:

What effects on our society do you think the following technological inventions will have?
  a. the electric car
  b. the television-telephone
  c. the laser beam
  d. the 2,000-mph jet
  e. central data storage
  f. disposable "paper" clothing
  g. interplanetary communication
  h. language-translation machines

Can you identify two or three ideas, beliefs, and practices that human beings will need to give up for their future well-being?

In case you are thinking that such questions as these are usable only in the higher grades, we want to assure you that young children (even third-graders) frequently provide imaginative and pointed answers to future-oriented questions, provided that the questions are suitably adapted to their level of understanding. Perhaps you can make it a practice to include future-oriented questions at least once a week in all your classes. It is especially important that this be done for young children. After all, by the time they have finished school, the future you have asked them to think about will be the present.

9. Anyone interested in helping students deal with the future (not to mention the present) would naturally be concerned, even preoccupied, with media of

communication. We recommend to you, of course, the books of Marshall McLuhan, especially *Understanding Media*. We think that the most productive way to respond to McLuhan's challenge (as he has suggested) is not to examine his statements but to examine the media. In other words don't dwell on the question "Is McLuhan right in saying such and such?" Instead, focus on the question "In what ways are media affecting our society?" Your answers may turn out to be better than McLuhan's. More important, if you allow your students to consider the question, their answers may be better than McLuhan's. And even more important than that, the process of searching for such answers, once learned, will be valuable to your students, throughout their lives.

Therefore, we suggest that media study become an integral part of all your classes. No matter what "subject" you are teaching, media are relevant. For example, if you are a history teacher, you can properly consider questions about the effects of media on political and social developments. If you are a science teacher, the entire realm of technology is open to you and your students, including a consideration of the extent to which technology influences the direction of the evolutionary process. If you are an English teacher, the role of media in creating new literatures, new audiences for literature, and new modes of perceiving literature is entirely within your province. In short, regardless of your subject and the age of your students, we suggest that you include the study of media as a normal part of the curriculum. You might bear in mind that your students are quite likely to be more perceptive and even more knowledgeable about the structure and meaning of newer media than you. For example, there are many teachers who haven't yet noticed that young people are enormously interested in poetry—the poetry that is now on LP records and sung by Joan Baez, Phil Ochs, and Bob Dylan; or that young people are equally interested in essays of social and political criticism as *heard* on records by Lenny Bruce, Bill Cosby, Godfrey Cambridge, Mort Sahl, et al.

10. Before making our final suggestion, we want to say a word of assurance about the revolution we are urging. There is nothing in what we have said that precludes the use, *at one time or another,* of any of the conventional methods and materials of learning. For certain specific purposes, a lecture, a film, a textbook, a packaged unit, even a punishment, may be entirely justified. What we are asking for is a methodological and psychological shift in emphasis in the roles of teacher and student, a fundamental change in the nature of the classroom environment. In fact, one model for such an environment already exists in the schools—oddly, at the extreme ends of the schooling process. A good primary-grade teacher as well as a good graduate-student

adviser operate largely on the subversive assumptions expressed in this book. They share a concern for process as against product. They are learner- and problem-oriented. They share a certain disdain for syllabi. They allow their students to pursue that which is relevant to the learner. But there is a 15-year gap between the second grade and advanced graduate study. The gap can be filled, we believe, by teachers who understand the spirit of our orientation. It is neither required nor desirable that *everything* about one's performance as a teacher be changed. Just the most important things.

11. Our last suggestion is perhaps the most difficult. It requires honest self-examination. Ask yourself how you came to know whatever things you feel are worth knowing. This may sound like a rather abstract inquiry, but when undertaken seriously it frequently results in startling discoveries. For example, some teachers have discovered that there is almost nothing valuable they know that was *told* to them by someone else. Other teachers have discovered that their most valuable knowledge was not learned in a recognizable sequence. Still others begin to question the meaning of the phrase "valuable knowledge" and wonder if anything they learned in school was "valuable." Such self-examination can be most unsettling as you can well imagine. English teachers have discovered that they hate Shakespeare; history teachers, that everything they know about the War of the Roses is useless; science teachers, that they really wanted to be druggists. The process, once begun, leads in many unexpected directions but most often to the question "Why am I a teacher, anyway?" Some honest answers that this question has produced are as follows:

- I can control people.
- I can tyrannize people.
- I have captive audiences.
- I have my summers off.
- I love seventeenth-century nondramatic Elizabethan literature.
- I don't know.
- The pay is good, considering the amount of work I actually do.

Obviously, none of these answers is very promising for the future of our children. But each in its way is a small act of positive subversion because it represents a teacher's honest attempt to know himself. The teacher who *recognizes* that he is interested, say, in exercising tyrannical control over others is taking a first step toward subverting that interest. But the question "Why am I a teacher, anyway?" also produces answers that are encouraging: for example, that one can participate in the making of intelligence and, thereby, in the development of a decent society. As soon as a teacher recognizes that this is, in fact, the reason he became a teacher, then the subversion of our existing educational system strikes him as a necessity. As we have been trying to say: we agree.

_____

Neil Postman (deceased) was an author and professor at the New School for Social Research.

Charles Weingartner (deceased) was a professor at Queen's College.

PART IV

What Do Good Schools Look Like?

Though a K–8 facility, Thayer is a small school with fewer than four hundred students attending this tasteful stone and brick building situated in a lovely, bucolic setting. As a bedroom community to one of the nation's largest cities, students at Thayer generally hail from homes of considerable affluence. Thayer boasts strong music and art programs, numerous after-school activities, including drama and the usual sports teams, computers with video streaming capabilities in every classroom, and an abundance of actively involved parent volunteers. The teachers at Thayer tend to be happy too. The average class size is under twenty students, and there is so little turnover in the staff that Thayer hasn't advertised a teaching position in years.

This year, like most years before it, students at Thayer Elementary School earned the distinction of having the highest test scores in the state. Tom Rogers, the principal at Thayer for the last six years, takes special pleasure in announcing this fact every year at the June Parent's Night meeting. He states, "Student performance on reading, writing, and math has been consistent enough for the State Department of Education to label the school 'high performing' and 'a model school where exemplary teaching and learning are the norm.'"

The Johnsons were thrilled to move to the Thayer district over the summer. And, when they arrived for their first Parent-Teacher Night in early September, they were brimming with anticipation when their daughter's teacher began her introduction.

"We've purchased a new basal reader for all sixth grade students," the teacher began. "We like this series because each reading is short and the text is accompanied by a teacher's edition that contains plenty of discussion questions, quizzes, and worksheets."

As their daughter's new teacher continued, the Johnsons thumbed through the basal readers. The Johnsons were crestfallen. Between the hard covers of the basal reader were no fewer than 25 great novels, each abridged into 5–10 page versions of the originals. More depressing, their daughter had already read most of the novels in their original form. The teacher continued and encouraged parents to walk around the room and examine student work from the previous year. The Johnsons wondered about the geography worksheets that required, for example, students to identify country names based upon longitude and latitude coordinates, the "A–Z List" which asked students to match Egypt-related vocabulary words with their definitions, and reams of math dittos. By the end of the evening, the Johnsons had serious questions about whether Thayer was the right place for their daughter.

Is Thayer a good school? What are the defining characteristics of a good school?

13

The Idea of Summerhill

A. S. Neill

This is a story of a modern school—Summerhill.

Summerhill was founded in the year 1921. The school is situated within the village of Leiston, in Suffolk, England, and is about one hundred miles from London.

Just a word about Summerhill pupils. Some children come to Summerhill at the age of five years, and others as late as fifteen. The children generally remain at the school until they are sixteen years old. We generally have about twenty-five boys and twenty girls.

The children are divided into three age groups: The youngest range from five to seven, the intermediates from eight to ten, and the oldest from eleven to fifteen.

Generally, we have a fairly large sprinkling of children from foreign countries. At the present time (1960) we have five Scandinavians, one Hollander, one German and one American.

The children are housed by age groups with a house mother for each group. The intermediates sleep in a stone building, the seniors sleep in huts. Only one or two older pupils have rooms for themselves. The boys live two or three or four to a room, and so do the girls. The pupils do not have to

NOTE: Copyright 1993 by A. S. Neill. From *Summerhill School: A New View of Childhood* by A. S. Neill. Reprinted by permission of St. Martin's Press, LLC.

stand room inspection and no one picks up after them. They are left free. No one tells them what to wear: they put on any kind of costume they want to at any time.

Newspapers call it a *Go-as-you-please* School and imply that it is a gathering of wild primitives who know no law and have no manners.

It seems necessary, therefore, for me to write the story of Summerhill as honestly as I can. That I write with a bias is natural; yet I shall try to show the demerits of Summerhill as well as its merits. Its merits will be the merits of healthy, free children whose lives are unspoiled by fear and hate.

Obviously, a school that makes active children sit at desks studying mostly useless subjects is a bad school. It is a good school only for those who believe in such a school, for those uncreative citizens who want docile, uncreative children who will fit into a civilization whose standard of success is money.

Summerhill began as an experimental school. It is no longer such; it is now a demonstration school, for it demonstrates that freedom works.

When my first wife and I began the school, we had one main idea: *to make the school fit the child*—instead of making the child fit the school.

I had taught in ordinary schools for many years. I knew the other way well. I knew it was all wrong. It was wrong because it was based on an adult conception of what a child should be and of how a child should learn. The other way dated from the days when psychology was still an unknown science.

Well, we set out to make a school in which we should allow children freedom to be themselves. In order to do this, we had to renounce all discipline, all direction, all suggestion, all moral training, all religious instruction. We have been called brave, but it did not require courage. All it required was what we had—a complete belief in the child as a good, not an evil, being. For almost forty years, this belief in the goodness of the child has never wavered; it rather has become a final faith.

My view is that a child is innately wise and realistic. If left to himself without adult suggestion of any kind, he will develop as far as he is capable of developing. Logically, Summerhill is a place in which people who have the innate ability and wish to be scholars will be scholars; while those who are only fit to sweep the streets will sweep the streets. But we have not produced a street cleaner so far. Nor do I write this snobbishly, for I would rather see a school produce a happy street cleaner than a neurotic scholar.

What is Summerhill like? Well, for one thing, lessons are optional. Children can go to them or stay away from them—for years if they want to. There is a timetable—but only for the teachers.

The children have classes usually according to their age, but sometimes according to their interests. We have no new methods of teaching, because we do not consider that teaching in itself matters very much. Whether a school has or has not a special method for teaching long division is of no significance, for long division is of no importance except to those who want to learn it. And the child who wants to learn long division will learn it no matter how it is taught.

Children who come to Summerhill as kindergartners attend lessons from the beginning of their stay; but pupils from other schools vow that they will never attend any beastly lessons again at any time. They play and cycle and get in people's way, but they fight shy of lessons. This sometimes goes on for months. The recovery time is proportionate to the hatred their last school gave them. Our record case was a girl from a convent. She loafed for three years. The average period of recovery from lesson aversion is three months.

Strangers to this idea of freedom will be wondering what sort of madhouse it is where children play all day if they want to. Many an adult says, "If I had been sent to a school like that, I'd never have done a thing." Others say, "Such children will feel themselves heavily handicapped when they have to compete against children who have been made to learn."

I think of Jack who left us at the age of seventeen to go into an engineering factory. One day, the managing director sent for him.

"You are the lad from Summerhill," he said. "I'm curious to know how such an education appears to you now that you are mixing with lads from the old schools. Suppose you had to choose again, would you go to Eton or Summerhill?"

"Oh, Summerhill, of course," replied Jack.

"But what does it offer that the other schools don't offer?"

Jack scratched his head. "I dunno," he said slowly; "I think it gives you a feeling of complete self-confidence."

"Yes," said the manager dryly, "I noticed it when you came into the room."

"Lord," laughed Jack. "I'm sorry if I gave you that impression."

"I liked it," said the director. "Most men when I call them into the office fidget about and look uncomfortable. You came in as my equal. By the way, what department did you say you would like to transfer to?"

This story shows that learning in itself is not as important as personality and character. Jack failed in his university exams because he hated book learning. But his lack of knowledge about *Lamb's Essays* or the French language did not handicap him in life. He is now a successful engineer.

All the same, there is a lot of learning in Summerhill. Perhaps a group of our twelve-year-olds could not compete with a class of equal age in handwriting or spelling or fractions. But in an examination requiring originality, our lot would beat the others hollow.

We have no class examinations in the school, but sometimes I set an exam for fun. The following questions appeared in one such paper:

Where are the following:—Madrid, Thursday Island, yesterday, love, democracy, hate, my pocket screwdriver (alas, there was no helpful answer to that one).

Give meanings for the following: (the number shows how many are expected for each)—Hand (3) . . . only two got the third right—the standard of measure for a horse. Brass (4) . . . metal, cheek, top army officers, department of an orchestra. Translate Hamlet's To-be-or-not-to-be speech into Summerhillese.

These questions are obviously not intended to be serious, and the children enjoy them thoroughly. Newcomers, on the whole, do not rise to the answering standard of pupils who have become acclimatized to the school. Not that they have less brain power, but rather because they have become so accustomed to work in a serious groove that any light touch puzzles them.

This is the play side of our teaching. In all classes much work is done. If, for some reason, a teacher cannot take his class on the appointed day, there is usually much disappointment for the pupils.

David, aged nine, had to be isolated for whooping cough. He cried bitterly. "I'll miss Roger's lesson in geography," he protested. David had been in the school practically from birth, and he had definite and final ideas about the necessity of having his lessons given to him. David is now a lecturer in mathematics at London University.

A few years ago someone at a General School Meeting (at which all school rules are voted by the entire school, each pupil and each staff member having one vote) proposed that a certain culprit should be punished by being banished from lessons for a week. The other children protested on the ground that the punishment was too severe.

My staff and I have a hearty hatred of all examinations. To us, the university exams are anathema. But we cannot refuse to teach children the required subjects. Obviously, as long as the exams are in existence, they are our master. Hence, the Summerhill staff is always qualified to teach to the set standard.

Not that many children want to take these exams; only those going to the university do so. And such children do not seem to find it especially hard to tackle these exams. They generally begin to work for them seriously at the age of fourteen, and they do the work in about three years. Of course they don't always pass at the first try. The more important fact is that they try again.

Summerhill is possibly the happiest school in the world. We have no truants and seldom a case of homesickness. We very rarely have fights—quarrels, of course, but seldom have I seen a stand-up fight like the ones we used to have as boys. I seldom hear a child cry, because children when free have much less hate to express than children who are downtrodden. Hate breeds hate, and love breeds love. Love means approving of children, and that is essential in any school. You can't be on the side of children if you punish them and storm at them. Summerhill is a school in which the child knows that he is approved of.

Mind you, we are not above and beyond human foibles. I spent weeks planting potatoes one spring, and when I found eight plants pulled up in June, I made a big fuss. Yet there was a difference between my fuss and that of an authoritarian. My fuss was about potatoes, but the fuss an authoritarian would have made would have dragged in the question of morality—right and wrong. I did not say that it was wrong to steal my spuds; I did not make it a matter of good and evil—I made it a matter of my spuds. They were *my spuds* and they should have been left alone. I hope I am making the distinction clear.

Let me put it another way. To the children, I am no authority to be feared. I am their equal, and the row I kick up about my spuds has no more significance to them than the row a boy may kick up about his punctured bicycle tire. It is quite safe to have a row with a child when you are equals.

Now some will say: "That's all bunk. There can't be equality. Neill is the boss; he is bigger and wiser." That is indeed true. I am the boss, and if the house caught fire the children would run to me. They know that I am bigger and more knowledgeable, but that does not matter when I meet them on their own ground, the potato patch, so to speak.

When Billy, aged five, told me to get out of his birthday party because I hadn't been invited, I went at once without hesitation—just as Billy gets out of my room when I don't want his company. It is not easy to describe this relationship between teacher and child, but every visitor to Summerhill knows what I mean when I say that the relationship is ideal. One sees it in the attitude to the staff in general. Rudd, the chemistry man, is Derek. Other members of the staff are known as Harry, and Ulla, and Pam. I am Neill, and the cook is Esther.

In Summerhill, everyone has equal rights. No one is allowed to walk on my grand piano, and I am not allowed to borrow a boy's cycle without his permission. At a General School Meeting, the vote of a child of six counts for as much as my vote does.

But, says the knowing one, in practice of course the voices of the grownups count. Doesn't the child of six wait to see how you vote before he raises his hand? I wish he sometimes would, for too many of my proposals are beaten. Free children are not easily influenced; the absence of fear accounts for this phenomenon. Indeed, the absence of fear is the finest thing that can happen to a child.

Our children do not fear our staff. One of the school rules is that after ten o'clock at night there shall be quietness on the upper corridor. One night, about eleven, a pillow fight was going on, and I left my desk, where I was writing, to protest against the row. As I got upstairs, there was a scurrying of feet and the corridor was empty and quiet. Suddenly I heard a disappointed voice say, "Humph, it's only Neill," and the fun began again at once. When I explained that I was trying to write a book downstairs, they showed concern and at once agreed to chuck the noise. Their scurrying came from the suspicion that their bedtime officer (one of their own age) was on their track.

I emphasize the importance of this absence of fear of adults. A child of nine will come and tell me he has broken a window with a ball. He tells me, because he isn't afraid of arousing wrath or moral indignation. He may have to pay for the window, but he doesn't have to fear being lectured or being punished.

There was a time some years back when the School Government resigned, and no one would stand for election. I seized the opportunity of putting up a notice. "In the absence of a government, I herewith declare myself Dictator. Heil Neill!" Soon there were mutterings. In the afternoon Vivien, aged six, came to me and said, "Neill, I've broken a window in the gym."

I waved him away. "Don't bother me with little things like that," I said, and he went.

A little later he came back and said he had broken two windows. By this time I was curious, and asked him what the great idea was.

"I don't like dictators," he said, "and I don't like going without my grub." (I discovered later that the opposition to dictatorship had tried to take itself out on the cook, who promptly shut up the kitchen and went home.)

"Well," I asked, "what are you going to do about it?"

"Break more windows," he said doggedly.

"Carry on," I said, and he carried on.

When he returned, he announced that he had broken seventeen windows. "But mind," he said earnestly, "I'm going to pay for them."

"How?"

"Out of my pocket money. How long will it take me?"

I did a rapid calculation. "About ten years," I said.

He looked glum for a minute; then I saw his face light up. "Gee," he cried, "I don't have to pay for them at all."

"But what about the private property rule?" I asked. "The windows are my private property."

"I know that but there isn't any private property rule now. There isn't any government, and the government makes the rules."

It may have been my expression that made him add, "But all the same I'll pay for them."

But he didn't have to pay for them. Lecturing in London shortly afterward, I told the story; and at the end of my talk, a young man came up and handed me a pound note "to pay for the young devil's windows." Two years later, Vivien was still telling people of his windows and of the man who paid for them. "He must have been a terrible fool, because he never even saw me."

Children make contact with strangers more easily when fear is unknown to them. English reserve is, at bottom, really fear; and that is why the most reserved are those who have the most wealth. The fact that Summerhill children are so exceptionally friendly to visitors and strangers is a source of pride to me and my staff.

We must confess, however, that many of our visitors are people of interest to the children. The kind of visitor most unwelcome to them is the teacher, especially the earnest teacher, who wants to see their drawing and written work. The most welcome visitor is the one who has good tales to tell—of adventure and travel or, best of all, of aviation. A boxer or a good tennis player is surrounded at once, but visitors who spout theory are left severely alone.

The most frequent remark that visitors make is that they cannot tell who is staff and who is pupil. It is true: the feeling of unity is that strong when children are approved of. There is no deference to a teacher as a teacher. Staff and pupils have the same food and have to obey the same community laws. The children would resent any special privileges given to the staff.

When I used to give the staff a talk on psychology every week, there was a muttering that it wasn't fair. I changed the plan and made the talks open to everyone over twelve. Every Tuesday night, my room is filled with eager youngsters who not only listen but give their opinions freely. Among the subjects the children have asked me to talk about have been these: The Inferiority Complex, The Psychology of Stealing, The Psychology of the Gangster, The Psychology of Humor, Why Did Man Become a Moralist?, Masturbation, Crowd Psychology. It is obvious that such children will go out into life with a broad clear knowledge of themselves and others.

The most frequent question asked by Summerhill visitors is, "Won't the child turn round and blame the school for not making him learn arithmetic or music?" The answer is that young Freddy Beethoven and young Tommy Einstein will refuse to be kept away from their respective spheres.

The function of the child is to live his own life—not the life that his anxious parents think he should live, nor a life according to the purpose of the educator who thinks he knows what is best. All this interference and guidance on the part of adults only produces a generation of robots.

You cannot make children learn music or anything else without to some degree converting them into will-less adults. You fashion them into accepters of the status quo—a good thing for a society that needs obedient sitters at dreary desks, standers in shops, mechanical catchers of the 8:30 suburban train—a society, in short, that is carried on the shabby shoulders of the scared little man—the scared-to-death conformist.

A. S. Neill (deceased) was the founder of the Summerhill School.

14

Success in East Harlem

How One Group of Teachers Built a School That Works

Deborah Meier

In the spring of 1991, Central Park East will graduate its first high school students. Some of them will have been with us since they were 4 years old. From age 4 to age 18, they will have attended a school—located in East Harlem in the midst of New York City's District 4—that many observers believe is as good as any school in the public or the private sector: A progressive school in the tradition of so many of New York's independent private schools, Central Park East is now firmly fixed within New York's school bureaucracy.

But it wasn't always so. We have had our share of luck, and we owe a great deal to many different people over the years. We know, too, that our success depended on the success of a districtwide effort to create a whole network of alternative schools. We are, in fact, just one of nearly 30 "options" that are available to families in District 4, aside from the regular neighborhood-zoned elementary schools.

In the fall of 1974 Anthony Alvarado, the new superintendent of District 4, initiated just two such alternatives: our elementary school and a middle school, the East Harlem School for the Performing Arts. Each year thereafter

NOTE: Reprinted with permission from the Fall 1987 issue of the *American Educator,* the quarterly journal of the American Federation of Teachers, AFL-CIO.

the district supported the launching of several more alternative schools—generally at the junior high level. These schools were rarely the result of a central plan from the district office, but rather tended to be the brainchildren of particular individuals or groups of teachers. They were initialed by the people who planned to teach in them.

It was the district's task to make such dreams come true. The details differed in each case. Most of these schools were designed around curricular themes—science, environmental studies, performing arts, marine biology. But they also reflected a style of pedagogy that suited their founders. They were always small, and, for the most part, staff members volunteered for duty in them. Finally, when the alternative schools outnumbered the "regulars," Alvarado announced that henceforth all junior high schools would be schools of "choice." By 1980 all sixth graders in the district chose where they would go for seventh grade. No junior high had a captive population.

On the elementary school level, neighborhood schools remain the norm, though the district handles zoning rather permissively. The only schools of choice on the elementary level are the Central Park East Schools, the East Harlem Block School (founded in the 1960s as a nonpublic, parent-run "free" school), and a network of bilingual elementary schools.

Today, Central Park East is, in fact, not one school but a network of four schools: Central Park East I, Central Park East II, and River East are elementary schools that feed into Central Park East Secondary School, which enrolls students from grades 7 through 12 and is affiliated with Theodore Sizer's* Coalition of Essential Schools.

The Central Park East schools were founded in 1974, during a time of great educational grief in New York City—just before the schools were forced to lay off more than 15,000 teachers and close elementary school libraries and at a time when the spirit of hope was crushed out of the parent movement and out of the struggles for decentralization, for teacher power and for structural change. Progressive educators suffered particularly, both because people began to claim that "openness" was "through" (and discredited) and because many of the young teachers and programs that had carried the progressive message were hardest hit by the layoffs.

In the spring of 1974, when Alvarado invited me to build a school in one wing of PS 171, it seemed a most unlikely offer. School District 4 served a dismal, bitterly torn, largely Hispanic community. Still, I accepted. Who

---

*Theodore Sizer is the author of *Horace's Compromise* and the founder of the Coalition of Essential Schools.

could refuse such an offer? After struggling for years to make my beliefs "fit" into a system that was organized on quite different principles, after spending considerable energy looking for cracks, operating on the margins, "compromising" at every turn, the prospect that the district bureaucracy would organize itself to support alternative ideas and practices was irresistible. I was being offered a chance to focus not on bureaucratic red tape, but on the intractable issues of education—the ones that really excited me and many of the teachers I knew.

But this was not a time for having large visions, and I didn't want to be disappointed. I met with Alvarado, began to collect some experienced teachers to help launch the effort, and gradually began to believe that he meant what he said. He offered to let us build a school just the way we wanted. The total allocation of funds (per-pupil costs) would have to be comparable to what was spent on any other school, and our teachers would have to meet the usual requirements of the city, the state, and the union contract. Nor could we be exempt from any city or state regulations. Beyond that, however, the district would support us in doing things our own way.

We began very small and very carefully. First there was the question of "we." Creating a democratic community was both an operational and an inspirational goal. While we were in part the products of what was called "open" education, our roots went back to early progressive traditions, with their focus on the building of a democratic community, on education for full citizenship and for egalitarian ideals. We looked upon Dewey, perhaps more than Piaget, as our mentor.

Virtually all of us had been educated in part at City College's Workshop Center under Lillian Weber. We came out of a tradition that was increasingly uneasy about the strictly individualistic focus of much of what was being called "open." We were also unhappy about the focus skills rather than content in many of the "modern," innovative schools— even those that did not embrace the "back-to-basics" philosophy. Many "open" classrooms had themselves fallen prey to the contemporary mode of breaking everything down into discrete bits and pieces skills that children could acquire at their own pace and in their own style. In contrast, we were looking for a way to build a school that could offer youngsters a deep and rich curriculum that would inspire them with the desire to know; that would cause them to fall in love with books and with stories of the past; that would evoke in them a sense of wonder at how much there is to learn. Building such a school required strong and interesting adult models—at home and at school—who could exercise their own curiosity and judgment.

We also saw schools as models of the possibilities of democratic life. Although classroom life could certainly be made more democratic than traditional schools allowed, we saw it as equally important that the school life of *adults* be made more democratic. It seemed unlikely that we could foster democratic values in our classrooms unless the adults in the school also had significant rights over their workplace.

We knew that we were tackling many difficult issues at once. Because of political considerations, planning time was insufficient, but the district tried to make up for this by being extra supportive. Looking back, we were so euphoric that we had the energy of twice our numbers.

We purposely started our school with fewer than a hundred students—in kindergarten, first grade, and second grade only. At the superintendent's request, we recruited outside of the usual district channels, in part so that we wouldn't threaten other schools in the district and in part because one of Alvarado's goals was to increase the pupil population of the district and thus guard against school closings.

One of our primary reasons for starting the school—although we didn't often say—was our personal desire for greater autonomy as teachers. We spoke a lot about democracy, but we were also just plain sick and tired of having to negotiate with others, worry about rules and regulations, and so on. We all came together with our own visions—some collective and some individual—of what teaching could be like if only we had control. Ours was to be a teacher-run school. We believed that parents should have a voice in their children's schooling, and we thought that "choice" itself was a form of power. We also believed that we could be professionally responsive to parents and that, since the school would be open to parents at all times and the staff would be receptive, there would be plenty of opportunity to demonstrate our responsiveness.

Good early childhood education, we believed, required collaboration between the school and the family. This was a matter not only of political principle but also of educational principle, and it motivated us from the start to work hard to build a family-oriented school. We wanted a school in which children could feel safe. Intellectual risk-taking requires safety, and children who are suspicious of a school's agenda cannot work up their potential. To create a safe school, we needed to have the confidence of parents, and children needed to know that their parents trusted us. It was that simple. Hard to create, perhaps, but essential.

We stumbled a lot in those early years. We fought among ourselves. We discovered that remaining committed to staff decision making was not easy.

It was hard, too, to engage in arguments among ourselves without frightening parents and raising doubts about our professionalism. We were often exhausted—some times by things that mattered least to us.

By the end of the second year, I had made some crucial decisions regarding the organization and structure of Central Park East. These involved my leaving the classroom to become a somewhat more traditional principal. We have never entirely resolved the tensions over who makes which decisions and how. But the staff continues to play a central role in all decisions, big and small. Nothing is "undiscussable," though we have learned not to discuss everything—at least not all the time. This has actually meant more time for discussing those issues that concern us most: how children learn, how our classes really work, what changes we ought to be making, and on what bases. We have also become better observers of our own practice, as well as more open and aware of alternative practices.

Today, we understand better the many, often trivial ways in which schools undermine family support systems, undercut children's faith in their parents as educators, and erode parents' willingness to assume their responsibilities as their children's most important educators. We have become more supportive of parents whose "home instruction" differs from ours. We give less advice on such topics as how not to teach arithmetic or how to be a good parent.

As we became more secure with ourselves and our program, the district was expanding its network of alternative schools. In the fall of 1974 we were one of two. Within a half-dozen years there were about 15 "alternative concept" schools, mostly glaringly broken down.

The district also dispensed with the assumption that one building equals one school. Instead, every building in the district was soon housing several distinct schools—each with its own leadership, parent body, curricular focus, organization, and philosophy. Most of the new junior highs were located in elementary school buildings. Former junior high buildings were gradually turned to multiple uses, as well. Sometimes three or more schools shared a single building. As a result, the schools were all small, and their staffs and parents were associated with them largely by choice.

By the late Seventies, Central Park East was so inundated with applicants that the district decided to start a small annex at PS 109, now known as Central Park East II. The district's decision was probably also motivated by the availability of federal funds for the purpose of school integration. While Central Park East has always had a predominantly black (45%) and Hispanic (30%) student population, it is one of the few district schools that has also maintained a steady white population, as large as about 25%. (The population of District 4 is about 60% Hispanic, 35% black, and 5% white.)

In the beginning, this ratio came about largely by chance, but the 25% white population in the school has been maintained by choice. In general, the school has sought to maintain as much heterogeneity as possible, without having too many fixed rules and complex machinery. The school accepts all siblings, as part of its family orientation. After siblings, priority goes to neighborhood families. In other cases, the school tries to be nonselective, taking in most of its population at age five strictly on the basis of parental choice, with an eye to maintaining a balanced student body. Well over half of the students have always qualified for free or reduced-price lunches and some 15% to 20% meet the state requirements for receiving special education funds.

The demand for spaces still far outstripped available seats, and, a few years later, the district decided to start a third elementary school. This one was named River East.

Thus by 1984 Central Park East had become three schools, each designed for about 250 students, each with its own individual style and character, yet united in basic ways. Then, in 1984, at the 10th anniversary celebration of our founding, Theodore Sizer congratulated the school for its impressive history and asked, "why not a Central Park East secondary school?" Why not keep the good things going through the 12th grade?

We agreed. Our own study of our sixth-grade graduates persuaded us that starting a secondary school was a good idea. Some of our critics had said that a secure and supportive elementary school would not prepare students to cope with the "real world." Our study of our graduates had proved them wrong. Regardless of race or social class, our graduates had handled the real world well. They had coped. The statistics we compiled amazed even us. Only one of our graduates, who were hardly an academic elite, had left school prior to earning a high school diploma. Furthermore, half of our graduates had gone on to college.

But our graduates had stories to tell. And their stories were not stories about being educated, but about survival. They told us stories that confirmed what Sizer had written about U.S. high schools in *Horace's Compromise*. But the stories our graduates told us were generally far worse than Sizer chronicled, since he was often describing wealthy or middle-class schools.

We began negotiations with the district and with the city. In the fall of 1985 we opened the doors to Central Park East Secondary School, which serves grades 7 through 12. We are now back where we began, starting something entirely new. However, the obstacles that block the path of reforming a high school are harder to budge than those that face elementary schools.

For instance, the idea that an "alternative" high school means a school for "difficult" kids is firmly entrenched in the tradition of New York City high schools, and the anxiety about preparing students for the "real world" is more pressing than in elementary schools. Moreover, the Regents exam, course requirements, college pressures, and the usual panic about dealing with adolescents and their problems combine to make the task even more complex—especially in light of New York's recently adopted Regents Action Plan, which runs counter to everything we and Coalition of Essential Schools believe. With its increased number of required courses and standardized examinations and its greater specificity about course content, the Regents Action Plan leaves far less room for initiative and innovation at the school level. There is little for us to learn from and not much of a network of teachers or teacher education institutions that can provide us with support, ideas, and examples.

But we have a lot going for us, too. We have our three sister elementary schools to lean on and draw support from. We have the Coalition of Essential Schools and a growing national interest in doing something about the appalling quality of many public secondary schools. And, under its current superintendent, Carlos Medina, the district continues to support the idea of alternative "schools of choice" for all children, all parents, and all staff members. We have also been receiving invaluable support from the citywide high school division and the alternative high school superintendent, who oversees a disparate collection of small high schools throughout New York City.

And we are determined. New York City's high schools are clearly in a state of crisis. The dropout rate is appalling, the fate of many who do not drop out officially is equally devastating, and the decline in college attendance by black and Hispanic students is frightening. Perhaps the time has come for progressive education to tackle the high school again, to demonstrate that giving adolescents and their teachers greater responsibility for the development of educational models is the key ingredient.

The notion of respect, which lies at the heart of democratic practice, runs counter to almost everything in our current high schools. Today's urban high schools express disrespect for teachers and students in myriad ways— in the physical decay of the buildings, in their size, in the anonymity of their students, and in the lack of control over decisions by those who live and work in them.

Although the reasons for the recent national concern over high schools may have little to do with democracy, the current reform mood offers an important opening—if we can resist the desire for a new "one best way." We cannot achieve true reform by fiat. Giving wider choices and more power to those who are closest to the classroom are not the kinds of reforms that appeal to busy legislators, politicians, and central board officials. They cannot be mandated, only facilitated. Such reforms require fewer constraints, fewer rules—not more of them. They require watchfulness and continuous documenting and recording, not a whole slew of accountability schemes tied to a mandated list of measurable outcomes.

Do we have the collective will to take such risks? Only if we recognize that the other paths are actually far riskier and have long failed to lead us out of the woods. Like democratic societies, successful schools can't be guaranteed. The merits of letting schools try to be successful schools can't be guaranteed. The merits of letting schools try to be successful are significant. But allowing them to try requires boldness and patience—not a combination that is politically easy to sustain.

What They Do and How They Do It

As teachers at Central Park East overhauled and rebuilt the traditional school structure, they kept one key aim in mind: to give teachers time to get to know each student and time to tailor the instructural program for each individual. Here are some examples of what they've done:

Time for Students

- To get the student load way down, all professional staff—including the librarian and the director—teach. Aside from one director, there are no supervisors.
- The high school is organized into Houses of 80 students, each with a faculty of four. The basic class is 20 students and the student load per teacher is never more than 80. If the teacher teaches two disciplines instead of one, the load is just 40.
- To maximize the personal relationship between students and teachers, students stay with the same teacher (or teachers) two years in a row.

Time for Teachers

- Each fall the staff plans a series of semi-monthly faculty meetings. One year, every other faculty meeting considered various approaches to writing. Sometimes, at a teacher's request, one student's progress or one teacher's curriculum is discussed.
- Once a week, the staff of each House takes an 80-minute lunch and discusses the progress of individual students and the overall work of the House.
- One morning a week, while students work in the community, teachers from each department can spend three uninterrupted hours designing, evaluating, and tinkering with the curriculum.

The Curriculum

The curriculum is designed by those who teach it. Teachers can opt to hire consultants.

- The seventh and eighth grade science sequence includes an interdisciplinary unit on "Light and Sight" that exposes students to both biology (optics) and physics (the properties of light).
- The eighth grade humanities sequence focuses on "power"—who has it, who doesn't, and how different people have gotten it. The first semester focuses on the English, French, and American revolutions; the second, on nonrevolutionary change in America.

Flexible Scheduling

Because the schedule is in the hands of teachers, the time allotted the revolutions could be increased when it was discovered that at least one student still thought Boston was in London.

Resources

Once a topic—such as the revolutions—has been chosen, all faculty haunt used-book shops to build a resource library on the subject. Teachers are thus not text bound, but have access to a variety of materials—some of which will interest every student.

Writing

Working in different settings with different "editors," students get plenty of practice with—and individual attention to—their writing. They write at least once a week in humanities and in a "writing work shop," plus four days a week in regularly reviewed journals.

Parent Conferences

Twice a year, parents must come to the school, review a portfolio of their child's work, and meet with the teacher *and* the student to discuss the student's progress. With everybody in the same room together, parents won't hear one version of events from the student and another from the teacher.

Deborah Meier is the principal of the Mission Hill Elementary School in Boston, Massachusetts.

15

When Learning Matters

Using Learning Plans to Educate One Student at a Time

Elliot Washor

One hundred years ago in *Atlantic Monthly*, William James wrote,

> In children we observe a ripening of impulses and interests in a certain deter-
> minate order. Creeping, walking, climbing, imitating, vocal sounds, con-
> structing, drawing, calculating, possess the child in succession. Of course, the
> proper pedagogic moment to work in skill and to clinch the useful habit is
> when the native impulse is most acutely present. Crowd on the athletic
> opportunities, the mental arithmetic, the verse-learning, the drawing, the
> botany, or what not, the moment you have reason to think the hour is ripe.

James' thoughts make me believe that when learning matters, schools are
student-centered. They are places that encourage, generate and sustain the
abilities and talents of every child. Our schools need to be places where

---

NOTE: Previously published in *Personalized Learning*, pp. 1–16, edited by Joseph DiMartino,
John Clarke, and Denise Wolk. Reprinted by permission of Scarecrow Education.

learning matters, but instead most of the time they are places where only what is being taught matters. From early on the content starts to matter more than learning it. This includes at what grade material is taught rather than what students are learning.

Ian Kelly, a first grade student living in Ireland, recently presented me with a telling riddle to ponder that went like this:

Question: Who's still talking when everyone has stopped listening?
Answer: The teacher

This riddle lets us in on the secret that every child knows—that in school, teaching matters more than learning.

This chapter will focus on the importance of creating student-centered learning environments using *Personalized Learning Plans* (PLPs) to engage students in their own learning experiences. I discuss my own experience with the difference between the PLPs used at the Met and the *Individualized Education Plans* (IEPs) that are commonly used for students with special needs. The importance of creating a supportive link between the student, family, advisor and mentors in creating a challenging and personalized educational plan for every student is crucial, and examples of how the process works at the Met are presented here. By allowing students the opportunity to learn using hands-on experience they are able to demonstrate proficiency through a variety of non-traditional methods. In the end, we have found that students with PLPs are able to utilize the experience they've gained to determine their future goals for college and beyond.

The Met

The Metropolitan Regional Career and Technical Center (the Met) is a five-year-old Rhode Island public high school with a mission to rethink and revamp the entire delivery of secondary school education. As researcher Adria Steinberg puts it, the Met "turns education on its head" by starting with the student instead of with a preset curriculum and classroom structured learning. The Met is a school that uses real world experiences to build skills and knowledge, one student at a time. By engaging its students in real projects with working adults, the Met prepares them for college, work, and citizenship. It demonstrates how effective a school can be when the entire community is a resource for education.

All Met students have their own Personalized Learning Plan based on their particular interests, which are continually updated by the student and her teacher, parents and mentors. Met students are intrinsically motivated to learn, because they have a say in choosing the work they do.

To carry out their learning plans, Met students establish a unique intern relationship called Learning Through Internship (LTI) with a mentor in the community. The LTI is based on the premise that adolescents need to learn in real world settings and interact effectively with adults. The primary function of the school is to provide the infrastructure that supports that learning. The student works on learning goals and develops a portfolio of work as evidence of achieving those goals. The mentor is a role model, content expert and learning resource.

Over the years, we have enhanced our work around learning plans so they have changed and evolved as we have changed. We have connected them and acculturated them into the Met as we grew from using them with incoming ninth graders to translating learning plans into a driving force for our students' entry into Senior Institute in the eleventh grade and as a resource for our innovative college transcript. The Met's evolution of the learning plan is a statement of what educators can do to make a community accountable for learning and engage families in learning if educators have students and families in mind.

All schools are mandated to use learning plans for children with Special Needs, but does this ensure that learning is personalized? Mandates do not ensure that learning plans are student-centered and that learning really matters. A student-centered environment is key to the success of learning plans that allow for accountability, flexibility and family engagement.

Michael's Story: IEP Versus PLP

The following story is my own account of my son Michael's Individualized Education Plan (IEP) meeting from a school he attended. Here I'm in the role of parent.

In his middle grades my son Michael was diagnosed with a language/reading disability. I will share here what transpired at a learning plan (Individualized Education Plan) meeting at his middle school. These meetings are mandatory for any child who is diagnosed as Special Needs.

As I went into the room you could see some of the testers talking with each other but keeping their distance from me. There were 8–10 people assembled in a circle. The group included the guidance counselor, special education teacher, school psychologist, two school testers, the assistant principal, and two of Michael's teachers. There were eight staff members from the school, and myself as a parent. It was quite intimidating.

The guidance counselor started the meeting. She introduced everyone and then asked the school psychologist to present and analyze the results of the test and observational data. It seems that the data showed Michael was easily distracted, tended to daydream, did a lot of drawing but was not a discipline problem. One tester said he fit into the average range of intelligence showing some deficits and confusion when it came to putting details together. Another said his issues in learning to write are that his fine motor coordination is below par. One by one, each person talked about Michael through the data either from formalized tests or his grades in school. As the meeting went on, one or two more of his teachers came in late and joined us around the circle. Each one pointed out Michael's deficits. It was a very uncomfortable feeling for everyone sitting around the table. I didn't know anyone there.

As they presented their evaluations and remediations, it was also clear that some were uncomfortable talking, some even broke out in hives, and others were displaying their discomfort through their body language.

From my perspective, it was uncomfortable as a parent to hear qualified educational experts talk about my child using test data and a smattering of observations. The intent is to somehow use scientific instruments that give a profile of a child but nothing can be further from the truth. I can't believe the original intent of any law was to mandate testing over really knowing a child well.

All the while I sat there listening, and I must confess I was doodling a bit to deal with my uneasiness. Finally, the guidance counselor said in summation, "So it seems everything is going along well. Michael is receiving some extra support in reading and language development. We are working on his writing. Thanks for coming. Do you have any questions?"

Now, no one in the room knew me, and they only learned that I was a principal because I told them that during our introductions. I said, "I have some things to say. First, all of you talked about Michael through your findings, but do you really know my son? Do any of you know he is a protégé jazz guitarist who practices three hours a night? Do you realize the tremendous intellectual focus, concentration and dexterity it takes to play an instrument at that level? Do you know that athletically he is the fastest student in the school? (So much for his fine or gross motor coordination issues.) And do you know that he is well liked and respected by other students and seems to get along well with all the teachers in the building? People on both sides of his family have been musicians and artists for generations. This may account for his doodling but maybe not. Maybe he is not connected to what he is doing in school. You said, he is easily distracted, and doodles. Do his doodles look anything like this?" I turned the paper I was doodling on around so all could see. I smiled and everyone was a bit relieved. I did this in a way that was not casting blame but opening up a conversation about looking at the strengths and weaknesses. As my friend Bill Ayers from Chicago says, "Our primary responsibility as teachers is to give hope."

After my comments we really started talking about Michael. It was apparent that these folks really do care about children, but there is no way in this system for people to really care. There was no way for these educators to really look at the whole child, strengths and weaknesses, and build learning environments that will use strengths to get at a weakness.

Like most systems, there is a distrust of parents as part of the educational planning where they can be used as a resource. The work of student learning is relegated to what has been mandated either as remedial plans or standards-based reform. These mandates take all the craft, art, and in many cases, even the technical components out of teaching and learning. It is exactly the idea Dewey warned us about when he stated, "All reforms which rest simply upon the enactment of law, or the threatening of certain penalties, or upon changes in mechanical or outward arrangements, are transitory or futile."

Michael graduated from the Met last year, and now attends Wheaton College where he is majoring in music and business. At the Met he had a learning plan where he, his parents, advisors/teachers and mentors were involved in his learning, and we all knew one another well. Everyone was encouraged to sit in on his learning plan meetings. His learning has evolved over the years to a place where things in Michael's life make sense for the person he is, where he wants to go, and what he wants to learn.

The Importance of Family Engagement

My voice is that of a parent and an educator when I agree with Cremin's (1976) statement " . . . the real message of the Coleman and Jencks studies of equal educational opportunities: not that the school is powerless but that the family is powerful." Family Engagement at the Met is very different than most schools and our learning plan meetings are a major part of the difference. The average family comes to the Met to learning plan meetings and exhibitions seven times a year. In the past, these families rarely went into their children's schools. In my own experience, I went to my son's school only for parent night, one or two events, and an IEP meeting. It was not that I didn't want to go to the school; it was that there was nothing for me to go to. As a matter of fact, one time I wanted to see the principal and the secretary told me I would have to wait three weeks for an appointment. The tipping point that gets families engaged at the Met is that families are used as a resource at learning plan meetings and are an important part of the learning process.

Families are not only participants in learning plans but at times are the topic of a project. A Met graduate who is now attending college in Rhode Island did a project on fibromyalgia, a condition with which her mom was diagnosed. This project illustrates the depth of the work that can be accomplished through an LTI, and how Met learning goals are woven into the academic needs of a student and agreed on at a Learning Plan meeting.

When Priscilla Santana came back to school in the fall of 10th grade, she had a new interest. Her mother had had carpal tunnel surgery over the summer and was doing physical therapy as part of her recovery. Priscilla's interest was awakened to physical therapy, and she decided that she wanted to learn more, both for herself and to help her mother. After searching, interviewing and job shadowing, she started an LTI with a mentor in a physical therapy clinic. At a learning plan meeting, Priscilla, her mentor, her parents, and her advisor, Rachel, identified a product that the clinic needed, and it became Priscilla's responsibility and the basis for her project.

The following is an excerpt from Priscilla's learning plan on the project proposal:

Product

An informational pamphlet for patients recently diagnosed with the condition fibromyalgia.

Investigation

First try: Why do there seem to be more cases of fibromyalgia diagnosed in Rhode Island than in Florida, as my mentor thinks from talking to another physical therapist down there? Is it doctor diagnosis and referral to physical therapy? Is it weather-related? Are there more retirees in Florida and therefore it's work-related? What accounts for the difference?

(Continued)

(Continued)

Second try: A thorough understanding of fibromyalgia, its causes, manifestations and various treatment options. Learn the "tender points" used to diagnose patients. Understand the physics of torque for biomechanics and how this translates to lifting objects.

Reflection:

(Synopsis of student's journal writing and student narrative)

The first investigation didn't work because fibromyalgia is a recently developed diagnosis and even the Centers for Disease Control had no information. I planned to survey doctors but when I tried to set up an interview with a doctor to look at my survey, he didn't respond. I had no idea that this kind of information might not be available yet and that it would be so hard to get doctors. This was frustrating and made me nervous because I was worried my project wouldn't be good. But then Rachel (my advisor) helped me see that it just meant sometimes projects don't go the way you plan and you have to be on top of it and make a change when you need to. So that's when we changed to the second investigation and I did all the research.

I was so surprised that I could read a lot of the medical journals and get the information I needed. My mentor also helped me by answering my questions to understand what I was reading about. I learned a lot of new terms like pressure points and bone names and what it meant that there might be a disease. I was also surprised to learn about how torque is measured in lifting objects. And when I had to put it all together, I learned how to use PageMaker to put it on a computer layout.

I learned so much in this project, not just about this syndrome, but also about myself and how I learn and how I do a project.

The concept of LTIs goes hand in hand with developing learning plans and portfolios for post high school goals, whether it's college, vocational school, apprenticeships or directly to work. From working on the learning plans, each student will have a portfolio that allows him or her to customize all of their experiences for application to each college or work situation.

Throughout this project Priscilla's parents, her mentor, and her teacher were all in agreement about her learning. Priscilla is now pursuing a college education. Her parents have been part of her education at the Met from her beginning enrollment. They have watched her develop interests in writing, poetry and nursing. They have questioned her on her learning journey as well as gotten to know her teacher Rachel, her mentors and her principals. The learning plan meeting is one of the key places where this forum takes place and everyone can be accountable.

Learning Plans and Accountability

The notion of high stakes accountability has been thrust on schools from the many varied constituencies that want schools to show what children are learning, and to be more precise, to see if what is being taught is being learned, and why it is not. Being accountable is one of those ideas that everyone agrees on, for surely students, schools, teachers, and parents must account for learning. For the most part, accountability has been measured by whether a child achieves a given content or skill standard by passing a test on a certain amount of information.

On the other hand, learning plans offer a way to account for student learning one student at a time, by literally bringing everyone to the table to agree upon what the goals for learning are in a given amount of time, and over an extended period of time. This is what happens at the Met. Our students demonstrate proficiency in what they have learned during student exhibitions that are held at least four times this year. Each student presents work and evidence of learning before a public panel of teachers, parents, mentors, students, and other community members who know him well or bring relevant field expertise. Panelists evaluate the student's work and presentation skills against criteria pre-determined by the teacher and student, and against the standards of their own field. Through these exhibitions, students demonstrate mastery of skills and knowledge. Because a student's work at the Met is not quantified by the use of traditional courses or credits, other methods are needed to document what is accomplished. One of these methods is the creation of a portfolio, a comprehensive collection of artifacts of student work. The contents vary among students, but they typically include final papers and drafts, photos of products, notes, videotape of exhibitions, artwork, narrative reports and other assessments, and a student-authored journal. In the end, Met students prove what they learned through a comprehensive demonstration of skills, not just by fielding questions on a standardized test.

A learning plan meeting is not always easy to facilitate or to participate in. Parents, students, and teachers may disagree but in order to connect everyone to learning, our teachers learn to facilitate and negotiate learning plans starting from student interest, and the skills and knowledge a student has. Then, they develop a way to bring that student toward reaching his/her goals. Learning plans have become part of our culture at the Met. Our accountability to our students, their families and to ourselves is to ensure our students graduate and are prepared to move on to forms of higher education and the workforce. After four years of learning plan meetings and LTIs, the Met's first graduating class had every student accepted to a post secondary institute. Students, their families, their mentors and teachers were involved through learning plan meetings every step of the way where education was planned one student at a time.

How LTIs Help Students Shape Their Own Future

We have students such as John who have amassed experiences in a wide variety of LTI situations. For the Met, John's family and for John, this is fine. John was born in New York City and came to Providence while he was in middle school. When he came to the Met in ninth grade at his first learning plan meeting, he expressed an interest in animation. His first year LTI was at a local graphic design studio, a start-up organization that is contracted by other businesses to do animation and multi-media presentations. He worked along side programmers and business managers alike and developed a flipbook of cartoons and a Claymation video. Simultaneously, he took a short acting class at a local theatre company and discovered he had an interest in theater. His interest led him to a summer job as the sound manager for a local theater group's production of "Fame."

When John returned to school in the fall of his 10th grade year, he found out about internship opportunities with the state judicial system. Just a little over a year before he had been involved with the legislative hearings for the opening of the Met and had testified before the House Finance Committee. This new opportunity interested him. At his 10th grade learning plan meeting, everyone agreed on an LTI at the Supreme and Superior Court of Rhode Island, where he honed in on the juvenile justice system and conducted an opinion survey of people in the court system about why juveniles commit crimes. At the end of 10th grade, John earned a Summer Search scholarship and spent 6 weeks in Colorado in a wilderness-training course and was certified as a lifeguard as well as a CPR instructor. This New York–born teen, in his own words, had trouble getting his feet back on city ground when he returned to Providence.

In 11th grade, John had an LTI with a dance choreographer/educator in the dance department in a local middle school. He worked on the technical aspects of performance and was the stage manager for a production of "Milan." Simultaneously, he, another student and a Met teacher rehearsed for a three person play written by a local playwright entitled "Slow Dance on the Killing Ground," scheduled to go on stage in the spring.

John already had a Summer Search scholarship lined up for the end of his 11th grade year, and had to decide between a performing arts program in London or a language program in Spain to help him develop better literacy in his family's first language, Spanish. The sum of all these experiences was a prelude to his senior year, when he began the process of selecting colleges.

John now attends a college near Worcester, Massachusetts, is majoring in criminal justice, and is still performing in school productions. He was recently on a TV show talking about his first year of college and how an innovative high school prepared him for his college experience.

There have been a few movies made in recent years about learning. One movie, *Billy Elliot*, is the story of a boy with an amazing gift as a dancer. The school he attended never recognized or cared about his interests and passions. In *October Sky*, another student has a passion for rockets and one teacher supported his interests in the face of family and school obstacles. What would it have been like for these children to have had learning plans that allowed them to pursue their interests at their school? I think we all know the answer. It is too scary to think, what if they don't?

Resources

Cotton, K. (1994). *School Size, Climate, and Student Performance*. Portland OR. Northwest Regional Laboratory, U.S. Dept. of Education.

Cremin, L. (1961). The Transformation of the School. *Progressivism in American Education*, 1876–1957. New York: Alfred A. Knopf.

Cremin, L. (1975). *Public Education*. New York: Basic Books, 1975.

Cremin, L. (1988). *American Education: The Metropolitan Experience, 1876–1980*. New York: Harper & Row.

Csikszentmihalyi, M. (1988). Motivation and Creativity: Toward a Synthesis of Structural and Energistic Approaches to Cognition. *New Ideas in Psychology*, 6(2), 159–176.

Csikszentmihalyi, M. (1988). *Optimal Experience*. New York: Cambridge University Press.

Csikszentmihalyi, M. (1990). *Flow*. New York: Harper & Row.

Dewey, J. (1916). *Democracy in Education*. New York: The MacMillan Company.

Dewey, J. (1933). *How We Think*, Second Revised Edition. New York: D.C. Heath & Co.

Hillman, J. (1996). *The Soul's Code*. New York: Random House.

James, W. (1958). *Talks to Teachers on Psychology and to Students on Some of Life's Ideals*. New York: W. W. Norton & Co. (originally published 1899).

Klonsky, M., & Ford, P. (1994, May). One Urban Solution: Small Schools. *Educational Leadership*, 64–66.

Levine, E. B. (2001). *One Kid at a Time: A Visionary High School Transforms Education*. New York: Teacher's College Press.

Littky, Dennis, & Allen, Farrel. Whole-School Personalization, One Student at a Time. *Educational Leadership*, September 1999.

Meier, D. (1995). *The Power of Their Ideas: Lessons For America From a Small School in Harlem*. Boston: Beacon Press.

Montessori, M. (1966). *The Secret of Childhood*. New York: Ballantine Books.

Sarason, S. (1990). *The Predictable Failure of School Reform*. San Francisco: Jossey-Bass.

Schank, R. (2000). *Coloring Outside the Lines: Raising a Smarter Kid by Breaking All the Rules*. New York: Harper Collins.

Steinberg, A. (1996). *Real Learning, Real Work*. New York: Routledge.

Wilson, F. R. (1998). *The Hand: How Its Use Shapes the Brain, Language, and Human Culture*. New York: Pantheon Books.

Elliot Washor is co-director of the Big Picture Company and a former teacher and school principal.

16

Beyond the Deficit Paradigm

An Ecological Orientation to Thriving Urban Schools

Kelly Donnell

Whether reading newspaper headlines or federal educational reforms, you, like many Americans, may have developed a sense that urban schools in our nation are in a state of crisis. This sense of crisis is related to a wide range of factors, some of which are legitimate and others, less so. Unfortunately, the intense attention to this perceived crisis belies the fact that many urban schools are thriving; they are effective, caring, just, and strive for success for all children, without exception. As a student of education you may marvel at or, perhaps, feel overwhelmed by the challenges and complexity of teaching and learning. However, beginning teachers just like you are succeeding in urban schools and their voices are woven throughout this article.

It is true that urban education has struggled, historically and today, with inefficient and dehumanizing bureaucracies; a lack of funding and appropriate staffing; wave upon wave of new reforms and initiatives; differences in the demographic profiles of teacher and student populations; the gaps in school achievement and completion rates among racial, cultural, and economic groups of students; and acute problems in the recruitment and retention of teachers for urban schools. These are real and daunting concerns. As

---

NOTE: Reprinted with kind permission from the author.

one beginning teacher commented, when teaching in an urban school, "you feel the weight of society on your shoulders."

Successful teaching requires recognition of these conditions and an understanding of how they influence urban schooling, particularly because an emphasis on the sense of crisis often both stems from and reinforces a deficit paradigm. The deficit paradigm is an orientation in which children and their families and communities are seen as deficient and blamed for lack of success. Those who engage in deficit thinking regard student failure as a result of alleged internal deficiencies, such as a lack of intelligence, or socially linked shortcomings such as dysfunctional family situations. The popular "at risk" construct views urban children and their families as responsible for urban school failure. The deficit paradigm is highly counterproductive and fails to capitalize on the positive and powerful opportunities available in urban education. When we acknowledge that there is nothing "wrong" with urban students or their families or their communities, we must ask if the problem has been in the type of schools we have been providing for them.

An alternative paradigm from which to understand the success of many urban schools is an ecological approach. This approach views school life and classroom teaching as occurring within interconnected webs of settings and institutions that transcend classroom and school borders. Schooling is considered to be embedded in, and therefore influenced by, socially and culturally organized environments. Ecological systems, more than isolated factors such as outdated textbooks or school violence, affect schooling. Systems (such as the students, the classroom, the family, the school, the community, the society) are nested within each other and have a cascading influence upon each other.

With regard to urban schools, an ecological view acknowledges that urban policy, structure, and customs are integrally related to what happens in urban classrooms. Urban schools function within an ecological web of interconnected social entities, beginning with children in classrooms extending out to schools, districts, and communities. These complex, layered contexts influence each other in bi-directional ways. Urban schools are embedded in a much larger context, one that requires multiple sectors of the community acting in concert. The teacher, students and their families, the school, or even the school district alone cannot bring about meaningful change in urban schools. But together they can create highly successful schools that ensure achievement for all students and that function as a service to the community.

"Loving, highly successful" urban schools may be more common than many citizens and educators alike would believe, given the pervasive nature of the deficit paradigm. Scheurich (1998) has researched schools that have operationalized a model that has become known as HiPass Schools (High Performance All Student Success). The model, which encompasses many of the concepts throughout this chapter, was developed at the grass-roots level by school-level educators, not by academics at the university or bureaucrats from school administration. The schools in Scheurich's study perform exceptionally well on state-based high stakes tests and they are deeply caring and child-centered.

If we consider the ecology of urban education as a web, at its center are the students. A critical thread in this ecological web is utilization of the wealth of diversity and of the cultural and personal resources that students and their families bring to urban schools. In thriving urban schools, children's cultural backgrounds, including their first language, are highly valued. Students bring essential "funds of knowledge" (Moll, 2000) to school; they bring rich cultural and cognitive resources that teachers use to provide meaningful learning that incorporates students' prior knowledge and experience. Below, one beginning teacher describes how she learned to integrate students' funds of knowledge while teaching a high school poetry unit:

> I wanted to introduce them to traditional poets, the classic, canonical poets. But at the same time I realized that that has not been working. I could not think of a creative way to engage them with learning about T. S. Eliot! And so, I thought I would start in a place I assumed they were. They all listen to music, but my primary assumption was that they listen to hip-hop or some form of rap. I just thought, how can I make it academic? So I picked rappers or hip-hop artists who talk about significant things, you know like historical events. And then I picked lyrics that use like metaphors and other things that I talk about on and on, like personification and all these things. Because the first thing we did we read this article about the need for revolution in contemporary hip hop, the need for like music to change and stop being so materialistic, misogynist, and all this stuff. And just within the text there was so much vocabulary that they hadn't encountered that I realized we needed to do vocab first. And the vocab took a week because so much discussion came out of the kinds of words that we used. . . . You know, it was amazing for me because the last three weeks we were doing my unit was the only time I had good attendance and actual engagement and students talking about what we did in class outside of class, you know, in a positive way. They actually asked me questions and they would call me. I took some of them to poetry readings.

In thriving urban schools, everyone associated with life in the school fiercely believes that each and every child can succeed at high academic levels. This is common rhetoric but is rarely enacted in practice. This belief is not rooted in the current discourse that high standards will address deficiencies in urban children, but in an understanding that children are naturally inclined to high engagement and achievement. Successful schools embrace a strong, shared vision and commitment to the idea that there are ways to engage in school so that everyone achieves, so long as everyone is willing to find that way. One beginning teacher put it this way:

> You have to walk into that classroom expecting to change all of them. If you go in saying, "Ok, some of them I'm just not going to reach," I think it's going to make you try less hard. When you get that resistance and a child is, like, putting up a wall, I think that if you are expecting failure, you are that much more likely to just be okay with that wall being there. Whereas if you go saying, "No way, my kids are succeeding by the end of the year," you are going to work to get over the wall.

Everyone acts on this deep commitment, asking not whether it can be done, but determining how. The entire ecology of school is focused on academic success and holistic well-being of the children.

In addition, all children are treated with compassion, care, and respect. This is not to say that successful urban schools are driven by a coddling notion of the primacy of self-esteem. Rather, the school focuses on building communities children want to go to in which they feel treasured:

> I couldn't teach without being who I am as a person. And who I am as a person is going to put myself out there with families. I think that's why I have the [positive] response that I have. Because they see that. My boss, it used to drive her nuts that I would hug my kids at the end of the night before they went home. That's who I am and my kids know me. You hug me before you go home for the day. That's it. That's how it goes. Because that way they know that no matter what happened during the day, "I'm not mad at you. You know, everything is fine. You made some mistakes. You made some bad choices. But you know what? Tomorrow is a new day."

In the words of another beginning teacher:

> I have to be able to say that the reason I'm teaching this class of kids or [am] there every day is because I care about the students. And I want them to reach their fullest potential. . . . . And I can always believe that that's right. Like those are very fundamental truths to teaching any classroom of kids. And so as long as I can really apply that to what I'm doing then I can know that at least that much is right.

Care and respect for children is viewed as ethical and moral accountability, not sentimentality.

The complex interrelatedness of the various stakeholders and environments in urban schools comes together in the concept of community. This key element is woven again and again throughout thriving urban schools. Community is emphasized in many capacities: through the perspective of the teacher, through the culture of the school, through partnerships with the actual local community. For example, Peter Murrell, from Northeastern University, has developed the concept of "the community teacher." At the core of a community teacher's educational practice is the development of his or her ecological knowledge—contextualized knowledge—of the urban culture, community, and identity of children and families. The community teacher sees learning as situated in particular contexts and settings and resists the separation of school and the everyday world of students. The community teacher views learning as a process of co-participation and activity with other people and human systems and works to create "communities of practice."

Successful urban schools are integral parts of their communities. There is very little separation between the two. The school is often the nerve center of the community:

> I think another critical thing about [this urban high school] is that their support services are incredible. They have a health center right in the school. They have a day care center at the high school. (Student teacher)

This nerve center is often built through partnerships with organizations in the community. There are many different types of partnerships. Schools find meaningful relationships with businesses, universities, youth organizations, service agencies, and faith-based organizations. Historically, many organizations in urban communities such as Boys and Girls Clubs, YMCAs, the Urban League, and Scouting have provided urban students with opportunities to connect with the larger society and have promoted a positive sense of purpose and participation. The roles of these organizations continue to evolve to meet the needs of students in urban schools. Because of their long-standing history they often have built relationships and cultural knowledge of local communities and their families.

Urban schools, just like their counterparts in other types of communities in our country, can and must be places where children and adults thrive and are cared for and where every single child achieves meaningful success. It is happening in urban schools across the country. And not only are these schools thriving, they are offering us all a window into how our participation in the ecology of our communities is essential. Scheurich (1998) suggests that the teachers and parents who created HiPass schools have given us a gift that is larger than just education, as vitally important as education is to our society. In terms of organizations and life in those organizations, these schools have given us living examples of a kind of organization that is wonderful to work within and that performs at the highest levels . . . the very idea that our work environments could be both loving and high performing is truly startling for most of us, given our typical experiences in organizations. . . . It would be ironic, indeed, if a better kind of organization has emerged from low-SES schools and communities of color. (p. 478)

Successful, caring urban schools will require recognition of and commitment to the importance of the entire ecology in which students are embedded. But as the HiPass schools attest, this is not hollow rhetoric or an idealistic dream; it is a thriving reality in many urban schools.

HiPass (High Performance All Student Success Schools)

High performance for each and every child, delivered in a passionately committed and loving way, is the only way. (Scheurich, 1998, p. 460)

- Cultural characteristics
- Loving, caring environment for adults and children
- Strong shared vision
- Collaborative, family-oriented
- Innovative, open to new ideas
- Hardworking, but not burning out
- Appropriate conduct is built into the organizational culture
- School staff as a whole hold themselves accountable for success of all children

The theme of the school is Who am I? Who are We? We want everything to be interdisciplinary and co-disciplinary. So in social studies we are going to be doing the geography of the continents but also independence movements. Relating it to a part of the mission of the school is being an engaged citizen and being an active person in your community. So for science and social studies it's a lot of connecting with your community. I want to introduce independence movements and then kind of connect it to current events and everyday life. (Student teacher, Summer 2003)

I found that letting the kids kind of give life to whatever the assignment was, even if it wasn't initially the direction I had planned, worked so much better. And it was really kind of exciting but also a little bit scary for me. I remember coming in with these really structured lessons. . . . But I had to incorporate the kids into them. (Student teacher, Spring 2003)

References

Gonzalez, N., Moll, L.C., and Amanti, C. (2005). *Funds of Knowledge: Theorizing Practices in Households and Classrooms.* Mahwah, NJ: Lawrence Erlbaum Associates.

Scheurich, J. J. (1998). Highly successful and loving public elementary schools populated mainly by low-SES children of color: Core beliefs and cultural characteristics. *Urban Education, 33,* 451–491.

***

Kelly Donnell is a professor of education at Roger Williams University.

PART V

How Should We
Assess Student Learning?

Mrs. Yan is puzzled. Shayla is one of the hardest working, most motivated students in her 11th-grade English class. Shayla participates actively, writes poetry and short fiction, and always offers the most astute insights when class discussion turns to the interpretation of literature.

And yet Shayla struggles on Mrs. Yan's exams and she can't seem to memorize even a simple soliloquy for the oral presentation requirement. In addition, she gets glassy-eyed whenever Mrs. Yan talks about the importance of learning vocabulary as part of SAT preparation.

When reviewing Shayla's performance for the semester, Mrs. Yan noticed that Shayla's poetry and her short fiction, often published in the school's literary magazine, was exemplary, as was her effort and classroom participation. But her performance on exams, research papers, and more formal, oral presentations was, more often than not, deficient.

Struck by these inconsistencies, Mrs. Yan decided that the only fair way to arrive at a final report card grade was to average all Shayla's marks together. However, there was something about this approach that made Mrs. Yan uncomfortable.

For her part, Shayla believes that her grade should reflect her exceptional fiction and poetry, her sophisticated interpretation of literature, and her active class participation. Shayla is not happy with Mrs. Yan's simple solution to the complex problem.

Why assess student learning? What is the purpose of assessment? What does good assessment look like?

17

A Mania for Rubrics

Thomas Newkirk

N ear the beginning of the film *Dead Poets Society*, the English teacher played by Robin Williams forces his students to read aloud—from the absurd preface to their anthology. Works of literature, the preface states, can be evaluated by graphing two qualities: importance and execution. Midway through the reading, Mr. Williams' character tells his students to rip out the offending pages. Art can never be so mechanically reduced.

This movie's warning is relevant today because we are now in the middle of a resurgence of mechanical instruction in writing. Driven by state testing, teachers are being pulled toward prompt-and-rubric teaching that bypasses the human act of composing and the human gesture of response.

Proponents of rubrics will claim that they are simply trying to be clear about criteria that are too often tacit and unexplained. By using rubrics, the argument goes, we are giving students more precise and analytic reasons for the evaluations they receive. By placing these criteria in the clear light of day, students will come to see evaluations as less subjective, less what the teacher "likes."

If this were truly the case, who could disagree? The crux of the issue is this: Do rubrics clarify the process of sensitive response? Or do they distort,

NOTE: Previously published in *Education Week*, September 2000. Reprinted with permission.

obscure, or mystify that response? And to answer that question, we need to think carefully about what we do when we read student work (when we are at our best)—and what we want from an evaluator.

Personally, I have never been able to use rubrics that establish predetermined weighting systems. I always cheat. I work backwards, determining the impression or sense I had of the writing, a unitary evaluative reaction. Then I jimmy the categories so that they fit my general reaction, hoping to escape detection. In other words, I am not thinking of multiple criteria (organization, detail, mechanics) as I read, parceling out my attention.

As I read, I feel myself in a magnetized field. I am drawn to—or released from—the text I am reading. Initially, this response is more physical than cognitive or analytic; when the text is working I feel more alert, and a good line or image propels me forward. At other times, I feel slack, unmagnetized, as if nothing is drawing me in, drawing me on. This lack of attraction may come from too little detail (or too much), from a lack of direction, absence of personality or voice, from dialogue that doesn't reveal character, but the immediate sensation is physical. The student's text has let me go.

Rather than reveal processes like the one I have described, rubrics conceal or mystify them. They fail to reveal the narrative, moment-by-moment process of evaluation. Their formal and categorical ratings belie—or worse, short-circuit—the work of the reader. Terms like "organization" fail to clarify (or even locate) the disruption in the reader's sense of continuity. Rubrics fail to provide a *demonstration* of the reading process that can later be internalized by the writer.

The very authoritative language and format of rubrics, their pretense to objectivity, hides the human act of reading. The key qualities of good writing (organization, detail, a central problem) are represented as something the writing *has*—rather than something the writing *does*.

All of this, of course, assumes that the purpose of rubrics is to convey response. More often, however, they are used to enforce uniformity of evaluation—as a preparation to test-taking. A striking example appeared in the February 2000 issue of *Educational Leadership,* describing the way kindergartners were prepped for a drawing test. I will quote from the article so that I might not be accused of exaggeration.

After the teacher explained what elements of the drawing were needed to get a score of 4, she said, "Notice that this drawing shows the ground colored green and brown. There are also a tree, the sky, some clouds, and the sun." She then showed a picture earning a 3, in which the tree, clouds, and sun were not as clearly defined. After this explanation, she asked each student to create "artwork that met the requirement of the level-4 drawing" and rate the artwork of a partner. Children spent the rest of class time "improving their drawings until all the student pictures either met the level-4 rubric or went up at least one level."

This is not *preparation*—it is capitulation. This developmentally inappropriate task is presented not as educational malpractice, but as a "success" for standards-based instruction. Which only goes to prove the education writer Alfie Kohn's point: that the standards movement is going to make satire obsolete.

Thomas Newkirk is a professor of English at the University of New Hampshire.

18

Grading

The Issue Is Not How But Why?

Alfie Kohn

Why are we concerned with evaluating how well students are doing? The question of motive, as opposed to method, can lead us to rethink basic tenets of teaching and learning and to evaluate what students have done in a manner more consistent with our ultimate educational objectives. But not all approaches to the topic result in this sort of thoughtful reflection. In fact, approaches to assessment may be classified according to their depth of analysis and willingness to question fundamental assumptions about how and why we grade. Consider three possible levels of inquiry:

Level 1. These are the most superficial concerns, those limited to the practical issue of how to grade students' work. Here we find articles and books offering elaborate formulas for scoring assignments, computing points, and allocating final grades—thereby taking for granted that what students do must receive *some* grades and, by extension, that students ought to be avidly concerned about the ones they will get.

NOTE: Copyright 1994 by Alfie Kohn. Reprinted from *Educational Leadership* with the author's permission. For more information, please see www.alfiekohn.org.

Level 2. Here educators call the above premises into question, asking whether traditional grading is really necessary or useful for assessing students' performance. Alternative assessments, often designated as "authentic," belong in this category. The idea here is to provide a richer, deeper description of students' achievement. (Portfolios of students' work are sometimes commended to us in this context, but when a portfolio is used merely as a means of arriving at a traditional grade, it might more accurately be grouped under Level 1.)

Level 3. Rather than challenging grades alone, discussions at this level challenge the whole enterprise of assessment—and specifically why we are evaluating students as opposed to how we are doing so. No matter how elaborate or carefully designed an assessment strategy may be, the result will not be constructive if our reason for wanting to know how students are doing is itself objectionable.

Grading Rationale I: Sorting

One reason for evaluating students is to be able to label them on the basis of their performance and thus to sort them like so many potatoes. Sorting, in turn, has been criticized at each of the three levels, but for very different reasons. At Level 1, the concern is merely that we are not correctly dumping individuals into the right piles. The major problem with our high schools and colleges, the argument goes, is that they don't keep enough students off the Excellent pile. (These critics don't put it quite this way, of course; they talk about "grade inflation.") Interestingly, most studies suggest that student performance does not improve when instructors grade more stringently and, conversely, that making it relatively easy to get a good grade does not lead students to do inferior work—even when performance is defined as the number of facts retained temporarily as measured by multiple-choice exams (Vasta and Sarmiento 1979, Abrami et al. 1980).

At Level 2, questions are raised about whether grades are reliable enough to allow students to be sorted effectively. Indeed, studies show that any particular teacher may well give different grades to a single piece of work submitted at two different times. Naturally, the variation is even greater when the work is evaluated by more than one teacher (Kirschenbaum et al. 1971). What grades offer is spurious precision, a subjective rating masquerading as an objective assessment.

From the perspective of Level 3, this criticism is far too tame. The trouble is not that we are sorting students badly—a problem that logically should be addressed by trying to do it better. The trouble is that we are sorting them at all. Are we doing so in order to segregate students by ability and teach them separately? The harms of this practice have been well established (Oakes 1985). Are we turning schools into "bargain-basement personnel screening agencies for business" (Campbell 1974, p. 145)? Whatever use we make of sorting, the process itself is very different from—and often incompatible with—the goal of helping students to learn.

Grading Rationale II: Motivation

A second rationale for grading—and indeed, one of the major motives behind assessment in general—is to motivate students to work harder so they will receive a favorable evaluation. Unfortunately, this rationale is just as problematic as sorting. Indeed, given the extent to which A's and F's function as rewards and punishments rather than as useful feedback, grades are counterproductive regardless of whether they are intentionally used for this purpose. The trouble lies with the implicit assumption that there exists a single entity called "motivation" that students have to a greater or lesser degree. In reality, a critical and qualitative difference exists between intrinsic and extrinsic motivation—between an interest in what one is learning for its own sake, and a mindset in which learning is viewed as a means to an end, the end being to escape a punishment or snag a reward. Not only are these two orientations distinct, but they also often pull in opposite directions.

Scores of studies in social psychology and related fields have demonstrated that extrinsic motivators frequently undermine intrinsic motivation. This may not be particularly surprising in the case of sticks, but it is no less true of carrots. People who are promised rewards for doing something tend to lose interest in whatever they had to do to obtain the reward. Studies also show that, contrary to the conventional wisdom in our society, people who have been led to think about what they will receive for engaging in a task (or for doing it well) are apt to do lower quality work than those who are not expecting to get anything at all.

These findings are consistent across a variety of subject populations, rewards, and tasks, with the most destructive effects occurring in activities that require creativity or higher-order thinking. That this effect is produced by the extrinsic motivators known as grades has been documented with students of different ages and from different cultures. Yet the findings are rarely cited by educators.

Studies have shown that the more students are induced to think about what they will get on an assignment, the more their desire to learn evaporates, and, ironically, the less well they do. Consider these findings:

• On tasks requiring varying degrees of creativity, Israeli educational psychologist Ruth Butler has repeatedly found that students perform less well and are less interested in what they are doing when being graded than when they are encouraged to focus on the task itself (Butler and Nissan 1986; Butler 1987, 1988).

• Even in the case of rote learning, students are more apt to forget what they have learned after a week or so—and are less apt to find it interesting—if they are initially advised that they will be graded on their performance (Grolnick and Ryan 1987).

• When Japanese students were told that a history test would count toward their final grade, they were less interested in the subject—and less likely to prefer tackling difficult questions than those who were told the test was just for monitoring their progress (Kage 1991).

• Children told that they would be graded on their solution of anagrams chose easier ones to work on—and seemed to take less pleasure from solving them—than children who were not being graded (Harter 1978).

As an article in the *Journal of Educational Psychology* concluded, "Grades may encourage an emphasis on quantitative aspects of learning, depress creativity, foster fear of failure, and undermine interest" (Butler and Nissan 1986, p. 215). This is a particularly ironic result if the rationale for evaluating students in the first place is to encourage them to perform better.

Grading Rationale III: Feedback

Some educators insist that their purpose in evaluating students is neither to sort them nor to motivate them, but simply to provide feedback so they can learn more effectively tomorrow than they did today. From a Level 2 perspective, this is an entirely legitimate goal—and grades are an entirely inadequate means of reaching it. There is nothing wrong with helping students to internalize and work toward meeting high standards, but that is most likely to happen when they experience success and failure not as reward and punishment, but as information (Bruner 1961, p. 26). Grades make it very difficult to do this. Besides, reducing someone's work to a letter or number simply is not helpful; a B+ on top of a paper tells a student nothing about what was impressive about that paper or how it could be improved.

But from Level 3 comes the following challenge: Why do we want students to improve? This question at first seems as simple and bland as baby food; only after a moment does it reveal a jalapeno kick: it leads us into disconcerting questions about the purpose of education itself.

Demand vs. Support

Eric Schaps (1993), who directs the Developmental Studies Center in Oakland, California, has emphasized "a single powerful distinction: focusing on what students ought to be able to do, that is, what we will demand of them—as contrasted with focusing on what we can do to support students development and help them learn." For lack of better labels, let us call these the "demand" and "support" models.

In the demand model, students are workers who are obligated to do a better job. Blame is leveled by saying students "chose" not to study or "earned" a certain grade—conveniently removing all responsibility from educators and deflecting attention from the curriculum and the context in which it is taught. In their evaluations, teachers report whether students did what they were supposed to do. This mind-set often lurks behind even relatively enlightened programs that emphasize performance assessment and—a common buzzword these days—outcomes. (It also manifests itself in the view of education as an investment, a way of preparing children to become future workers.)

The support model, by contrast, helps children take part in an "adventure in ideas" (Nicholls and Hazzard 1993), guiding and stimulating their natural inclination to explore what is unfamiliar; to construct meaning; to develop a competence with and a passion for playing with words, numbers, and ideas. This approach meshes with what is sometimes called "learner-centered" learning, in which the point is to help students act on their desire to make sense of the world. In this context, student evaluation is, in part, a way of determining how effective we have been as educators. In sum, improvement is not something we require of students so much as something that follows when we provide them with engaging tasks and a supportive environment.

Supportive Assessment

Here are five principles of assessment that follow from this support model:

1. Assessment of any kind should not be overdone. Getting students to become preoccupied with how they are doing can undermine their interest in what they are doing. An excessive concern with performance can erode curiosity—and, paradoxically, reduce the quality of performance. Performance-obsessed students also tend to avoid difficult tasks so they can escape a negative evaluation.

2. The best evidence we have of whether we are succeeding as educators comes from observing children's behavior rather than from test scores or grades. It comes from watching to see whether they continue arguing animatedly about an issue raised in class after the class is over, whether they come home chattering about something they discovered in school, whether they read on their own time. Where interest is sparked, skills are usually acquired. Of course, interest is difficult to quantify, but the solution is not to return to more conventional measuring methods; it is to acknowledge the limits of measurement.

3. We must transform schools into safe, caring communities. This is critical for helping students to become good learners and good people, but it is also relevant to assessment. Only in a safe place, where there is no fear of humiliation and punitive judgment, will students admit to being confused about what they have read and feel free to acknowledge their mistakes. Only by being able to ask for help will they be likely to improve.

Ironically, the climate created by an emphasis on grades, standardized testing, coercive mechanisms such as pop quizzes and compulsory recitation, and pressure on teachers to cover a prescribed curriculum makes it more difficult to know how well students understand—and thus to help them along.

4. Any responsible conversation about assessment must attend to the quality of the curriculum. The easy question is whether a student has learned something; the far more important—and unsettling—question is whether the student has been given something worth learning. (The answer to the latter question is almost certainly no if the need to evaluate students has determined curriculum content.) Research corroborates what thoughtful teachers know from experience: when students have interesting things to do, artificial inducements to boost achievement are unnecessary (Moeller and Reschke 1993).

5. Students must be invited to participate in determining the criteria by which their work will be judged, and then play a role in weighing their work against those criteria. Indeed, they should help make decisions about as many elements of their learning as possible (Kohn 1993). This achieves several things: It gives them more control over their education, makes evaluation feel less punitive, and provides an important learning experience in itself. If there is a movement away from grades, teachers should explain the rationale and solicit students' suggestions for what to do instead and how to manage the transitional period. That transition may be bumpy and slow, but the chance to engage in personal and collective reflection about these issues will be important in its own right.

And If You Must Grade . . .

Finally, *while conventional grades persist, teachers and parents ought to do everything in their power to help students forget about them.* Here are some practical suggestions for reducing the salience.

- *Refrain from giving a letter or number grade for individual assignments,* even if you are compelled to give one at the end of the term. The data suggest that substantive comments should replace, not supplement, grades (Butler 1988). Make sure the effect of doing this is not to create suspense about what students are going to get on their report cards, which would defeat the whole purpose. Some older students may experience, especially at first, a sense of existential vertigo: a steady supply of grades has defined them. Offer to discuss privately with any such student the grade he or she would probably receive if report cards were handed out that day. With luck and skill, the requests for ratings will decrease as students come to be involved in what is being taught.

- *Never grade students while they are still learning something and, even more important, do not reward them for their performance at that point.* Studies suggest that rewards are most destructive when given for skills still being honed (Condry and Chambers 1978). If it is unclear whether students feel ready to demonstrate what they know, there is an easy way to find out: ask them.

- *Never grade on a curve.* The number of good grades should not be artificially limited so that one student's success makes another's less likely. Stipulating that only a few individuals can get top marks regardless of how well everyone does is egregiously unfair on its face. It also undermines collaboration and community. Of course, grades of any kind, even when they are not curved to create artificial scarcity—or deliberately publicized—tend to foster comparison and competition, an emphasis on relative standing. This is not only destructive to students' self-esteem and relationships but also counterproductive with respect to the quality of learning (Kohn 1992). As one book on the subject puts it: "It is not a symbol of rigor to have grades fall into a normal distribution; rather, it is a symbol of failure: failure to teach well, to test well, and to have any influence at all on the intellectual lives of students" (Milton et al. 1986, p. 225).

• *Never give a separate grade for effort.* When students seem to be indifferent to what they are being asked to learn, educators sometimes respond with the very strategy that precipitated the problem in the first place: grading students' efforts to coerce them to try harder. The fatal paradox is that while coercion can sometimes elicit resentful obedience, it can never create desire. A low grade for effort is more likely to be read as "You're a failure even at trying." On the other hand, a high grade for effort combined with a low grade for achievement says, "You're just too dumb to succeed." Most of all, rewarding or punishing children's efforts allows educators to ignore the possibility that the curriculum or learning environment may have something to do with students' lack of enthusiasm.

References

Abrami, P. C., W. J. Dickens, R. P. Perry, and L. Leventhal. (1980). "Do Teacher Standards for Assigning Grades Affect Student Evaluations of Instruction?" *Journal of Educational Psychology* 72: 107–118.

Bruner, J. S. (1961). "The Act of Discovery." *Harvard Educational Review* 31: 21–32.

Butler, R. (1987). "Task-Involving and Ego-Involving Properties of Evaluation." *Journal of Educational Psychology* 79: 474–482.

Butler, R. (1988). "Enhancing and Undermining Intrinsic Motivation." *British Journal of Educational Psychology* 58 (1988): 1–14.

Butler, R., and M. Nissan. (1986). "Effects of No Feedback, Task-Related Comments, and Grades on Intrinsic Motivation and Performance." *Journal of Educational Psychology* 78: 210–216.

Campbell, D. N. (October 1974). "On Being Number One: Competition in Education." *Phi Delta Kappan:* 143–146.

Condry, J., and J. Chambers. (1978). "Intrinsic Motivation and the Process of Learning." In *The Hidden Costs of Rewards: New Perspectives on the Psychology of Human Motivation,* edited by M. R. Lepper and D. Greene. Hillsdale, NJ: Lawrence Erlbaum.

Grolnick, W. S., and R. M. Ryan. (1987). "Autonomy in Children's Learning: An Experimental and Individual Difference Investigation." *Journal of Personality and Social Psychology* 52: 890–898.

Harter, S. (1978). "Pleasure Derived from Challenge and the Effects of Receiving Grades on Children's Difficulty Level Choices." *Child Development* 49: 788–799.

Kage, M. (1991). "The Effects of Evaluation on Intrinsic Motivation." Paper presented at the meeting of the Japan Association of Educational Psychology, Joetsu, Japan.

Kirschenbaum, H., R. W. Napier, and S. B. Simon. (1971). *Wad-Ja-Get?: The Grading Game in American Education.* New York: Hart.

Kohn, A. (1992). *No Contest: The Case Against Competition.* Rev. ed. Boston: Houghton Mifflin.

Kohn, A. (September 1993). "Choices for Children: Why and How to Let Students Decide." *Phi Delta Kappan:* 8–20.

Milton, O., H. R. Pollio, and J. A. Eison. (1986). *Making Sense of College Grades.* San Francisco: Jossey-Bass.

Moeller, A. J., and C. Reschke. (1993). "A Second Look at Grading and Classroom Performance." *Modern Language Journal* 77: 163–169.

Nicholls, J. C., and S. P. Hazzard. (1993). *Education as Adventure: Lessons from the Second Grade.* New York: Teachers College Press.

Oakes, J. (1985). *Keeping Track: How Schools Structure Inequality.* New Haven: Yale University Press.

Schaps, E. (October 1993). Personal communication.

Vasta, R., and R. F. Sarmiento. (1979). "Liberal Grading Improves Evaluations But Not Performance." *Journal of Educational Psychology* 71: 207–211.

Alfie Kohn is an author, speaker, and social critic.

19

The Standards Fraud

William Ayers

The goals of school reform—to provide every child with an experience that will nourish and challenge development, extend capacity, encourage growth, and offer the tools and dispositions necessary for full participation in the human community—are simple to state but excruciatingly difficult to enact. Hannah Arendt once argued, "Education is the point at which we decide whether we love the world enough to assume responsibility for it and by the same token save it from that ruin which, except for renewal, except for the coming of the new and the young, would be inevitable . . . and where we decide whether we love our children enough not to expel them from our world and leave them to their own devices, nor to strike from their hands their chance of undertaking something new, something unforeseen by us, but to prepare them in advance for the task of renewing a common world." That's a lot, much of it dynamic and ever-changing, much of it intricately interdependent. Yet it is what we must seek, if our ideal is education in a democracy.

Today, there is no more insistent or attractive distraction from that ideal than the "standards movement" that Deborah Meier takes on. This conservative push, dressed up as a concern for standards, is at its heart a fraud. It promotes a shrill and insistent message, simple and believable in its own right, while

NOTE: From *Will Standards Save Public Education?* by Deborah Meier, copyright 2000. Reprinted with permission from Beacon Press.

it subtly shifts responsibility away from the powerful, making scapegoats of the victims of power.

High academic standards (as well as social and community standards) are essential to good schools, and such standards, in part, demonstrate a commitment to high expectations for all students. A watered-down curriculum, vague or meaningless goals, expectations of failure—these are a few of the ingredients of academic ruin, and they have characterized urban schools for too long. Standards exist, whether or not we are explicit about them, and standards of some sort are everywhere. I'm all for clarity of standards, for a more explicit sense of what we expect from students. The questions, however, are: What do we value? What knowledge and experience are of most worth? How can we organize access to that worthwhile knowledge and experience? When we look at this school or classroom, what standards are being upheld? Who decides? These kinds of deep and dynamic questions are never entirely summed up, never finished; they are forever open to the demands of the new. Standards setting, then, should not be the property of an expert class, the bureaucrats, or special interests. Rather, standard setting should be part of the everyday vocation of schools and communities, the heart and soul of education, and it should engage the widest public. Standard setting means systematically examining and then reexamining what we care about, what we hope for, what the known demands of us next. Standard setting, often by other names, is already the work of successful schools and many, many effective classrooms.

The "standards movement" is flailing at shadows. All schools in Illinois, for example, follow the same guidelines: These standards apply to successful schools as well as collapsing ones. These written, stated standards have been in place for decades. And yet Illinois in effect has created two parallel systems—one privileged, adequate, successful, and largely white; the other disadvantaged in countless ways, disabled, starving, failing, and African-American. Some schools succeed brilliantly while others stumble and fall. Clearly something more is at work here.

The American school crisis is neither natural nor uniform, but particular and selective; it is a crisis of the poor, of the cities, of Latino and African-American communities. All the structures of privilege and oppression apparent in the larger society are mirrored in our schools. Chicago public school students, for example, are overwhelmingly children of color and children of the poor. More than half of the poorest children in Illinois (and over two thirds of the bilingual children) attend Chicago schools. And yet Chicago schools must struggle to educate children with considerably fewer human and material resources than neighboring districts have. For example,

Chicago has fifty-two licensed physics teachers in the whole city, and a physics lab in only one high school. What standard does that represent?

In the last two years, 50,000 kids attended summer school in Chicago in the name of standards. Tens of thousands were held back a grade. It is impossible to argue that they should have been passed along routinely has been the cynical response for years. But failing that huge group without seriously addressing the ways school has failed them—that is, without changing the structures and cultures of those schools—is to punish those kids for the mistakes and errors of all of us. Further, the vaunted standard turns out to be nothing more than a single standardized test, a relatively simpleminded gate designed so that half of those who take it must not succeed.

The purpose of education in a democracy is to break down barriers, to overcome obstacles, to open doors, minds, and possibilities. Education is empowering and enabling; it points to strength, to critical capacity, to thoughtfulness and expanding capabilities; it leads to an ability to work, to contribute, to participate. It aims at something deeper and richer than simply imbibing and accepting existing codes and conventions, acceding to whatever is before us. The larger goal of education is to assist people in seeing the world through their own eyes, interpreting and analyzing through their own experiences and thinking, feeling themselves capable of representing, manifesting, or even, if they choose, transforming all that is before them. Education, then, is linked to freedom, to the ability to see and also to alter, to understand and also to reinvent, to know and also to change the world as we find it. Can we imagine this at the core of all schools, even poor city schools?

If city schools are to be retooled, streamlined, and made workable, and city schools are to become palaces of learning for all children (and why shouldn't they be?), then we must fight for a comprehensive program of change. Educational resources must be distributed fairly. Justice—the notion that all children deserve a decent life, and that those in the greatest need deserve the greatest support—must be our guide. There is no single solution to the obstacles we face. But a good start is to ask what each of us wants for our own children. What are our standards? I want a teacher in the classroom who is thoughtful and caring, not a mindless clerk or deskilled bureaucrat but a person of substance, depth, and compassion. I want my child to be seen, understood, challenged, and nourished. I want to be able to participate in the community, to have some voice and choice in the questions the school faces.

And so the set of principles outlined by Meier are useful. A small school—as metaphor and practice—is a good starting point. Better yet, one where school people find common cause with students and parents, remaking schools by drawing on strengths and capacities of communities rather than their deficiencies and difficulties. Such a school must focus on shared problems, and find solutions that are collective and manageable. It must talk of solidarity rather than "services," people as self-activated problem solvers and citizens rather than passive "clients" or "consumers." And it must focus on the several deep causes of school failure: the inequitable distribution of educational resources, the capacity of a range of self-interested bureaucracies to work against the common good, and the profound disconnect between schools and the communities they are supposed to serve.

The solutions to the problems we face in a democracy are, as Meier appropriately puts it, more democracy. If the standards guiding schools today are weak or watery—and in many instances they are—the answer is not silence, credulousness, and passivity, but a broader and deeper and more lively engagement with the widest possible public. This is messy and complicated, but true to the ideal of letting the people decide. School is a public space where the American hope for democracy, participation, and transformation collides with the historical reality of privilege and oppression, the hierarchies of race and class. We should all work to raise expectations for our children, to reform and restructure schools, to prepare all students for a hopeful and powerful future, to drive resources to the neediest communities, to demand successful and wondrous learning environments for everyone, to involve teachers, parents, and communities— the public in public schools—in the discussion of what's important for kids to know and experience. At that point the conservative "standards movement," geared to simple, punitive, one-size-fits-all solutions, can be swept aside for something so much better.

William Ayers is a Distinguished Professor of Education and Senior University Scholar at the University of Illinois at Chicago.

20

Learning to Love Assessment

Carol Ann Tomlinson

From judging performance to guiding students to shaping instruction to informing learning, coming to grips with informative assessment is one insightful journey.

When I was a young teacher—young both in years and in understanding of the profession I had entered—I nonetheless went about my work as though I comprehended its various elements. I immediately set out to arrange furniture, put up bulletin boards, make lesson plans, assign homework, give tests, compute grades, and distribute report cards as though I knew what I was doing.

I had not set out to be a teacher, and so I had not really studied education in any meaningful way. I had not student taught. Had I done those things, however, I am not convinced that my evolution as a teacher would have been remarkably different. In either case, my long apprenticeship as a student (Lortie, 1975) would likely have dominated any more recent knowledge I might have acquired about what it means to be a teacher. I simply "played school" in the same way that young children "play house"—by mimicking what we think the adults around us do.

The one element I knew I was unprepared to confront was classroom management. Consequently, that's the element that garnered most of my attention during my early teaching years. The element to which I gave least attention was assessment. In truth, I didn't even know the word *assessment* for a good number of years. I simply knew I was supposed to give tests and grades. I didn't much like tests in those years. It was difficult for me to move beyond their judgmental aspect. They made kids nervous. They made me nervous. With no understanding of the role of assessment in a dynamic and success-oriented classroom, I initially ignored assessment when I could and did it when I had to.

Now, more than three decades into the teaching career I never intended to have, it's difficult for me to remember exactly when I had the legion of insights that have contributed to my growth as an educator. I do know, however, that those insights are the milestones that mark my evolution from seeing teaching as a job to seeing teaching as a science-informed art that has become a passion.

Following are 10 understandings about classroom assessment that sometimes gradually and sometimes suddenly illuminated my work. I am not finished with the insights yet because I am not finished with my work as a teacher or learner. I present the understandings in something like the order they unfolded in my thinking.

The formulation of one insight generally prepared the way for the next. Now, of course, they are seamless, interconnected, and interdependent. But they did not come to me that way. Over time and taken together, the understandings make me an advocate of informative assessment—a concept that initially played no conscious role in my work as a teacher.

Understanding 1: Informative Assessment Isn't Just About Tests

Initially I thought about assessment as test giving. Over time, I became aware of students who did poorly on tests but who showed other evidence of learning. They solved problems well, contributed to discussions, generated rich ideas, drew sketches to illustrate, and role-played. When they wanted to communicate, they always found a way. I began to realize that when I gave students multiple ways to express learning or gave them a say in how they could show what they knew, more students were engaged. More to the point, more students were learning.

Although I still had a shallow sense of the possibilities of assessment, I did at least begin to try in multiple ways to let kids show what they knew. I used more authentic products as well as tests to gain a sense of student understanding. I began to realize that when one form of assessment was ineffective for a student, it did not necessarily indicate a lack of student success but could, in fact, represent a poor fit between the student and the method through which I was trying to make the student communicate. I studied students to see what forms of assessment worked for them and to be sure I never settled for a single assessment as an adequate representation of what a student knew.

Understanding 2: Informative Assessment Really Isn't About the Grade Book

At about the same time that Understanding 1 emerged in my thinking, I began to sense that filling a grade book was both less interesting and less useful than trying to figure out what individual students knew, understood, or could do. My thinking was shifting from assessment as judging students to assessment as guiding students. I was beginning to think about student accomplishment more than about student ranking (Wiggins, 1993).

Giving students feedback seemed to be more productive than giving them grades. If I carefully and consistently gave them feedback about their work, I felt more like a teacher than a warden. I felt more respectful of the students and their possibilities (Wiggins, 1993). I began to understand the difference between teaching for success and "gotcha" teaching and to sense the crucial role of informative assessment in the former.

Understanding 3: Informative Assessment Isn't Always Formal

I also became conscious of the fact that some of the most valuable insights I gleaned about students came from moments or events that I'd never associated with assessment. When I read in a student's journal that his parents were divorcing, I understood why he was disengaged in class. I got a clear picture of one student's misunderstanding when I walked around as students worked and saw a diagram she made to represent how she understood the concept we were discussing. I could figure out how to help a student be more successful in small groups when I took the time to study systematically, but from a distance, what he did to make groups grow impatient with him.

Assessment, then, was more than "tests plus other formats." Informative assessment could occur any time I went in search of information about a student. In fact, it could occur when I was not actively searching but was merely conscious of what was happening around me.

I began to talk in more purposeful ways with students as they entered and left the classroom. I began to carry around a clipboard on which I took notes about students. I developed a filing system that enabled me to easily store and retrieve information about students as individuals and learners. I was more focused in moving around the room to spot-check student work in progress for particular proficiencies. I began to sense that virtually all student products and interactions can serve as informative assessment because I, as a teacher, have the power to use them that way.

Understanding 4: Informative Assessment Isn't Separate From the Curriculum

Early in my teaching, I made lesson plans. Later on, I made unit plans. In neither time frame did I see assessment as a part of the curriculum design process. As is the case with many teachers, I planned what I would teach, taught it, and then created assessments. The assessments were largely derived from what had transpired during a segment of lessons and ultimately what had transpired during a unit of study. It was a while before I understood what Wiggins and McTighe (1998) call *backward design*.

That evolution came in three stages for me. First, I began to understand the imperative of laying out precisely what mattered most for students to know and be able to do—but also what they should understand—as a result of our work together. Then I began to discover that many of my lessons had been only loosely coupled to learning goals. I'd sometimes (often?) been teaching in response to what my students liked rather than in response to crucial learning goals. I understood the need to make certain that my teaching was a consistent match for what students needed to know, understand, and be able to do at the end of a unit. Finally, I began to realize that if I wanted to teach for success, my assessments had to be absolutely aligned with the knowledge, understanding, and skill I'd designated as essential learning outcomes. There was a glimmer of recognition in my work that assessment was a part of—not apart from—curriculum design.

Understanding 5: Informative Assessment Isn't About "After"

I came to understand that assessments that came at the end of a unit—although important manifestations of student knowledge, understanding, and skill—were less useful to me as a teacher than were assessments that occurred during a unit of study. By the time I gave and graded a final assessment, we were already moving on to a new topic or unit. There was only a limited amount I could do at that stage with information that revealed to me that some students fell short of mastering essential outcomes—or that others had likely been bored senseless by instruction that focused on outcomes they had mastered long before the unit had begun. When I studied student work in the course of a unit, however, I could do many things to support or extend student learning. I began to be a devotee of *formative assessment*, although I did not know that term for many years.

It took time before I understood the crucial role of preassessment or diagnostic assessment in teaching. Likely the insight was the product of the embarrassment of realizing that a student had no idea what I was talking about because he or she lacked vocabulary I assumed every 7th grader knew or of having a student answer a question in class early in a unit that made it clear he already knew more about the topic at hand than I was planning to teach. At that point, I began to check early in the year to see whether students could read the textbook, how well they could produce expository writing, what their spelling level was, and so on. I began systematically to use preassessments before a unit started to see where students stood in regard to prerequisite and upcoming knowledge, understanding, and skills.

Understanding 6: Informative Assessment Isn't an End in Itself

I slowly came to realize that the most useful assessment practices would shape how I taught. I began to explore and appreciate two potent principles of informative assessment. First, the greatest power of assessment information lies in its capacity to help me see how to be a better teacher. If I know what students are and are not grasping at a given moment in a sequence of study, I know how to plan our time better. I know when to reteach, when to move ahead, and when to explain or demonstrate something in another way. Informative assessment is not an end in itself, but the beginning of better instruction.

Understanding 7: Informative Assessment Isn't Separate From Instruction

A second and related understanding hovered around my sense that assessment should teach me how to be a better teacher. Whether I liked it or not, informative assessment always demonstrated to me that my students' knowledge, understanding, and skill were emerging along different time continuums and at different depths. It became excruciatingly clear that my brilliant teaching was not equally brilliant for everyone in my classes.

In other words, informative assessment helped me solidify a need for differentiation. As Lorna Earl (2003) notes, if teachers know a precise learning destination and consistently check to see where students are relative to that destination, differentiation isn't just an option; it's the logical next step in teaching. Informative assessment made it clear—at first, painfully so—that if I meant for every student to succeed, I was going to have to teach with both singular and group needs in mind.

Understanding 8: Informative Assessment Isn't Just About Student Readiness

Initially, my emergent sense of the power of assessment to improve my teaching focused on student readiness. At the time, I was teaching in a school with a bimodal population—lots of students were three or more years behind grade level or three or more years above grade level, with almost no students in between. Addressing that expansive gap in student readiness was a daily challenge. I was coming to realize the role of informative assessment in ensuring that students worked as often as possible at appropriate levels of challenge (Earl, 2003).

Only later was I aware of the potential role of assessment in determining what students cared about and how they learned. When I could attach what I was teaching to what students cared about, they learned more readily and more durably. When I could give them options about how to learn and express what they knew, learning improved. I realized I could pursue insights about student interests and preferred modes of learning, just as I had about their readiness needs.

I began to use surveys to determine student interests, hunt for clues about their individual and shared passions, and take notes on who learned better alone and who learned better in small groups. I began to ask students to write to me about which instructional approaches were working for them and which were not. I was coming to understand that learning is multidimensional and that assessment could help me understand learners as multidimensional as well.

Understanding 9: Informative Assessment Isn't Just About Finding Weaknesses

As my sense of the elasticity of assessment developed, so did my sense of the wisdom of using assessment to accentuate student positives rather than negatives. With readiness-based assessments, I had most often been on the hunt for what students didn't know, couldn't do, or didn't understand. Using assessment to focus on student interests and learning preferences illustrated for me the power of emphasizing what works for students.

When I saw "positive space" in students and reflected that to them, the results were stunningly different from when I reported on their "negative space." It gave students something to build on—a sense of possibility. I began to spend at least as much time gathering assessment information on what students *could* do as on what they couldn't. That, in turn, helped me develop a conviction that each student in my classes brought strengths to our work and that it was my job to bring those strengths to the surface so that all of us could benefit.

Understanding 10: Informative Assessment Isn't Just for the Teacher

Up to this point, much of my thinking was about the teacher—about me, my class, my work, my growth. The first nine understandings about assessment were, in fact, crucial to my development. But it was the 10th understanding that revolutionized what happened in the classrooms I shared with my students. I finally began to grasp that teaching requires a plural pronoun. The best teaching is never so much about me as about us. I began to see my students as full partners in their success.

My sense of the role of assessment necessarily shifted. I was a better teacher—but more to the point, my students were better learners—when assessment helped all of us push learning forward (Earl, 2003). When students clearly understood our learning objectives, knew precisely what success would look like, understood how each assignment contributed to their success, could articulate the role of assessment in ensuring their success, and understood that their work correlated with their needs, they developed a sense of self-efficacy that was powerful in their lives as learners. Over time, as I developed, my students got better at self-monitoring, self-managing, and self-modifying (Costa & Kallick, 2004). They developed an internal locus of control that caused them to work hard rather than to rely on luck or the teacher's good will (Stiggins, 2000).

Assessing Wisely

Lorna Earl (2003) distinguishes between assessment of learning, assessment for learning, and assessment as learning. In many ways, my growth as a teacher slowly and imperfectly followed that progression. I began by seeing assessment as judging performance, then as informing teaching, and finally as informing learning. In reality, all those perspectives play a role in effective teaching. The key is where we place the emphasis.

Certainly a teacher and his or her students need to know who reaches (and exceeds) important learning targets—thus summative assessment, or assessment of learning, has a place in teaching. Robust learning generally requires robust teaching, and both diagnostic and formative assessments, or assessments for learning, are catalysts for better teaching. In the end, however, when assessment is seen as learning—for students as well as for teachers—it becomes most informative and generative for students and teachers alike.

It was difficult to move beyond the judgmental aspect of tests. They made kids nervous. They made me nervous.

I began to grasp that teaching requires a plural pronoun. The best teaching is never so much about "me" as about "us."

If I meant for every student to succeed, I was going to have to teach with both singular and group needs in mind.

Informative assessment is not an end in itself, but the beginning of better instruction.

References

Costa, A., & Kallick, B. (2004). *Assessment strategies for self-directed learning.* Thousand Oaks, CA: Corwin.

Earl, L. (2003). *Assessment as learning: Using classroom assessment to maximize student learning.* Thousand Oaks, CA: Corwin.

Lortie, D. (1975). *Schoolteacher: A sociological study.* Chicago: University of Chicago Press.

Stiggins, R. (2000). *Student-involved classroom assessment* (3rd ed.). Upper Saddle River, NJ: Prentice-Hall.

Wiggins, G. (1993). *Assessing student performance: Exploring the purpose and limits of testing.* San Francisco: Jossey-Bass.

Wiggins, G., & McTighe, J. (1998). *Understanding by design.* Alexandria, VA: Association for Supervision and Curriculum Development.

Carol Ann Tomlinson is Professor of Educational Leadership, Foundation, and Policy at the University of Virginia in Charlottesville; cat3y@virginia.edu.

PART VI

How Does One
Develop a Critical Voice?

It's August 26th and, together with my colleagues, I'm gearing up for yet another—in a seemingly endless series—professional development workshop designed to tell me how to "do it right." Every year, usually right before school begins, the district brings in a math consultant, or a behavior specialist, or a literacy coach, or a curriculum expert, or an assessment guru or . . . for goodness sake, who knew there were so many authorities on teaching that don't have their own classrooms, may never have worked with kids?

Dutifully, I attend the scheduled sessions anyway, as I always do. There are no surprises. The other teachers have gotten too used to the routine. The district has brought in a consultant for the day to train us to use newly established reading standards. We take our seats and thumb through our resource packages as the consultant makes a PowerPoint presentation on the importance of the standards, exactly how they will be implemented, and how the state assessment will monitor student reading achievement. We listen attentively. There are a few questions and the consultant does her best to answer concerns. Most concerns are deflected with the statement, "This is the direction that everybody is heading." After lunch, small grade-level focus groups meet. The discussions are collegial, cordial; as teachers we are all compliant. Time well spent. Very professional. Everyone agrees. I guess I better start modifying my plans to align with the new district approach.

How should a teacher respond? If a teacher disagrees, then what words should he or she use? What shall be the tone?

21

Teachers as Transformative Intellectuals

Henry Giroux

The call for educational reform has gained the status of a recurring national event, much like the annual Boston Marathon. There have been more than 30 national reports since the beginning of the 20th century, and more than 300 task forces have been developed by the various states to discover how public schools can improve educational quality in the United States.[1]But unlike many past educational reform movements, the present call for educational change presents both a threat and challenge to public school teachers that appears unprecedented in our nation's history. The threat comes in the form of a series of educational reforms that display little confidence in the ability of public school teachers to provide intellectual and moral leadership for our nation's youth. For instance, many of the recommendations that have emerged in the current debate either ignore the role teachers play in preparing learners to be active and critical citizens, or they suggest reforms that ignore the intelligence, judgment and experience that teachers might offer in such a debate. Where teachers do enter the debate, they are the object of educational reforms that reduce them to the status of high-level technicians carrying out dictates and objectives decided by "experts" far removed from the everyday realities of classroom life.[2] The message appears to be that teachers do not count when it comes to critically examining the nature and process of educational reform.

The political and ideological climate does not look favorable for teachers at the moment. But it does offer them the challenge to join in a public debate with their critics as well as the opportunity to engage in a much-needed self-critique regarding the nature and purpose of teacher preparation, inservice teacher programs and the dominant forms of classroom teaching. Similarly, the debate provides teachers with the opportunity to organize collectively so as to struggle to improve the conditions under which they work and to demonstrate to the public the central role that teachers must play in any viable attempt to reform the public schools.

In order for teachers and others to engage in such a debate, it is necessary that a theoretical perspective be developed that redefines the nature of the educational crisis while simultaneously providing the basis for an alternative view of teacher training and work. In short, recognizing that the current crisis in education largely has to do with the developing trend towards the disempowerment of teachers at all levels of education is a necessary theoretical precondition in order for teachers to organize effectively and establish a collective voice in the current debate. Moreover, such a recognition will have to come to grips not only with a growing loss of power among teachers around the basic conditions of their work, but also with a changing public perception of their role as reflective practitioners.

I want to make a small theoretical contribution to this debate and the challenge it calls forth by examining two major problems that need to be addressed in the interest of improving the quality of teacher work, which includes all the clerical tasks and extra assignments as well as classroom instruction. First, I think it is imperative to examine the ideological and material forces that have contributed to what I want to call the proletarianization of teacher work; that is, the tendency to reduce teachers to the status of specialized technicians within the school bureaucracy, whose function then becomes one of managing and implementing curricula programs rather than developing or critically appropriating curricula to fit specific pedagogical concerns. Second, there is a need to defend schools as institutions essential to maintaining and developing a critical democracy and also to defending teachers as transformative intellectuals who combine scholarly reflection and practice in the service of educating students to be thoughtful, active citizens. In the remainder of this essay, I will develop these points and conclude by examining their implications for providing an alternative view of teacher work.

Toward a Devaluing and Deskilling of Teacher Work

One of the major threats facing prospective and existing teachers with the public schools is the increasing development of instrumental ideologies that emphasize a technocratic approach to both teacher preparation and classroom pedagogy. At the core of the current emphasis on instrumental and pragmatic factors in school life are a number of important pedagogical assumptions. These include: a call for the separation of conception from execution; the standardization of school knowledge in the interest of managing and controlling it; and the devaluation of critical, intellectual work on the part of teachers and students for the primacy of practical considerations.[3]

This type of instrumental rationality finds one of its strongest expressions historically in the training of prospective teachers. That teacher training programs in the United States have long been dominated by a behavioristic orientation and emphasis on mastering subject areas and methods of teaching is well documented.[4] The implications of this approach, made clear by Zeichner, are worth repeating:

> Underlying this orientation to teacher education is a metaphor of "production," a view of teaching as an "applied science" and a view of the teacher as primarily an "executor" of the laws and principles of effective teaching. Prospective teachers may or may not proceed through the curriculum at their own pace and may participate in varied or standardized learning activities, but that which they are to master is limited in scope (e.g., to a body of professional content knowledge and teaching skills) and is fully determined in advance by others often on the basis of research on teacher effectiveness. The prospective teacher is viewed primarily as a passive recipient of this professional knowledge and plays little part in determining the substance and direction of his or her preparation program.[5]

The problems with this approach are evident in John Dewey's argument that teacher training programs that emphasize only technical expertise do a disservice both to the nature of teaching and to their students.[6] Instead of learning to reflect upon the principles that structure classroom life and practice, prospective teachers are taught methodologies that appear to deny the very need for critical thinking. The point is that teacher education programs often lose sight of the need to educate students to examine the underlying nature of school problems. Further, these programs need to substitute for the language of management and efficiency a critical analysis of the less obvious conditions that structure the ideological and material practices of schooling.

Instead of learning to raise questions about the principles underlying different classroom methods, research techniques and theories of education, students are often preoccupied with learning the "how to," with "what works," or with mastering the best way to teach a *given* body of knowledge. For example, the mandatory field-practice seminars often consist of students sharing with each other the techniques they have used in managing and controlling classroom discipline, organizing a day's activities and learning how to work within specific time tables. Examining one such program, Jesse Goodman raises some important questions about the incapacitating silences it embodies. He writes:

> There was no questioning of feelings, assumptions, or definitions in this discussion. For example, the "need" for external rewards and punishments to "make kids learn" was taken for granted; the educational and ethical implications were not addressed. There was no display of concern for stimulating or nurturing a child's intrinsic desire to learn. Definitions of *good kids* as "quiet kids," *workbook work* as "reading," *on task time* as "learning," and *getting through the material on time* as "the goal of teaching"—all went unchallenged. Feelings of pressure and possible guilt about not keeping to time schedules also went unexplored. The real concern in this discussion was that everyone "shared."[7]

Technocratic and instrumental rationalities are also at work within the teaching field itself, and they play an increasing role in reducing teacher autonomy with respect to the development and planning of curricula and the judging and implementation of instruction. This is most evident in the proliferation of what has been called "teacher-proof" curriculum packages.[8] The underlying rationale in many of these packages reserves for teachers the role of simply carrying out predetermined content and instructional procedures. The method and aim of such packages is to legitimate what I call management pedagogies. That is, knowledge is broken down into discrete parts, standardized for easier management and consumption, and measured through predefined forms of assessment. Curricula approaches of this sort are management pedagogies because the central questions regarding learning are reduced to the problem of management, i.e., "how to allocate resources (teachers, students and materials) to produce the maximum number of certified . . . students within a designated time."[9] The underlying theoretical assumption that guides this type of pedagogy is that the behavior of teachers needs to be controlled and made consistent and predictable across different schools and student populations.

What is clear in this approach is that it organizes school life around curricular, instructional and evaluation experts who do the thinking while teachers are reduced to doing the implementing. The effect is not only to deskill teachers, to remove them from the processes of deliberation and reflection, but also to routinize the nature of learning and classroom pedagogy. Needless to say, the principles underlying management pedagogies are at odds with the premise that teachers should be actively involved in producing curricula materials suited to the cultural and social contexts in which they teach. More specifically, the narrowing of curricula choices to a back-to-basics format, and the introduction of lock-step, time-on-task pedagogies operate from the theoretically erroneous assumption that all students can learn from the same materials, classroom instructional techniques and modes of evaluation. The notion that students come from different histories and embody different experiences, linguistic practices, cultures and talents is strategically ignored within the logic and accountability of management pedagogy theory.

Teachers as Transformative Intellectuals

In what follows, I want to argue that one way to rethink and restructure the nature of teacher work is to view teachers as transformative intellectuals. The category of intellectual is helpful in a number of ways. First, it provides a theoretical basis for examining teacher work as a form of intellectual labor, as opposed to defining it in purely instrumental or technical terms. Second, it clarifies the kinds of ideological and practical conditions necessary for teachers to function as intellectuals. Third, it helps to make clear the role teachers play in producing and legitimating various political, economic and social interests through the pedagogies they endorse and utilize.

By viewing teachers as intellectuals, we can illuminate the important idea that all human activity involves some form of thinking. In other words, no activity, regardless of how routinized it might become, can be abstracted from the functioning of the mind in some capacity. This is a crucial issue because by arguing that the use of the mind is a general part of all human activity we dignify the human capacity for integrating thinking and practice, and in doing so highlight the core of what it means to view teachers as reflective practitioners. Within this discourse, teachers can be seen not merely as "performers professionally equipped to realize effectively any goals that may be set for them. Rather [they should] be viewed as free men and women with a special dedication to the values of the intellect and the enhancement of the critical powers of the young."[10]

Viewing teachers as intellectuals also provides a strong theoretical critique of technocratic and instrumental ideologies underlying an educational theory that separates the conceptualization, planning and design of curricula from the processes of implementation and execution. It is important to stress that teachers must take active responsibility for raising various questions about what they teach, how they are to teach, and what the larger goals are for which they are striving. This means that they must take a responsible role in shaping the purposes and conditions of schooling. Such a task is impossible within a division of labor in which teachers have little influence over the ideological and economic conditions of their work. This point has a normative and political dimension that seems especially relevant for teachers. If we believe that the role of teaching cannot he reduced to merely training in the practical skills, but involves, instead, the education of a class of intellectuals vital to the development of a free society, then the category of intellectual becomes a way of linking the purpose of teacher education, public schooling and inservice training to the very principles necessary for developing a democratic order and society.

I have argued that by viewing teachers as intellectuals those persons concerned with education can begin to rethink and reform the traditions and conditions that have prevented schools and teachers from assuming their full potential as active, reflective scholars and practitioners. It is imperative that I qualify this point and extend it further. I believe that it is important not only to view teachers as intellectuals, but also to contextualize in political and normative terms the concrete social functions that teachers perform. In this way, we can be more specific about the different relations that teachers have both to their work and to the dominant society.

A fundamental starting point for interrogating the social function of teachers as intellectuals is to view schools as economic, cultural and social sites that are inextricably tied to the issues of power and control. This means that schools do more than pass on in an objective fashion a common set of values and knowledge. On the contrary, schools are places that represent forms of knowledge, language practices, social relations and values that are representative of a particular selection and exclusion from the wider culture. As such, schools serve to introduce and legitimate *particular* forms of social life. Rather than being objective institutions removed from the dynamics of politics and power, schools actually are contested spheres that embody and express a struggle over what forms of authority, types of knowledge, forms of moral regulation and versions of the past and future should be legitimated and transmitted to students. This struggle is most visible in the demands, for example, of right-wing religious groups currently trying to institute school prayer, remove certain books from the school library, and include certain forms of religious teachings in the science curricula. Of course, different demands are made by feminists, ecologists, minorities and other interest groups who believe that the schools should teach women's studies, courses on the environment, or black history. In short, schools are not neutral sites, and teachers cannot assume the posture of being neutral either.

In the broadest sense, teachers as intellectuals have to be seen in terms of the ideological and political interests that structure the nature of the discourse, classroom social relations and values that they legitimate in their teaching. With this perspective in mind, I want to conclude that teachers should become transformative intellectuals if they are to subscribe to a view of pedagogy that believes in educating students to be active, critical citizens.

Central to the category of transformative intellectual is the necessity of making the pedagogical more political and the political more pedagogical. Making the pedagogical more political means inserting schooling directly into the political sphere by arguing that schooling represents both a struggle to define meaning and a struggle over power relations. Within this perspective, critical reflection and action become part of a fundamental social project to help students develop a deep and abiding faith in the struggle to overcome economic, political and social injustices, and to further humanize themselves as part of this struggle. In this case, knowledge and power are inextricably linked to the presupposition that to choose life, to recognize the necessity of improving its democratic and qualitative character for all people, is to understand the preconditions necessary to struggle for it.

Making the political more pedagogical means utilizing forms of pedagogy that embody political interests that are emancipatory in nature; that is, using forms of pedagogy that treat students as critical agents; make knowledge problematic; utilize critical and affirming dialogue; and make the case for struggling for a qualitatively better world for all people. In part, this suggests that transformative intellectuals take seriously the need to give students an active voice in their learning experiences. It also means developing a critical vernacular that is attentive to problems experienced at the level of everyday life, particularly as they are related to pedagogical experiences connected to classroom practice. As such, the pedagogical starting point for such intellectuals is not the isolated student but individuals and groups in their various cultural, class, racial, historical and gender settings, along with the particularity of their diverse problems, hopes and dreams.

Transformative intellectuals need to develop a discourse that unites the language of critique with the language of possibility, so that social educators recognize that they can make changes. In doing so, they must speak out against economic, political and social injustices both within and outside of schools. At the same time, they must work to create the conditions that give students the opportunity to become citizens who have the knowledge and courage to struggle in order to make despair unconvincing and hope practical. As difficult as this tack may seem to social educators, it is a struggle worth waging. To do otherwise is to deny social educators the opportunity to assume the role of transformative intellectuals.

Notes

1. K. Patricia Cross, "The Rising Tide of School Reform Reports," *Phi Delta Kappan*, 66:3 (November 1984), p. 167.

2. For a more detailed critique of the reforms, see my book with Stanley Aronowitz, *Education Under Siege* (South Hadley, MA: Bergin and Garvey Publishers, 1985); also see the incisive comments on the impositional nature of the various reports in Charles A. Tesconi, Jr., "Additive Reforms and the Retreat from Purpose," *Educational Studies* 15:1 (Spring 1984), pp. 1–11: Terrence E. Deal, "Searching for the Wizard: The Quest for Excellence in Education," *Issues in Education* 2:1 (Summer 1984), pp. 56–67; Svi Shapiro, "Choosing Our Educational Legacy: Disempowerment or Emancipation?" *Issues in Education* 2:1 (Summer 1984), pp. 11–22.

3. For an exceptional commentary on the need to educate teachers to be intellectuals, see John Dewey, "The Relation of Theory to Practice," in John Dewey, *The Middle Words, 1899–1924*, edited by Jo Ann Boydston (Carbondale: Southern Illinois University Press, 1977) [originally published in 1904]. See also, Israel Scheffler, "University Scholarship and the Education of Teachers," *Teachers College Record*, 70:1 (1968), pp. 1–12; Henry A. Giroux, *Ideology, Culture, and the Process of Schooling* (Philadelphia: Temple University Press, 1981).

4. See, for instance, Herbert Kliebard, "The Question of Teacher Education," in D. McCarty (ed.), *New Perspectives on Teacher Education* (San Francisco: Jossey-Bass, 1973).

5. Kenneth M. Zeichner, "Alternative Paradigms on Teacher Education," *Journal of Teacher Education* 34:3 (May–June 1983), p. 4.

6. Dewey, op. cit.

7. Jesse Goodman, "Reflection and Teacher Education: A Case Study and Theoretical Analysis," *Interchange* 15:3 (1984), p. 15.

8. Michael Apple, *Education and Power* (Boston: Routledge & Kegan Paul, Ltd., 1982).

9. Patrick Shannon, "Mastery Learning in Reading and the Control of Teachers and Students," *Language Arts* 61:5 (September 1984), p. 488.

10. Israel Scheffler, op. cit., p. 11.

Henry Giroux is the Global Television Network Chair in English and Cultural Studies at McMaster University.

22

Resistance and Courage

A Conversation With Deborah Meier

Alan Canestrari: What does teaching require these days?

Deborah Meier: First of all, any kind of teaching requires toughness. You have to have firm convictions about a whole lot of stuff that you are not, in fact, always so sure about. But, if a kid asks can he sharpen his pencil or go to the bathroom, you have to exercise a judgment pretty fast and firmly even if more than one good answer might make sense, or even be the right one. You have to be tough on yourself, so that at the end the day you're left with a bunch of unanswered questions of the "Could I have . . . ?" or "Maybe next time . . ." or even, "Did I just blow a great moment for . . . ?" And, you need to carve out of an exceedingly unleisurely profession, time to think . . . enough time to think about these sticky matters over time, realizing that all the odd living and reading you do can help you in finding the answers. And then, you need to be tough enough to stick to it.

Bruce Marlowe: Suppose your way of doing your work, exercising judgment—about those little things you mention like going to the bathroom or the big things about what's worth teaching—is very different than your colleagues' ways? Or very different from what the principal, school district, or state is invested in?

NOTE: This reading consists of a conversation between the editors and Deborah Meier. Reprinted with permission.

Meier: Now that's tougher still. And, these days, that's what many of us are struggling with—the plethora of external regulation about what our work is and how we do it. But of course in fact with rare exceptions, those of us involved all our lives in public education have rarely been in situations where we have had to deal with anything less.

Today, though, we are witnessing something new. And there are some tough choices facing us in the teaching field as a result. After a decade or more of considerable "laissez-faire" between the mid-70s and the early 90s (it varied by locale) we're witnessing a retightening of the screws—with more of the screws coming from higher and more remote places, in a setting in which technology makes it harder to hide. The culture of privacy has been ripped apart—for reasons both good and bad. Thus, the kind of quiet, behind-closed-doors resistance that flourished during my earliest teaching years is more problematic. Today, the standardized curriculums and lesson plans which were always part of the traditional public schools—even when ignored—are being republished and reissued, in even greater detail. The old regime has been reinstalled, plus.

Canestrari: So, what lessons would you offer new teachers?

Meier: Number one is: How to survive. It probably helps to remember that this is not new. The technology to enforce it [teacher compliance] is more brutal, but the intent is old and familiar. And, it has, unfortunately, been accepted by too many men and women of good will as a necessity if all children are to meet "high standards."

When I first arrived in New York City there was a loosely enforced grade-by-grade curriculum, and fairly decent guides for carrying it out step-by-step. We survived in part by figuring out where we had space to deviate and where we didn't. In Head Start I was told teaching the names of numbers, letters, and colors was what we'd be tested on in June; but I figured if we did modestly well at that I could spend 90 percent of my time exploring more important stuff like the properties of real life. I realized I never met a kid of 8 who didn't know his colors—unless he was color blind and then drilling colors at age 4 was worse than useless. And the same would be true of the names of letters unless we persisted in teaching them to read formally too early and insisted that we use the names of the letters as a key way into such early instruction. Survival, in other words, depends on making some decisions about what's important, and living by them—most of the time.

Canestrari: Can teachers be effective in changing their conditions?

Meier: Of course, once they learn to survive. The second strategy is to organize—join with others. It starts with being a good colleague in one's own schools. Not easy work. Another way is through teacher and staff organizations. The power of solidarity among working people is still, or once again, obviously vital. As fewer unions exist nationwide, natural allies among other working people have lessened. But teacher unions also provide us with links to other organized working people.

But it's important to remember that it's not just joining with the teachers. For example, you may also be a parent. Don't hesitate to speak out in that role also, without feeling that somehow it's unfair or unwise. Not at all. We listen to what doctors say about the kind of medicine they want for their own kids. So you are doubly powerful in this dual role. But even if you decide to be just a parent in your child's school, be a loud one on behalf of the things you believe are good for all kids and teachers.

And then work, within both roles—as teacher and parent—for the strongest and loudest alliance between these two self-interested and power-ful groups. If parents and teachers were truly able to use their strength in even a semi-united way, they'd overcome. But, we've allowed a rift to exist between us that serves others, but neither parents nor teacher. This is a time in history when we have to put the issues that unite us to the fore, and agree to disagree on others.

Then there's using your voice. I don't just mean your teacherly voice, but your broader professional voice. Find every way you can to hone your skills as a writer and speaker—to little audiences and big ones, letters to the editors included. And, not just on contentious reform issues. Speak out and write out as an expert on reading, or science, or classroom management, or children's aspirations. Insist on the idea that you are a theorist and an expert, not only a practitioner; don't make it easy to be seen as hardwork-ing, dedicated, loving but a wee bit weak in the head and too prone to sentimentality, or likely to only see the faces in front of you, to miss the important systemic problems!

Then comes the last course of action. For those who can't find any of the above individual or group strategies feasible, and begin to find it hard to face themselves each morning in the mirror, it may be best to change schools, move to another less draconian locale, or even, dare I say it, quit teaching. There is other important work to be done in the world, including work on behalf of children. And, if and when you leave, don't miss the opportu-nity; don't go quietly and don't go blaming your former colleagues, families, or kids.

Marlowe: Any final advice for new teachers?

Meier: In each and every way that you work in the field, bring the best of yourself as a parent, citizen, and passionate learner into your work, and put "getting along" in perspective. Getting along helps smooth the way, no mean goal, and it makes for more allies, and it makes your voice more effective. Assuming that your colleagues (like the families whose kids you teach) want similar things, acting out of their best intentions is the place to begin. But, watch out when getting along starts becoming a way of life, and other people's good intentions begin to undermine your own. The "courage" you need is the courage to not excuse yourself too often for failing to do what needs doing, for pretending that bad practice—including your own—is good practice, or for seeing yourself and your colleagues as the enemy—or the victims. Victims don't make good teachers—because above all we want our kids to see themselves as competent actors who have learned how to be competent citizens from teachers who saw themselves as that—citizens of their schools and communities.

Deborah Meier is the principal of the Mission Hill Elementary School in Boston, Massachusetts.

23

Speaking in a Critical Voice

Marilyn Page

Three Vignettes

Stan

Last month, a newly crowned Doctor of Education interviewed for a position in social studies teacher education at a large university in the Northeast. He had taught in the elementary grades for twenty-five years and was now hoping to move to a university professorship. He presented his research involving post-Standards changes to geography education and then fielded questions from the audience. When asked what it meant to him to be a teacher in a democracy, he became flustered and skirted the question with responses that didn't relate at all. Here was a social studies teacher who could not define the role of a teacher in a democracy. When asked how teachers in his school were responding to the new learning Standards and to state-mandated testing, he explained that his state was preparing lessons, and directions for delivering all lessons, for all teachers in the state and that the teachers would do exactly what they were told to because they didn't have a union and therefore wouldn't do anything they weren't supposed to do for fear of losing their jobs.

NOTE: Reprinted with kind permission from the author.

Mary

As a second semester doctoral student, Mary enrolled in the Research in Social Studies Education class at a large mid-Atlantic university. Mary had taught for five years at the elementary level and had obtained a Master's Degree in Education from a Midwestern university known for its first-class reputation in teacher education. In response to an assignment to write a literature review and to analyze the materials critically, Mary confessed: "I don't know what critical thinking is"; "I have never done it"; "I have never learned about it."

John and Jenni

John had been teaching eighth grade for fifteen years. Jenni was a brilliant preservice teacher completing her first student teacher practicum. She had the ability to develop dynamic learning plans, conduct in-depth and purposeful learning experiences, and assess student understanding and content knowledge in multiple ways. During the first four weeks of her five week practicum, she led eighth grade students in an exploratory adventure through the Civil War. The students became the investigators after several stalling tactics usually couched in the terms: "We can't do that"; "It's too hard"; "We've never done that before." The students not only triumphed in the investigatory process but realized exemplary content proficiency, deep comprehension of cause and effect, ability to analyze using different perspectives, ability to relate current issues in the country, and ability to draw and support conclusions. But John, the classroom teacher, could think only of the upcoming tests. He sent Jenni to the library for a day so he could "teach" the students the necessary information to pass the test—information he was sure they had missed because they had not been involved in the traditional rote/recovery mode of instruction and evaluation.

What Is Critical Voice?

One of the similarities among Stan, Mary, and John is the lack of understanding, development, and/or use of critical voice. In Stan's case, he and his fellow teachers were afraid to speak up to state powers concerning the state mandates and prescribed lesson plans. Mary didn't even know what critical voice/thinking meant, let alone how to use it. John was willing to let Jenni try some active learning approaches but then didn't have the belief in the methods or students' ability to learn from anything other than his traditional approach. None of the three teachers spoke up to administrators, state officials, or school boards. They did what they were told, what they had been taught, or what they themselves had experienced in their schooling.

To develop a critical voice, a teacher has to take the time to analyze directives, mandates, and messages from whatever the source and then use that analysis to speak up about issues willingly and strongly to the power sources. To be able to think critically or analytically does not mean to criticize. It means to look at messages and materials through different lenses and from many perspectives; it means to be able to recognize propaganda regardless of its origin; it means to be able to "detect crap" (Postman & Weingartner, 1969); it means to pull apart materials, sort them, question them, reorganize them mentally, and then synthesize the pieces into a coherent understanding and whole.

Teachers and Their Critical Voices

A teacher has to ask herself if she has a critical voice. If she believes she already has a critical voice, then she needs to think about how she will use it. When? Why? And what will happen if she does? What will happen if she doesn't? What is her responsibility in using this voice? If a teacher does not have a critical voice, or like Mary, has not experienced critical thinking or ever heard of it, then that teacher has work to do.

Assumptions About Teaching and Learning

Every teacher has to have a solid grasp of his assumptions about how people learn (Marlowe & Page, 1998) and how that translates into the kind of environment the teacher will provide. Without a grounded philosophy or theory, a new teacher will end up like John or Stan—doing whatever the administration or the state tells him to do. The teacher will not have a base for figuring out the problems in the classroom and will look to a power figure to handle the issue. If a teacher strongly believes in whatever the latest mandate for teaching and learning is and knows why he believes in it, that is one thing. On the other hand, if he doesn't know what his own beliefs are about teaching and learning, he shouldn't be teaching at all.

Since all mandates are generated by or attached to political agenda, every teacher in a democracy has a responsibility to analyze every new mandate in terms of educational validity and to raise his critical voice if he does not agree with the mandate. Teachers need to be able and willing to separate the politics from the mandates. Without thinking teachers, we do not have thinking schools. Without thinking schools, we do not have thinking students or future citizens who can think. Teachers who timidly follow and obey mandates without considering the pros and cons and political agendas attached to the mandates are dangerous. Thinking and questioning teachers will not only tweak and improve our school systems but will work to improve our democracy and model the responsibilities of all citizens.

Stan and John epitomize teachers who, for whatever reason, either do not know how to think critically or if they do, cannot act on their analyses. They should not be teachers in our democracy. They model what is the most dangerous threat to our society—the inability to speak in critical voice. It is hard to believe that Mary received a master's degree and never came in contact with the concept of critical thinking and speaking. But if a teacher does somehow escape these concepts or any discussion about responsibility of a teacher in a democracy, he needs to begin to look at all messages and mandates in-depth as there is no meaning in a message without knowing its origin (i.e., the sender) and without knowing its destination (i.e., the recipient). For example, if a teacher, Mr. Caron, consistently grades students with either A's or B's and another teacher, Ms. Smith, rarely thinks any work is worthy of an A or B, and Johnny goes home with an A from Ms. Smith and an A from Mr. Caron, how might Johnny and his parents translate what those two A grades mean? Now, add to that the information that Johnny is a student who rarely receives an A or B. How does that change the interpretation of the message?

Responsible citizens and especially teachers, given the power they hold in relation to hundreds of future citizens, must continually consider the source of messages, the medium used to deliver the messages, and the recipients, often themselves. A teacher without the ability to think critically or to translate that thinking into a critical voice does a disservice to teaching, to learning, to students, and to our democracy.

Self-Diagnosis: Do You Have and Use Critical Voice?

1. Will you do whatever your principal tells you to do without discussion or question?

2. Will you do whatever your principal tells you to do, but gripe in the teachers' room?

3. Do you fear having to spend most of your time preparing students for standardized tests?

4. If so, will you speak up?

5. Will you sheepishly adhere to new mandates so that you will not lose your job?

6. Are you worried that your students will not have standardized scores as high as other students?

7. Do you have a solid theory/philosophy about how students learn best?

8. If you do and it contradicts what the administration is demanding that you do, will you write a rationale for developing plans that your theory supports?

9. Have you ever written proposals to recommend changes in action or procedure?

10. Are you prepared to go before a school board and argue your point of view?

NOTE: "Yes" answers to questions 1–3 and 5–6 and "no" answers to 4 and 7–10 indicate lack of critical voice.

Stan, Mary, and John were not thinking in any way that would represent their responsibility in a democracy; that is, to prepare students to be critically empowered thinkers and to use their (the teachers') own critical voices to further the discussion and understanding of how students learn best and how this relates to whatever is the most recent mandate. It takes a teacher who has a grounding in theory and philosophy and who has developed his own critical voice to produce dynamic learning environments that provide students the opportunities to create their own critical voices. Any teacher who cannot or does not develop and speak in critical voice needs to be in a different profession.

References

Gardner, H. (1991). *The unschooled mind: How children think and how schools should teach*. New York: Basic Books.

Kohn, A. (1993). *Punished by rewards: The trouble with gold stars, incentive plans, A's, praise, and other bribes*. Boston: Houghton Mifflin.

Marlowe, B., & Page, M. (1998). *Creating and sustaining the constructivist classroom*. Thousand Oaks, CA: Corwin Press.

Pestalozzi, J. H. (1801/1898). *How Gertrude teaches her children* (L. E. Holland & F. C. Turner, Trans.). New York: C. E. Bardeen.

Postman, N., & Weingartner, C. (1969). *Teaching as a subversive activity*. New York: Dell Publishing.

Marilyn Page consults on novice teacher, reform, classroom management, and technology issues in education. She is the author, most recently, of *You Can't Teach Until Everyone Is Listening: 6 Simple Steps to Preventing Disorder, Disruption, and General Mayhem*.

24

From Silence to Dissent

Fostering Critical Voice in Teachers

Alan S. Canestrari

Bruce A. Marlowe

In today's top-down school structures, new teachers need to develop capacities for critical reflection during pre-service training.

Despite their sense of expectation, enthusiasm, and energy, new teachers too often become assimilated into school cultures that are character- ized by cynicism, resignation, and, ultimately, compliance. As Albert Shanker once famously remarked, it only takes about six weeks for new teachers to look like old ones. The reasons for this sad state of affairs are obviously complex, but we believe that such resignation is, at least in part, due to a lack of pre-service opportunity for potential teachers to think criti- cally about the most salient characteristics of American public education.

Teacher preparation programs seem to cover every conceivable facet of teaching. However, in their breadth and their depoliticized, neutral stand on every question, they perpetuate what Tyack and Cuban (1995) refer to as the

NOTE: "Silence to Dissent: Fostering Critical Voices in Teachers" by Alan S. Canestrari and Bruce A. Marlowe. In *Encounter: Education for Meaning and Social Justice, 18*(4). Used with permission.

"grammar of schooling." That is, there is plenty of expository, rhetorical discourse describing the management of student behavior, methods of instruction, the construction of curricula, and the assessment of students. And, there is narrative too: for example, about what it is like to be a teacher. But there is virtually no critical discourse. As a result, the tone and level of student engagement with such programs rarely moves beyond the prosaic. Worse, when teacher preparation programs take a critical stance about current practices or provide examples of alternative models of teaching and learning, they do so in a way that invariably marginalizes these approaches as radical, impractical, or, at the very least, controversial. In part, this framing of the critical stance as extreme occurs because teachers no longer set the agenda.

In fact, teachers today have lost almost all control over their work. Few are capable of standing up to state-mandated, top-down curricular and instructional mandates. They are tightly constrained by school districts seeking compliance and higher test scores. We need critically literate teachers capable of challenging the technocratic demands of state-mandated curricula. Preparing such teachers must begin at the *pre-service* level; otherwise new teachers will find themselves looking very much like the old ones, mindlessly going through the motions without question or reflection.

But even when new teachers know that the top-down system is wholly inadequate, they lack clear direction as to how to move purposefully in another direction, to ask questions and challenge assumptions. But what questions should teachers ask? What answers should teachers accept? We hope new teachers will consider asking whether their instruction promotes the status quo. New teachers need models of critical reflection (and even dissent) in order to help them develop their *own* critical questions, their *own* voice, by being given the opportunity to engage in serious conversations about learning and teaching in the context of increasing pressures for accountability and uniformity of instruction.

Serious discussions with our students about teaching and learning inevitably begin with what we have begun to call the "Yes, but . . ." question because this is how the conversation inevitably begins. That is, after introducing common sense—and research-based—notions about teaching and learning we frequently hear, for example,

- Yes, but . . . won't I have to teach to the test if the district demands that scores on statewide assessments improve?
- Yes, but . . . what if the principal requires that all second grade classrooms work on math at 9:15, regardless of my kids' needs or interests on a particular day?
- Yes, but . . . what if the school district adopts basal readers and requires that we use them to the exclusion of other approaches and instructional activities?
- Yes, but . . . what if the schoolwide discipline policy requires that kids stay in for recess if they don't finish their homework?

On several occasions we have used these "Yes, but. . ." questions as a point of departure, and after simply asking what our students thought about all of this, we taped the discussion that ensued. The conversations are invariably thoughtful, reflective, and insightful, and the occasional debate—between students—addresses exactly the kinds of questions new teachers should be contemplating. These include the kinds of teacher decisions that rise to the level of moral imperatives, about how we got where we are, about whether teachers should even make decisions about curriculum, and about the role teachers can, and should, play in the shaping of broader educational policy and decision making.

Imagine how our schools might be different if in-service teachers engaged in regular discussions like the one below about whether the mandates they face are consistent with their view of what is in the best interest of their students.

JANE:	But, what do we do when we are asked to do something we know isn't right, or is contrary to what we've learned in some of our classes here? I just had a class in literacy where we talked about how research indicates that "Round Robin" reading is not best practice. And yet, the classroom I'm in now as a student teacher, that's all they do. It's the whole reading program.
MAYA:	As a new person, as a first year teacher I wouldn't say anything. I mean you don't have any credibility. You're the new kid on the block and you have to go along at first.
MARLOWE:	Will it be the same as a tenth year teacher? How long do you wait to do what you see as the right thing?
TED:	One thing we can count on is that what's wrong today will be right tomorrow. School reforms come in waves.
CANESTRARI:	So will you allow yourself to be swept in and out with the tide?
KATE:	Yeah, but I agree with Maya. You want the job, right? You're not going to say, "See ya later," because, I mean, good luck finding another job. There aren't that many out there so you do have to swim with the tide.
ALEX:	Should you risk losing your job by raising questions? Don't you have a larger responsibility to your family? I mean what do we really know about teaching anyway? We're new. I agree with Maya too. We have to go along at first. After a while, maybe then you can say something. But, definitely not at first.

MARLOWE: Is there a point at which you stop saying to yourself, "I'm just going to hold my tongue, and I'm not going to say a thing?" Okay, Jane mentioned round-robin reading. The stakes seem relatively low here. But, what about practices that you view as actually harmful? Is there a point at which you will respond to a principal's directive with "No, I won't do that"?

RONALD: I would. I would absolutely refuse if I thought morally or educationally something I was asked to do was wrong.

KATE: You need to be respectful though. Whether you agree or not, you are the rookie. So you can disagree I guess, but be tactful. Something like, "I know the test scores are down, and I realize that you want more seat time to help my students prepare for the tests, but I'm thinking about doing it a little differently. I've looked into the research. . . ." Something like that, where you go into the discussion with the principal with a knowledge base, with some preparation. Then, maybe he will give a little bit too.

SALLY: Isn't there a happy medium here where you can do something of yours and also what the curriculum might dictate? Just so that it's not completely one way or the other. You get to do some of what you want, what you know is right, what will work with kids, and you do some of what they want too.

RONALD: So, it's OK to do the harmful stuff, as long as you do the good stuff too?

SALLY: Yeah, well, I mean . . . to some extent, maybe. No, I guess I wouldn't do the bad stuff. That doesn't make sense. I'm thinking there is stuff that needs to be taught that addresses the standards, but I guess actually, no, I won't do it if it's wrong.

We liken this evolving conversation to "spinning plates." As students formulate their positions and develop their own insights, they are forced to consider the ideas of others through this dialectical exchange, thereby positioning another "plate" to be spun, another thought that must be considered. It is this emerging complexity that allows insights to move toward solutions. Notice how the following excerpt concerning teaching-to-the-test evolves with increasing clarity.

JANE: As a student teacher, I'm going to be in a predicament next semester. I'm going into a fourth grade class and I've already been told that we will be making a final push to prepare students for statewide assessments in the spring. Here, in our program, we're all told that we're not supposed to teach to the test, but I mean, my cooperating teacher couldn't have made it any clearer to me.

CANESTRARI: Testing has become a yearly event. The results are published in the paper and the schools are ranked from low to high performing. Do you have to pay attention to these results, or should you simply teach the way you know is best for your students?

RYAN: Well, again, as a beginning teacher, if I'm told that it's imperative that we do better on the tests, I would highly recommend that you teach more to the test. But, obviously, I mean you could maintain your teaching and still address the test issue.

JANE: Do I drop social studies? Science? My cooperating teacher didn't say specifically, "We're going to drop science," but there's no doubt in my mind that's what she meant when she said, "We need to prepare the students for the test."

RONALD: If we teach the right way won't students be prepared for the test anyway?

KATE: No. If there's a statewide assessment in 5th grade in mathematics, and your job is to prepare students to do well on this test, what do you have to give up to do that? I agree that you can do lots of things the right way that will help them in math, but even if you do everything well to teach them math, but drop the rest of the curriculum to prepare for the math test, are you serving your students well?

Although not always sure of why these conversations are important, all of the students, as you will see in the exchange below, are certain that such conversations are a critical part of teacher education, and perhaps more importantly, should be part and parcel of the on-going professional development of in-service teachers as well. In fact, students are so certain of the importance of these conversations that once given the opportunity it is like the opening of the flood gates.

MEGAN: Isn't this what it's really about, carefully listening to and analyzing each other's views? I mean do real teachers do this? Do they ever really get to reflect on their practice, or do they just go through the motions?

TED: I know I'm only beginning my student teaching, but I don't see this happening in my school. Is this what faculty meetings are like?

RYAN: I've been a long-term substitute for a whole semester and I've never been in a faculty meeting where there was a conversation like this. And I don't get it. Shouldn't teachers be engaged in this kind of discussion? Isn't this what should happen in a faculty meeting?

This exchange, and many more like it, underscores the perceived importance—even urgency—of addressing the "Yes, but . . ." question. The taped transcripts reveal not only deep student reflection about weighty educational issues, but also important insights. Further, there is clearly an evolution in thinking unfolding here that underscores the value of engaging teachers in the kind of dialectical process advocated in the past by notable educators like Dewey (1938) and today by a whole host of critical theorists (e.g., Giroux 1985; Zeichner 1983).

Our students also came to some important conclusions about how deliberate attempts at creating a chorus of teachers' voices may be the profession's greatest hope for continuous renewal—a discussion that echoes an interview we conducted with Deborah Meier earlier last year. When asked, "Can teachers be effective in changing their conditions?" Meier responded:

Of course, once they learn to survive. The second strategy is to organize—join with others. It starts with being a good colleague in one's own schools. Not easy work. Another way is through teacher and staff organizations. The power of solidarity among working people is still, or once again, obviously vital. . . . Teacher unions also provide us with links to other organized working people. But, it's important to remember that it's not just joining with the teachers. For example, you may also be a parent. Don't hesitate to speak out in that role also. . . . Then, there's using your professional voice. I don't just mean your teacherly voice, but your broader professional voice. (See Meier, Reading 22)

And, here is what our students had to say after a similar question.

CANESTRARI: How do good teachers get heard when they have a different vision than the administration about what a classroom should look like?

MIKE: You are teaching a science kit lesson and you decide that it is going really well and so you ask the principal to sit in. Everybody is interactive, it's going great, learning is taking place or maybe someone else in the school is interested in a demonstration, and so you invite them into the room.

RONALD: Or you teach together. Let's try something here and approach this unit all from the same standpoint, teaching across content areas.

RYAN: Teaming through integration is powerful. . . . building consensus, doing things even across grade levels by showing what really works.

CARISSA: I think change requires one person first, and then you talk with someone else, and you have a partner and then it grows. Soon, collectively, you can make a push. At some point when districts will realize that it's come to the point where you have pockets of teachers yelling so loudly that you can't cover your ears up any more and even legislators, people dictating policy, administrators . . . they're going to have to start listening to what we know about good teaching.

As we probed further about how the "Yes, but . . ." conversation should be initiated, students expanded the focus of the discussion to larger questions about who should participate in such discussions and where they should occur. It was during this part of the conversation that many students realized for the first time that those above them face pressures too. We probed further, "Don't educational leaders have the most and best opportunities to engage in critical discourse?" Together, we came to some important conclusions. Like teachers, educational leaders can also cave in to internal and external pressures. These collapses are often exacerbated by hierarchical school cultures that have evolved into sorts of feudalistic protectorates where each layer of authority protects the layer below it; superintendents protect principals, principals protect teachers, in return for loyalty, compliance, and silence.

It also didn't take long for our students to see the very real ways in which the mandates they will soon face as teachers mirror those that we face as professors. This became abundantly clear as we pushed our students to reflect more deeply about exactly why they thought the discussion was so fruitful. Students were quick to point out that even at the post-secondary level mandatory assessment and grading policies often interfere with learning. As Schap has argued (in Kohn 1994) grading policies interfere with learning when teachers use them as a way to assess the extent to which students have complied with their demands as opposed to using grades as supportive feedback to help guide student learning, to inform instruction, and to help teachers understand whether or not their pedagogy is effective. Discussing this demand versus support model of grading was eye-opening for many students; while they expressed discomfort with many of their grading experiences, they had never before really reflected on how, and for what purposes, grades might be employed. Some expressed surprise, and relief, that our discussion was ungraded. Because after reflection, the number of instructional activities students identified in their program that were explicitly evaluated struck many as inconsistent with what professors were telling them about good teaching and learning for its own sake. The fact that this activity was not graded was unique, even liberating. But, like our students who will soon be teachers, we too often have little say about whether to give grades. Similarly, as university professors in a teacher education program, we must worry about how our students will fare on standardized tests, as the state will make judgments about our program based on our students' performance. But assessment information based on standardized tests is often misleading and can be used to make dubious claims about how much students are actually learning or about the success of academic programs. It is for these reasons that we too perpetually face the "Yes, but . . ." question, a revelation for many students.

CANESTRARI: What's different about the conversation we're having now compared to discussions in other classes? What accounts for this very high level of engagement?

STEVE: Look at the situation. Is this high risk or low risk? Are we getting graded? No, we're just having a conversation with no stakes attached and we're really learning the most in this kind of setting. Everyone wants to get involved. Remember what we read about the affective filter? [Laughter in class] To get back to the original question, yeah there is a place for this we need this at both the undergraduate and graduate level. Look how everyone gets involved.

RONALD: In this university setting where everything is graded, everything is assessed, how can you maintain this level of engagement given a threatening environment? I mean we're still in a classroom where every experience, every paper, every assignment is graded and analyzed and evaluated and then we have pre-evals, in-process evals, post-evals . . . I just realized something!!! This is why kids hate school. Because the energy, the enthusiasm for learning gets sucked right out of them with all the obsessive focus on assessment.

CARISSA: So you're really in the same position as we will soon be in as teachers. You have people above you telling you that you must give grades, as just one example. You don't really have a choice either.

The students that we engaged in conversation were junior and senior undergraduates and graduate master's degree students that were very close to their final field placements. Ironically, it is at the end of the program, when they are closest to classrooms of their own, that our students become less secure as they reflect on the incongruity between what they are learning at the university and what they are seeing in public school classrooms. At a time when our students should be feeling more confident, more certain about the skills they have acquired, the dispositions they have adopted, they are instead feeling increasingly adrift; dissonance abounds. The "Yes, but . . ." question dominates their thinking and causes them to second guess their education and their good instincts.

Have we prepared our future teachers for the challenges that await them? Do our teacher education programs have enough emphasis on scholarship and tolerance for differing viewpoints? Have we engaged students in a way that allows them to think critically? Have we given them substantial preparation in articulating what's right in a way that either facilitates or causes others to rethink their classrooms? Have we prepared them in the art of resistance and dissent? Our suspicion is that we have not and our conviction is that these questions must frame teacher education.

But, perhaps, there is hope for those teachers who are prepared differently. Hope for those who have internalized Freire's (1970) desire for liberation in the form of "problem-posing education" or Giroux's (1985) insistence that teachers think of themselves as "transformative intellectuals" or even Postman and Weingartner's (1969) urging that teachers be vigilant "crap" detectors. Ohanian (2004) warns us that teachers must be educated rather than trained, that offering recipes leads only to the deskilling of teachers, that teaching practice be informed by philosophy and art and music rather than simply by experts "who promise the keys to classroom control and creative bulletin boards, along with 100 steps to reading success."

It was through the back and forth of our conversation, the student-to-student exchange, the horizontal communication between faculty and students where all participants were peers, that reminded us all of the importance and power of these kinds of discussions to inform teaching and learning.

References

Canestrari, A., and B. A. Marlowe. 2004. *Educational foundations: An anthology of critical readings.* Thousand Oaks, CA: Sage.

Dewey, J. 1938. *Experience and education.* New York: Touchstone.

Freire, P. 1970. *Pedagogy of the oppressed.* New York: Continuum International Publishing Group.

Giroux, H. 1985, May. Teachers as transformative intellectuals. *Social Action.*

Kohn, A. 2004. Grading: The issue is not how, but why. *Educational Leadership* 52(2): 38–41.

Marlowe, B. A., and M. L. Page. 1998. *Creating and sustaining the constructivist classroom.* Thousand Oaks, CA: Corwin.

Ohanian, S. 2004. On stir and serve recipes for teaching. In *Educational foundations: An anthology of critical readings,* edited by A. Canestrari and B. A. Marlowe. Thousand Oaks, CA: Sage.

Postman, N., and C. Weingartner. 1969. *Teaching as a subversive activity.* New York: Delacorte.

Spinner, H., and B. J. Fraser. 2002. Evaluation of an innovative mathematics program in terms of classroom environment, student attitudes, and conceptual development. (ERIC Document Reproduction Service Number ED464829)

Tyack, D., and L. Cuban. 1995. *Tinkering toward utopia: A century of public school reform.* Cambridge: Harvard University Press.

Zeidmer, K. M. 1983, May–June. Alternative paradigms of teacher education. *Journal of Teacher Education* 34(3): 4.

25

The Quest

Achieving Ideological Escape Velocity—Becoming an Activist Teacher

Ann Gibson Winfield

Where We Are

In the fourth century B.C., Chinese philosopher Motse wrote:

> When nobody in the world loves any other, naturally the strong will over-power the weak, the many will oppress the few, the wealthy will mock the poor . . . (quoted in Heubner, 1999, p. 78)

Clearly, we are still struggling with what Motse observed in the fourth century B.C.! How can teachers contribute to changing this state of affairs? Teachers must advocate for their students' right to empowered lives, and must envision a society that values, supports, encourages, and revels in every student's talent, curiosity, and creativity. There is a heavy pressure to conform, to stay quiet, to obey and even to promote policies and practices that are damaging but are so deeply engrained in the system that they have become the "hidden curriculum" (Giroux 2004). A transformative, activist teacher does not submit to this pressure because they know that to do so is "not only unprincipled, deeply cynical and cowardly, it's suicidal, a slippery slope with lots of miserable historical precedent" (Ayers).

NOTE: Reprinted with kind permission from the author.

Where We Might Go

So, you ask, what do activist teachers do? Activist teachers understand that much of what is commonly assumed about education is a relic of the past, that these assumptions are socially constructed and are therefore open to be reconstructed. Activist teachers understand that schools are contexts where meaning is actively made by students, teachers, and administrators on a daily basis and that therefore those meanings can change and be a source of transformation. Activist teachers analyze school policies and practices in relation to the economic, political, social, and cultural forces that shape, and are in turn shaped by them. They consider race, class, gender, ethnicity, sexual orientation, language, religion, and physical and mental abilities and disabilities as social relations of power that often differentially determine school experiences and individual and collective identities.

Activist teachers also ask big questions and reflect on how and why U.S. schools continue to contribute to the reproduction of unequal educational opportunities and outcomes for our children. Activist teachers are, first and foremost, self-reflective. They do not blame students, their families, or their environments for any perceived lack. Instead, they continually strive to identify, evaluate, and critique their own assumptions, teaching practices, and willingness to conform by putting the interests of their students and a vision of a socially just society as the goal that supersedes all other goals.

You might be wondering at this point how one goes about achieving all this, and such a question is an example of the residue we all carry from our own experience in the educational system. We must resist the desire for a quick fix, a synopsis, or a recipe that will allow us to suddenly understand what it takes to become a transformative teacher. Rest assured that this is a lifelong process, an orientation toward the future if you will, that develops and grows over time. There is no doubt that every individual will have their own version of how to proceed, and it is in that spirit that I suggest the cultivation of the following habits:

- Read often, and deeply. As Appelbaum says, we read "because reading helps us to experience what is necessary to reconsider what we think to be true about our personal worlds of experience, for imagination, interpretation, and insight" (p. 12). From quick scans of thin newspaper coverage to the kinds of books you have to keep re-reading sentences in order to understand, read as much as possible. There is no substitute for exposure. Read book reviews and books, historical fiction and things written by and about people and places that are unfamiliar. When you aren't sure about something, look it up. Talk to people about what you read. Think about what you read. Write about what you read.

• Expose yourselves to as much art, theatre, music, and literature as possible, as often as possible. We are most free to recognize and support creativity, imagination, and multiple forms of expression in our students when we have an appreciation of the possibilities. Find and cultivate your own artistic talents.

• Seek out a variety of sources for the news, and change back and forth frequently. As you do this, you will begin to recognize the assumptions, biases, and ideological residue that pervade the media. Become a media critic, unearth hidden (intended or otherwise) messages, and teach your students to do the same.

• When you are unsure about what to do, always put your students' well being at the forefront of anything you are considering—when you do that, the answer usually becomes much clearer. Also, become comfortable with ambiguity—it is an authentic, thoughtful place to be that provides room for growth and change.

• Interact, examine, explore, compare, and critique with your colleagues as much as possible, but be a savvy judge of character and avoid toxicity, negativity, or anything that disrespects, denigrates, or puts limitations on students and their families.

• Never lose sight of the big picture; context is essential. It is never frivolous to ask difficult or seemingly unanswerable questions. What do schools teach? What should schools teach? Who should decide what schools teach? Is the primary aim of education to instill basic skills or to foster critical thinking? Should education aim to mold future citizens, create an efficient workforce, engender personal development, or inspire academic achievement? Must education have an aim? What beliefs, values, or attitudes are learned from classroom practice? What lessons are acquired but taken for granted, taught but not planned?

Good teachers are, to use Giroux's term, "transformative intellectuals," practicing theoreticians, willing and able to reflect the fluid nature of the world around them. Resist any implication that teaching is not a profession, that teaching doesn't require a special form of genius, that teaching is a skill that can be easily measured and monitored. Activism, or the commitment to progressive education and a socially just society that recognizes and values all people, occurs in the small things—activism is embedded in the questions you ask, in the pause before you respond, in the strategic building of knowledge, experience and insight, in the patience, in the security that your path is right and that the right answers are available, in the resistance to rest on one's laurels, to self-congratulate, to cling to old fears. Activism is the recognition that we are all connected. It means demanding of our democracy the representation, the ideals, and the vision contained in our founding documents.

What We Might See

We are all understandably reticent to ask questions and pursue goals that undermine the bedrock of our society—the status quo. We do not want to believe that societal institutions may not reflect our deepest beliefs about a just society. We want to get along, we are afraid of conflict, of being "wrong," of not knowing what to do. This, though, is an evasion of the fundamental responsibility for the lives of students that teachers take on. As Ayers (2006) has suggested, good teachers "must embody a profound threat to the status quo" by challenging "the imposition of labels and all the simple-minded metrics employed to describe student learning and rank youngsters in a hierarchy of winners and losers."

Teachers, good teachers, teachers who recognize, appreciate, respect, and embolden their students; those teachers do not have the luxury of failing to interrogate their own assumptions, nor the assumptions embedded in the institutional policies and practices that surround them at every turn. Teachers are morally obligated to do no harm (someone should write a Hippocratic Oath for teachers), and in order to achieve that they embark upon a quest to understand that is unflinching, lifelong, and metabolic.

This is no easy task. It requires that you create within *yourself* the kind of learner that reflects your aspirations for your students. Human beings are born with an insatiable curiosity and any experience for a child, educational or otherwise, that damages, hinders, or deflects the passion for more and more knowledge is unacceptable. It is just here that the motivation to engage in the constant disassembly of assumptions and a relentless pursuit of knowledge comes.

As teachers we must adhere ourselves to something more, something deeper, something that withstands political, economic, and ideological winds.

References

Appelbaum, P. (2008). *Children's Books for Grown-Up Teachers: Reading and Writing Curriculum Theory*. New York, NY: Routledge.

Ayers, W. (2006). Love me, I'm a Liberal. *Monthly Review*.

Dewey, J. (1933). *The Quest for Certainty*. Capricorn Books.

Giroux, H. A. (2004). Teachers as Transformative Intellectuals. In A. S. Canestrari and B. A. Marlowe (eds.), *Educational Foundations: An Anthology of Critical Readings*. Thousand Oaks, CA: Sage Publications.

Heschel, A. J. (1966/1959). *The Insecurity of Freedom: Essays on Human Existance.* Philadelphia, PA: Jewsish Publication Society.

Heubner, D. (1999). *The Lure of the Transcendent: Collected Essays by Dwayne E. Heubner.* Mahwah, NJ: Lawrence Erlbaum.

Ann Gibson Winfield is a professor of education at Roger Williams University in Bristol, Rhode Island, and the author of *Eugenics and Education in America: Institutionalized Racism and the Implications of History, Ideology and Memory* (Peter Lang, 2007).

Index

Supporting researchers for more than 40 years

Research methods have always been at the core of SAGE's publishing program. Founder Sara Miller McCune published SAGE's first methods book, *Public Policy Evaluation*, in 1970. Soon after, she launched the *Quantitative Applications in the Social Sciences* series—affectionately known as the "little green books." Always at the forefront of developing and supporting new approaches in methods, SAGE published early groundbreaking texts and journals in the fields of qualitative methods and evaluation.

Today, more than 40 years and two million little green books later, SAGE continues to push the boundaries with a growing list of more than 1,200 research methods books, journals, and reference works across the social, behavioral, and health sciences. Its imprints—Pine Forge Press, home of innovative textbooks in sociology, and Corwin, publisher of PreK–12 resources for teachers and administrators—broaden SAGE's range of offerings in methods. SAGE further extended its impact in 2008 when it acquired CQ Press and its best-selling and highly respected political science research methods list.

From qualitative, quantitative, and mixed methods to evaluation, SAGE is the essential resource for academics and practitioners looking for the latest methods by leading scholars.

For more information, visit **www.sagepub.com**.